CONTENTS

Introduction ix

Contributors xv

PART I: BIBLICAL FRAMEWORK

1. Moving beyond Warfare: Biblical Imagery and
   the Conduct of Mission. 3
   Dwight P. Baker

2. Spiritual Realities in the Gospels and Implications for
   Discipleship among Oral Learners in Northeast Thailand 25
   Mark Caldwell

3. Buddhist Spiritual Realities:
   Divining and Discerning the Future 43
   Alex G. Smith

4. Transforming Power Encounters into People Movements
   in the Buddhist World and Beyond 69
   David S. Lim

PART II: CULTURAL PRACTICES

5. How Buddhist Spirituality Influences and Shapes
   Asian Cultural Practices: Missiological Implications 101
   Sheryl Takagi Silzer

6. The Impact of Buddhism on Ancestor Veneration
   in Vietnam: Harmless Cross-Cultural Assimilation
   or Dark Spiritual Influence? 123
   Tin Nguyen

132005

7. "I Believe for 50%": Negotiating Spiritual and Scientific
   Realities in Contemporary Thai Cosmologies 141
   Daniëlle Koning

8. Rituals for Blessing and Destruction among
   the Rgyalrongwa of Sichuan, China 155
   David Burnett

9. An Evangelical Christian Analysis of Theravada Buddhist
   Spirituality Expressed in the Almsgiving Ceremony 173
   G. P. V. Somaratna

PART III: MISSION STRATEGY

10. A Post-3/11 Paradigm for Mission in Japan 193
    Hiroko Yoshimoto, Simon Cozens, Mitsuo Fukuda,
    Yuji Hara, Atsuko Tateishi, Ken Kanakogi, Toru Watanabe

11. Spiritual Realities in the Folk Buddhist Worldview
    of Sri Lanka 205
    Ravin Caldera

12. Signs and Wonders: Necessary but Not Sufficient 239
    Alan R. Johnson

13. Christian Response to Burmese *Nat* Worship in Myanmar 255
    Peter Thein Nyunt

14. People of Power: Becoming an "Alongsider" in
    Thailand and Beyond 277
    John P. Lambert

Index 305

Scripture Index 315

FIGURES

Figure 1: Folk Chinese worldview................................. 71

Figure 2: Folk Filipino-Chinese worldview 72

Figure 3: Paper money offered at family and territorial
deity altar, taken at a hotel lobby in Hanoi, 2012............ 125

Figure 4: Religious distribution in Vietnam...................... 128

Figure 5: Sources of Sri Lankan folk Buddhism.................208

Figure 6: The Buddhist interpretation of cosmology
according to Pali Canon 210

Figure 7: Folk Buddhist cosmological thinking.................. 211

Figure 8: Four categories of deities in folk Buddhism 212

Figure 9: The evolution of traditional guardians 214

Figure 10: Folk Buddhist demonology......................... 216

Where can I go from your Spirit?
Where can I flee from your presence?
If I go up to the heavens, you are there;
if I make my bed in the depths, you are there.
If I rise on the wings of the dawn,
if I settle on the far side of the sea,
even there your hand will guide me,
your right hand will hold me fast.
Psalm 139:7–11

INTRODUCTION

The Psalmist tells us that God's Spirit is present everywhere. While full recognition and complete submission to that presence may not be evident in any human context, the existence of God does not change. The spiritual reality of a creator and sustainer does not depend on our ability to comprehend or explain the divine. In the same way, the purposes of God are not limited by our lack of awareness of them.

Buddhism claims no god, yet spiritual realities abound in popular practice. What are these realities? What do they mean to the practitioners? How can understanding these realities inform Christ-followers seeking to communicate the good news of Jesus in ways that all can understand and relate to it? In answer to these and other questions, SEANET proudly presents its twelfth volume, *Seeking the Unseen: Spiritual Realities in the Buddhist World*. Christian practitioners from thirteen different Buddhist cultures and regions share insights gained from their wide-ranging experiences and perspectives. From Sri Lanka to Japan, from China to the Philippines, these women and men, Asian and Western, present on a topic that is often missing in mission literature today. And for readers seeking personal insight into the growing spiritual complexities of their own place in the post-modern world, lessons from these authors will guide you with practical principles from engaging, firsthand cultural experiences.

Most will readily acknowledge the existence of a spiritual realm even though it cannot be proven empirically. Every individual inherently possesses a spiritual dimension embodied in the physical.

This spirituality is vital to personal identity and to linking with higher powers. Even within Buddhism where there is no personification of higher powers, connections with the spiritual realm are widely pursued. *Seeking the Unseen* is a collective reflection on what those spiritual realities mean to practitioners with application to people of all faiths or none.

Mission practitioners are by nature pragmatic people. We desire to see lives changed and societies transformed. The desire for a new world is not simply a dream for the future but a way of life. Accused of being cultural destroyers for too long, most of us involved in Christian mission are committed to dealing with the injustices in our world here and now and not simply focusing on preaching religious concepts about a dim and distant future. We see the Creator's presence in the beautiful diversity of the world's cultures but also the impact of fallen humanity. We believe that the good news of God's desire for reconciliation must be lived out and impact all levels of society and creation for the better. The good news must impact all facets of life or it is not truly good! Yet, in the approaches moving towards that goal of transformation, there is often an unrecognized blindness among eager practitioners to the complex spiritual realities that already exist on many levels for those in the societies where God has called us. The physical and economic needs of a culture are so visible that the realm of the unseen (but clearly impactful) cultural manifestations of pre-existing spiritual realities is relegated to the margins of ministry.

The irony, of course, is that although cognitively we know (and verbally we preach) that the ultimate source of any worldview change and lasting social transformation comes only through God's spiritual empowerment, we who are involved in intercultural Christian witness tend to interpret the spiritual realities of cultures unfamiliar to us as evil. If we see them at all we view them through our own outsider lenses. Our modernist training has taught us to explain away the phenomenal as simply psychosomatic. What we don't understand we often ignore. While this may be necessary in some cases, God's mission is at work in ways un-orchestrated and even misunderstood by missionaries. Those involved in Christian mission cannot ignore the spiritual realities of their new host cultural context that has existed before they ever arrived. Our Buddhist sisters and brothers can actually teach Christian missionaries much about the power of spiritual realities, perhaps even more than most Christ followers have ever personally experienced.

One Thai Christian evangelist is fond of provoking thought by asking the question, "Do Christians believe in ghosts?" This is a popular topic among Thai Buddhists who are engaged in spiritual realities but one rarely raised among the Christian community. After a period of awkward silence, this man will answer his own question with, "Absolutely! We believe in the Holy Ghost!" Entire worldview systems revolve around recognizing and dealing with spiritual realities—both positive and negative. Many western post-enlightenment missionaries do not have the tools to integrate forms of spiritual realities unknown to them into the conversations, scriptural interpretations and missiological methods they employ. The spiritual power vacuum created by a modernist view of the gospel reinforces a bifurcated faith where the message of Christ is not enough for those who have experienced something different. Even philosophical Buddhism has adapted its focus from the need to separate from all desires found in the temporal to the pursuit of personal empowerment in the spiritual realm for success in the here and now. This is familiar to many practitioners of Buddhist traditions. Christians can learn much from this interchange.

This volume is divided into three sections. The first section includes four chapters building a Biblical framework for defining, understanding, and dealing with spiritual realities through the lens of scripture. Dwight Baker begins this section with a wakeup call to view mission in terms other than that of warfare. While clearly recognizing the spiritual realities in the task at hand he pleads for a broader look at what the Bible says helping us to recognize the impact that our imagery has upon mission practice. Mark Caldwell reviews three passages from the ministry of Jesus that model approaches to discipleship in cultures where spiritual realities abound. Alex Smith shows how divination is handled in certain Buddhist contexts with implications for intercultural Christian workers. David Lim continues this theme by showing how the spiritual realities of power encounter translates into multiplying movements of Christ-centered communities.

The second section, "Cultural Practices," details five different perspectives on the hidden cultural values of five unique Buddhist contexts. Sheryl Silzer draws out missiological implications from a study of how Buddhist spirituality influences and shapes Asian cultural practices. Tin Nguyen addresses a topic central to the Mahayana Buddhist of ancestor veneration looking in depth at responses to a cultural worldview need often ignored by Christians. The complexities of Thai cosmologies are engagingly described by Daniëlle Koning addressing the seemingly contradictory realities of spiritual experiences. David Burnett gives a thorough anthropological description with missiological insights of the revival of blessing and destruction rituals among the Rgyalrongwa of Sichuan, China. Somaratna's evangelical Christian analysis of Theravada Buddhist spirituality focuses on the Sri Lankan Almsgiving Ceremony.

The final section addresses what Christian practitioners are doing in Mission Strategy regarding these unseen spiritual realities. From Japan, a group of Christians share their experiences in this realm following the 3/11 Tsunami in their country. Drawing inspiration from the beautiful cultural expressions from his context Ravin Caldera explains the impact of expressing deep worldview values from Sri Lanka. No text on this topic would be complete without addressing the topic of signs and wonders. But are they enough to bring about worldview change? Alan Johnson addresses this question from his ministry experience in urban Thailand. Finally, Peter Thein Nyunt looks at the Christian contextualized response to Burmese *Nat* Worship in his home context of Myanmar.

Creating a work such as the one you are reading requires the contributions of many whose names are not written on the cover but without whom this book could never have been put into print. All who were part of this collective effort should be honored but there are more than can be named here. The editor wishes to recognize some of these who were especially helpful in the final creation of this work. First of all, I would like to recognize the hard work of my faithful and hardworking assistant, Christopher Hoskins. His hand is present on every page having personally connected with each author before these works came to print. Without his keen eye and sharp questioning mind, this volume would not stand together as completely as it does. Others who are unseen but should be recognized are all of the staff of William Carey Library Publishers. Special thanks go to Jeff Minard, managing editor for his encouragement and support of SEANET volumes over the years, to the two hardworking Melissas (Hicks and Hughes) for all your helpful communication, to copyeditor Brad Koenig for the thoroughness of his work, and to graphic designer Josie Leung for her vision and artistic ability seen on the cover. Gratitude in advance from all future readers who will search this book topically and scripturally must go to Rose Lee-Norman for creating the indices. Each of the authors whose names appear under the contributors section must be thanked for their hard work in taking the time to put their missiological reflections on complex cultural issues into writing. Thanks to all of the SEANET steering committee for their many contributions. Thanks also to Dwight Martin and the team at eSTAR Foundation in Chiang Mai for printing the first edition in Thailand. Any errors in this volume, both seen and unseen, are the fault of this editor and no one else.

Finally, credit must be given most of all to the Unseen Writer of every volume, the Inspirer of every God-honoring creative act and production, the One in whom and through whom we live and move have our being. May the deeper relational reality with that Unseen One be the desire of our heart and the purpose of our existence for we are all the offspring of this One.

Paul H. de Neui

CONTRIBUTORS

Dwight P. Baker was associate editor of the *International Bulletin of Missionary Research* from 2002–15. Prior to retirement in 2011, he also served as program director and then associate director of the Overseas Ministries Study Center, New Haven, Connecticut. Before that he was director of the World Christian Foundation's study program at the U.S. Center for World Mission in Pasadena, California. A United States citizen and ordained in the Evangelical Covenant Church, he earned a PhD in anthropology at Purdue University, an MDiv at North Park Theological Seminary, and an MA in English at Bemidji State University. He and his wife reside in Connecticut.

David Burnett has a particular interest in how religions function within societies, which was first stimulated by the year he taught in a Bible institute in India. He went on to study mission and cultural studies, and taught related subjects at All Nations Christian College in the United Kingdom where he was Academic Dean. He was awarded a PhD in anthropology at the School of Oriental and African Studies, University of London. Later he was invited to join the staff of a university in the west of China as professor of anthropology, involved in various research projects undertaken by the Institute of Multicultural Education. This allowed him the unique opportunity to engage with minority people in the eastern region of the Tibetan plateau. David and his wife Anne now live in the UK where David continues with his writing, teaching, and research.

Ravin D. Caldera is a lecturer and an assistant academic dean of Colombo Theological Seminary. He is from a Buddhist background and for more than a decade has planted churches in the urban Buddhist context. He holds a Bachelor's degree from Colombo Theological Seminary and M.A. in Biblical Studies from Dallas Theological Seminary. He is an ordained minister of Living Christ Church and currently assisting the house church movement among Buddhists. He is also a local preacher in the Methodist Church of Sri Lanka. His passion is to research and develop context-penetrating methods for reaching Sinhalese Buddhists in Sri Lanka.

Mark Caldwell grew up in the southeastern area of the United States. Mark has an MDiv from Golden Gate Theological Seminary, and is presently working on completing a doctorate of missiology at Malaysia Baptist Theological Seminary. Mark was in ministry in African-American contexts in Chicago, San Francisco, and Sacramento, California prior to going to Thailand with the International Mission Board. He has worked as a church planter and planter coach among the Isaan people of northeast Thailand. Spiritual realities have become a passion for Mark as a disciple of Christ who longs for Christ to be incarnated among the Isaan people. He is married with three children, and two grandchildren.

Simon Cozens is a missionary in Kyoto and has been planting house churches since 2011.

Paul de Neui is an ordained minister with the Evangelical Covenant Church. He and his wife served as missionaries with church planting and community development organizations in northeast Thailand from 1987–2005. He completed his PhD in Intercultural Studies at Fuller Theological Seminary. Paul has been involved in SEANET for over ten years. Presently he is the professor of Missiology and Intercultural Studies and the director of the Center for World Christian Studies at North Park Theological Seminary in Chicago, Illinois.

Mitsuo Fukuda is president of Bonton Inc., which has provided personnel development services in some Asian countries. After finishing at the Graduate School of Theology at Kwansei Gakuin University, he researched contextualization and cultural anthropology at Fuller

Theological Seminary as a Fulbright graduate student and received a doctorate degree in intercultural studies.

Alan R. Johnson is from Seattle and serves as a missionary to Thailand with the Assemblies of God. His doctoral research was an ethnographic study of social influence processes in a slum community in Bangkok done through the Oxford Centre for Mission Studies and University of Wales. Johnson serves as the secretary of the Missions Commission of the World Assemblies of God Fellowship that seeks to foster Majority World sending. He is a member of the Assemblies of God World Missions (AGWM) Missiology Think Tank; serves on the global leadership team for the Asia Pacific Region of AGWM and served for one year as the Hogan Chair of World Missions at the Assemblies of God Theological Seminary (AGTS). He serves as an adjunct professor at AGTS in their doctoral program in intercultural studies. He and his wife have been married thirty-six years and have two grown children and five grandchildren.

Daniëlle Koning is from the Netherlands. She has a PhD in anthropology/sociology of religion from VU University in Amsterdam, focusing on mission dynamics in so-called "immigrant churches" in the Dutch capital. Currently she works as both a researcher and mission practitioner in northeastern Thailand for Adventist Frontier Missions, a supportive ministry of the Seventh-day Adventist church. Her current research centers on how Thai Buddhists appropriate Bible texts, or, put more broadly, what "learning Christianity" looks like for this group.

John Lambert served as a missionary to North and Northeast Thailand before working with Frontier Ventures, formerly known as the U.S. Center for World Mission, in Pasadena, CA. John is a writer for Mission Frontiers magazine, teaches in the Perspectives on the World Christian Movement course, and is featured in the DVD Practical Tools and Insights for Reaching Buddhist People published by YWAM's Create International. John currently serves with Liberty Network International, a network of missionaries and ministers, based in Pensacola, FL.

David S. Lim is from the Philippines. He has served as academic dean at Asian Theological Seminary in the Philippines and Oxford Centre for Mission Studies in the UK. His PhD in New Testament Theology was earned from Fuller Theological Seminary. He now serves as the president of the Asian School of Development and Cross-cultural Studies, president of China Ministries International- Philippines, board chair of Lausanne Philippines, and coordinator of the Asian House Church Movement. He has authored several books and articles on non-Western missiology, theological contextualization, and transformational development.

Tin Nguyen was born and raised in Vietnam and educated in Canada and the USA. He holds a bachelor's and master's degree in computer science and worked for several years as a software design engineer. He holds a doctoral degree in Intercultural Studies from Western Seminary in Portland, Oregon where he also received a ThM in Systematic Theology and an MA in Exegetical Theology. Nguyen has served as a missionary to Vietnamese migrant workers in Malaysia. He has a mission-training ministry for pastors, missionaries and lay people in Vietnam, where ancestor worship and Buddhism are two of the most prominent religions. His research interests include apologetics, methods for theological education, contextualization and its application to Asian contexts, and strategies for developing churches in the persecuted world. He is the pastor of the Vietnamese Living Water Church in Portland, Oregon. Nguyen currently lives with his wife and son in Oregon.

Sheryl Takagi Silzer is a multicultural consultant with SIL International. She is a third generation Japanese American whose ancestors were Buddhist. Her paternal grandfather became a Christian through his immigration experience in the early 1910s and passed on his faith to his family. Sheryl leads cultural self-discovery workshops for multicultural teams working in cross-cultural ministries. She also teaches as an adjunct professor at Talbot School of Theology in Asian American ministry. Her specialty is the influence of Asian religious thought on Asian cultural practices. Sheryl received a PhD in Intercultural Studies at Fuller School of World Mission. She and her husband Pete served for several years with SIL in the Asia-Pacific area as Bible translators. They have two married sons and five grandchildren.

Alex G. Smith was born and raised in Australia until twenty-one. In Canada he graduated from Prairie Bible College and later the International Institute of Christian Communication in Kenya, Africa. In the USA he earned the DMiss and MA degrees at Fuller Theological Seminary and an MDiv from George Fox Evangelical Seminary. Veteran missionary to Thailand, he founded the Thailand Church Growth Committee, and co-founded SEANET (South, East, Southeast, and North Asia Network). He served as adjunct faculty at Multnomah University for eighteen years. Presently he is advocate in the Buddhist World for OMF International, under which he has worked for fifty years. He has published numerous books and articles on ministry in the Buddhist world. His Asian church planting experiences deepened the conviction that multiplying contextualized local indigenous fellowships and training local lay pastors are priority strategies for mission. He resides with his American wife, Faith, in the USA. They have three adult sons and four grandchildren.

G. P. V. Somaratna is from Sri Lanka. He has a PhD in South Asian history from the University of London. He served as head of the department of history and political science, professor of modern history at the University of Colombo, Sri Lanka, and is now serving as senior research professor at Colombo Theological Seminary. He also served as adjunct professor at Trinity Theological College and as post doctoral fellow at the Hebrew University of Jerusalem and at the Global Research Institute of Fuller Theological Seminary. He has published numerous articles and books on the history of Sri Lanka and the impact of Christianity upon Sri Lankan Buddhism. He is widely regarded as one of Sri Lanka's leading scholars on Ceylonese history.

Peter Thein Nyunt is a former Buddhist monk. He has a BA in Bible, MDiv in Theology, MTh in Missiology, and a PhD in Missiology. For several years he served in pastoral ministry and evangelism with the Rakhine in Buddhist communities in Myanmar. He is the vice principal of Myanmar Evangelical Graduate School of Theology, associate secretary of Myanmar Evangelical Christian Alliance, director of the Rakhine Missions Band for Christ, and the senior pastor of Bethel Assemblies of God Church. He is married and the father of three children.

Hiroko Yoshimoto is a housewife, residing in Tokyo, Japan. Earlier, she had spent several years in Central Asia, working in a Muslim context. After the disasters of March 2011, along with **Mitsuo Fukuda**, **Yuji Hara** and **Ken Kanakogi**, she traveled frequently to the tsunami affected areas.

PART I

BIBLICAL FRAMEWORK

*"If my people, who are called by my name,
will humble themselves and pray and seek
my face and turn from their wicked ways,
then I will hear from heaven, and I will
forgive their sin and will heal their land."*
2 Chronicles 7:14

"That which you seek is seeking you."
Rumi

*"For the Son of Man came
to seek and to save the lost."*
Luke 19:10

CHAPTER 1

MOVING BEYOND WARFARE: BIBLICAL IMAGERY AND THE CONDUCT OF MISSION[1]

DWIGHT P. BAKER

Poets may be, as the nineteenth-century Romantic poet Percy Bysshe Shelley declared, the unacknowledged legislators of humankind; deeper still, imagery and images are the unrecognized wellsprings of thought and action. They are fecund, vivifying, and energizing—and they have entailments. They touch the deepest roots of human motivation; an image aptly chosen moves us more profoundly than can either command or axiom. And the imagery we invoke speaks volumes about who or what we conceive ourselves to be.

Throughout history, Christian mission, sad to say, has often been pleased to be the beneficiary of overt warfare and the course of empire. Though few evangelicals today might care to embrace a territorial conception of the church or endorse war as a means of advancing the faith, in recent years seriously intentioned evangelicals have possibly been the most avid in embracing warfare terminology for articulating their understanding of Christian doctrine and Christian mission. They engage in spiritual warfare. They seek out prayer warriors. In mission they plan campaigns, develop strategies, establish beachheads, and target peoples. They call for a wartime lifestyle. They create manuals, even encyclopedias, of spiritual warfare. They view ordinary disappointments and setbacks of life through the lens of spiritual battle, seeing

---

1   This chapter is a modified version of the article "Beyond Warfare: Biblical Imagery and the Conduct of Mission," *Covenant Quarterly* 49: 3–4 (August–November 2011): 79–94. Used with permission.

in them evidence that spiritual forces have singled them out for direct personal attack.

Warfare terminology and imagery is widespread in the evangelical mission enterprise. The late Ralph Winter, cofounder of the U.S. Center for World Mission, Pasadena, California, advocated adoption of "a wartime, not a peacetime, lifestyle" (Winter and Hawthorne 2009, 210). In speaking to USCWM staff in 1999, he evoked the experience of Admiral Spruance in sending pilots to near certain death during the decisive World War II battle at Midway, using this story to elucidate the weight he felt as a mission leader who had to make decisions regarding mission personnel. The well-known pastor of Bethlehem Baptist Church in Minneapolis, John Piper (1993, 41), writes that "prayer is primarily a wartime walkie-talkie for the mission of the church" that invests the church with "the significance of front-line forces." Earlier, L. E. Maxwell (1977), longtime president of Prairie Bible Institute, titled his book *World Missions: Total War*. Before him Orville D. Jobson (1957) published *Conquering Oubangui-Chari for Christ*, an incongruous title for a Brethren missionary. More recently, Peter Wagner expounded the "power of strategic-level spiritual warfare" (1996), conjuring up an image of a squadron of high-flying B-52s, while Stephen Womack, in recruiting for the Wycliffe Bible Translators, keeps his feet on the ground by calling for "a participating, active, stepping-out-in-faith, *invasionary force of militant priests* in joint enterprise with Almighty God" (2000, 8; italics added).

Imagery plays a vital role in the New Testament documents, and this includes warfare imagery. Warfare and militaristic imagery is used to depict the activity of God against Satan and everything tainted by him, to speak of the struggle between God's Spirit and evil desires deeply embedded in the human heart, and to indicate the vigilance Christ's followers should exercise against Satan's attacks and the fortitude with which they should bear hardships and burdens in Christ's service. But two observations: first, that is about the sum total of the New Testament's use of warfare imagery. Second, the question posed below is whether the military model is optimal for describing the organization of the church and the lines along which its activities should be conducted. Specifically, are the organizational structure and ethos of mission agencies best patterned along military lines? Let's be clear: there *is* a war going on. God is at war, whether Gregory Boyd (1997) has all the angles quite right or not. There is war, not just on earth, but in heaven also (e.g., Rev 12:7–17). And as "Onward, Christian Soldiers" shows, martial images and music stir a response. But does the church's core identity really lie with war? What about other New Testament images for the Christian life, other images for the nature of the church, and other metaphors for the conduct of mission endeavors? If there are advantages to warfare rhetoric, what disadvantages or deficits come with militaristic imagery? Very importantly, does war rhetoric inherently constrain, in undesirable ways, the affective stance of those who use it within the missionary enterprise?

What follows consists of four steps: first, a reminder that, in our handling of it, mission's relation to war has been diverse and not always seemly; second, a reminder that war itself has worn different faces at different times and in different places; third, a look at imagery used for the church in Acts through Revelation; and, fourth, a set of reflections that question reliance upon military organization and ethos as models for the organization and conduct of mission agencies.

MISSION IN RELATION TO WAR

Mission or missions and war is a huge topic, as is the related topic of mission and empire (e.g., Stanley 1990; Porter 2004). All that can be done here is to place some markers to indicate high points of the terrain to be covered. (The specter of crusade as mission—often buttressed by appeals to the Hebrew Scriptures and to the church as the new Israel— raises another large cluster of topics. They deserve extended attention, but unfortunately will have to be left to another occasion. Suffice it to say that the church has not been given a mandate to impose obedience to the gospel by political triumph and still less by military conquest.)

Heavenly War

As mentioned, there *is* a war on a cosmic scale, dramatized in the book of Revelation. All of heaven and earth becomes the stage on which the battle is fought. The forces of God and Satan, good and evil, crisscross the tableau as scene follows scene in this first Christian drama. In this heavenly war, the Lamb slain before the foundation of the world stands victorious. He is our champion. We participate as followers in his train, exulting in his victory.

War Expanding the Frontiers of Christendom

The banner of Christendom down through the centuries has too frequently matched progress with the ensigns of war and imperialism, sometimes profiting from the tides of battle, sometimes spurring war on.

To pick a "successful" example, in "the most naked use of armed force for the spread of the faith which Christianity had yet seen," Charlemagne spent more than a quarter century in "converting" (that is, subjugating) the Saxons. It became deadly dangerous to be a Saxon and remain unbaptized (Latourette 1975, 350; Neill 1986, 68–69). Church growth advocate Donald McGavran apparently was able to contemplate Charlemagne's "crude" but ultimately effective methods sanguinely: they worked, did they not? (1972, 62). Or did they? Wilbert Shenk (1995, 54), citing studies conducted by Emmanuel-Célestin Suhard, bishop of Paris, reminds us that in France the very areas of forced conversion are the ones that today are the most resistant to the gospel.

Spain and Portugal's drive into Central and South America, carried out in the name of gold, glory, and the gospel, planted a pre–Counter Reformation version of Roman Catholicism there at the expense of the native inhabitants. Happily, some Christians such as Bartolomé de las Casas protested the extermination and enslavement of the local inhabitants (Wright 1970; Rivera 1992). Russian Orthodoxy rode eastward across northern Asia on the back of ethnic Russian military conquest and imperial expansion. Bribery and coercion, mixed with "heroic zeal, apostolic simplicity, willingness to suffer and to die," marked the church's advance to the Pacific. Neither story is wholly edifying, to speak kindly (Neill 1986, 181–87).

Europe's wars of religion can be viewed as a drawn-out contest to see whether various patches of Christendom would end up Catholic or Protestant—and, therefore, as not strictly missions—but it is worth remembering that the extended battle zones of Europe's post-Reformation conflicts over religion mark the fault lines along which the worst outbreaks of the European witch craze erupted. "That this recrudescence of the witch-craze in the 1560s was directly connected with the return of religious war is clear. It can be shown from geography" (Trevor-Roper 1972, 143).

Military, commercial, political, and missionary factors intertwined in the penetration and partitioning of Africa. The story is covered with sweeping strokes by Roland Oliver (1952) in *The Missionary Factor in East Africa* and, for colonial and missionary penetration along the Congo and Ubangi Rivers, in more fine-grained fashion by William Samarin (1989). Examples are unending. The question to be raised is whether the church has even yet sorted out the consequences of "linkage"; that is, seeking to capture an advantage for the gospel through conjunction with military conquest and as a partner to strategies for gaining political and commercial advantage.

Military Models for Mission Organizations

Linkage between mission and war can take another tack. Should mission organizations be structured after a military model? Some, following the lead of Ralph Winter (1974), would strip the church down to two structures, a parish modality and a mission sodality, that derive, respectively, from Roman civil administration and military organization. In this understanding, medieval Christendom's diocesan structure was adapted from the basic territorial unit of Roman civil administration, while its monastic and mission structures copied a nonterritorial, freely shifting, commander-centric, Roman military model of organization. But even if this reading of their pedigree is correct, does a military model provide the best pattern for mission organizations today and in the future? Even enthusiastic advocates would, I think, quickly find limits. The Knights Templar may have been slandered when they were suppressed in 1307 (Froude 1972), but the record of those orders that took the adjective "military" to heart is not wholly encouraging.

Issues of Motivation

John Kotter and James Heskett (1992), writing in *Corporate Culture and Performance*, stress the need for business leaders to create a sense of crisis if leadership is going to move a body of people in a particular direction. Later, Kotter identifies "establishing a sense of urgency" as the *sine qua non* for leading change (1996). What better image of crisis and urgency than war, where all, including life itself, is at stake? In war all resources are to be poured into the cause. No expense is to be spared. No hesitation or question can be tolerated. No divided loyalties can be countenanced. All must take up arms at once and enter the fray. Those who are not with us are against us. Onward to battle!

Social pressure is a great organizer of people's outlook, constraining them to hew to a common path. A half century ago, Anthony Wallace (1956a, 1956b) speculated that in times of intense pressure, individuals or societies enter a state of psychological malleability in which their conceptual orientation can undergo all-encompassing reorganization. He called this process "mazeway resynthesis." Such resynthesis happens best when pressure is not just high, but too high, beyond bearing. In a similar fashion, elements of the physical universe, under intense heat or cold or pressure, exhibit novel physical appearance or behavior. What of the spiritual sphere? If spiritual redirection is desired, is war the means? Is war itself, or at least war rhetoric, the way to raise the stakes and channel the randomness of individualistic Western psyches towards a common goal?

War as an Eye Opener

I was born toward the end of the Second World War, and a frequent feature in mission reports of my youth was the United States soldier who had seen the world in a new way during his extended World War II tour of duty overseas. American GIs saw the world with new eyes, and they saw new parts of the world. God uses information to open hearts. To that end, war *can* be useful just by moving some persons around, from where they thought they wanted to be to where they were unlikely to have gone had their preferences been consulted. In going, they gain new perspectives and insight. In addition to the large number of ex-GIs who returned as missionaries to the theaters of war where they had served, a number of new Western mission agencies were founded in the years following World War II. Of the seven hundred U.S. mission agencies listed in the *Mission Handbook: 1998–2000* (Siewert and Valdez 1997), ninety-four began in the span from 1944 to 1954. Many of these were specialist service agencies: World Relief (1944), Mission Aviation Fellowship (1945), Mustard Seed (1948), Trans World Radio

(1949), and World Vision (1950). Others opened new fields to the gospel. From evil, God can bring good, but should we therefore embrace war or militarism?

War as Convenient Precursor

What of war—or famine or peril or nakedness or epidemic—as God's plow to break up fallow ground? Is war something to be pushed far away with our lips, but secretly hugged close to our hearts as a favor from God because it seems to yield easy pickings in the conversion sweepstakes? Is that the impression we wish to convey to outsiders? To insiders? To intended beneficiaries of our witness? To searching observers and critics, inside or outside the church? If so, surely it is time to rethink our motivation, methods, and goals in mission.

IMAGERY OF WAR

In terms of imagery, war can convey a picture of utmost brutality: slaughter, conquest, vanquishment of an enemy (recalling Roman senator Cato the Elder's refrain: "Carthage must be destroyed"), utter annihilation. It can also be used in a more "refined," detached fashion, such as the following:

- *War as strategy.*
  The ultimate chess game in which the winner indeed takes all, including life and resources.
- *War as a practical laboratory for testing the comparative strength and efficacy of technological innovations.*
  The longbow in the hands of English yeomen in 1346 at Crécy, France, who mowed down the cream of French knighthood and thereby made a way of life as well as a particular method of war obsolete in a single battle (Tuchman 1978, 85–89; Zook and Higham 1966, 75–76; Ellis 1978, 64–65).
- *War as a test of strength between competing forms of economic and industrial organization.*
  The Union versus the Confederacy in the U.S. Civil War. The United States versus the Soviet Union in the Cold War.

- *War as a test of discipline and ability to perform between different forms of social organization.*
  The disciplined regiment that, though it does not always triumph over the unruly mob or acephalous horde, is still the one to bet on.
- *War as a monopoly of the state.* In the twentieth century, as Paul Johnson (1991, 783) observes, states did not dispose of this power well. He writes, "By the 1990s, state action had been responsible for the violent or unnatural deaths of some 125 million people during the century, more perhaps than it had succeeded in destroying during the whole of human history up to 1900."

In sum, war lends itself in many different ways to rhetorical usage. Perhaps most central is the image of total commitment because the cause is ultimate.

Is this the language of commitment and set of associations followers of Christ wish to appropriate to themselves for characterizing God's mandate of grace and their involvement in the world? I repeat: there is a war; God is at war. We are assailed by the enemy of our souls and by thrones, powers, and what not else in league with him. The Lamb slain before the foundation of the world acting as our champion has brought about our enemy's sure defeat—accomplished at the Cross, being made effective day by day, and with utmost certainty to be fully realized at his appearing. For this, hallelujah and all praise. But do we wish in any way to assume a warlike stance or rhetoric toward our co-assailees, those whom God is calling to himself—that is, people (whether American neopagans, nonregenerate "Christians" attending churches from time to time, adherents of traditional religions, secularists, Buddhists, Hindus, or Muslims, among many others) who are, like us, under attack by Satan?

BIBLICAL IMAGERY

Biblical images are not static, some sort of self-contained, stand-alone sources of inherent and timeless meaningfulness. They are dynamic. Their potency arises from the relationships they enter into. They draw upon both the persons and activities of which they speak and the larger body of narrative and didactic material of which they form a part. But no flags are posted, identifying the limits to their appropriate use. Images call for discretion and judgment. Readers of Scripture still have to apply themselves and to think. If Christ's disciples are salt or light, one must always ask: when, in what way, and for whom? We need to ask how New Testament images of the church function. What is being stated or shown or related through them? To what aspect of life do they apply? What semantic domains do they call into play? The following classification can only hint at the richness and profusion of New Testament imagery related to the church. The examples shown are drawn from a much larger corpus compiled in the course of my research. Though I am aware of the work of Paul S. Minear (1961, David W. Bennett (1993), and John Driver (1997), my research has been undertaken independently and on its own plan of approach; I especially recommend Stanley H. Skreslet, *Picturing Christian Witness: New Testament Images of Disciples in Mission* (2006). If the role, status, character, and manner of functioning of the church are central, the many images that refer to attitudes, actions, and relationships of individual believers form a rich circle of support around them.

Agonistic imagery
  Athletic: 1 Corinthians 9:24–27
  Military/martial/soldierly/armor: 2 Corinthians 10:2–5;
    Ephesians 6:10–18
  Self-discipline/endurance/self-control: Hebrews 12:7
  Struggle/contending/resistance/defeat: Philippians 1:27,28
  Suffer/suffering: 1 Peter 4:12–16
  Flight/pursuit: 1 Timothy 6:11
  Stand/standing firm: 1 Corinthians 16:13
  Overcoming: 1 John 5:4,5
Nurturing imagery
  Parenting: 1 Corinthians 4:14–16
  Teacherly/training: 2 Timothy 1:11
  Maturation / growing up: Ephesians 4:12–14
  Comforting: 2 Corinthians 7:6,7
  Strengthening/encouraging: Romans 15:4,5
  Birth / new birth / infancy: Ephesians 4:14

Organism/body/vitalistic/agricultural imagery
  Body: Romans 12:4,5
  Life/live: Colossians 2:13
  Agricultural: 1 Corinthians 3:6–8
Structural imagery
  Structure/building/component: 1 Peter 2:4,5
  Building / act of constructing / craftsmanship / artistry:
    1 Corinthians 3:10–13
Sensory imagery
  Olfactory: 2 Corinthians 2:14–16
  Gustatory: 1 Peter 2:2,3
  Sign/signal/flag/emblem/marker: Philippians 1:27,28
  Optical/light/darkness/day/night: Ephesians 5:8–14
  Awake/asleep: 1 Thessalonians 5:6,7
  Seeing/vision/appear/witness/look/perceive/imagine: 1
    Corinthians 13:12
Affiliation / social organization imagery
  Family: Romans 8:14–18
  Sister/brother/brothers/brotherly: Acts 15:23
  Affiliation by descent: 1 John 3:9
  Household: Ephesians 2:19
  Friend/friends: 1 Peter 2:11
  Kinship/nation/citizen: Ephesians 2:12–19
  Excluded / different citizenship / followers of a different
    lord: 1 Peter 2:11
Status / role assignment imagery
  Kings/royalty/ruler / kingly priests: 1 Peter 2:9
  Shepherd/caretaker/steward: 1 Peter 5:2
  Workman / fellow worker: Philippians 4:3
  Servant/slave: 2 Corinthians 4:5
  Renderer of service to God or the saints: Revelation 2:19
  Freeman: 1 Peter 2:16
  Prisoner/condemned: 1 Corinthians 4:9
Miscellaneous imagery
  Religious: Philippians 2:17
  Commercial: 2 Corinthians 1:21,22

With such an abundance, Paul Minear (1961, 222) justly states that no single image can establish itself as *the* baseline image of the church. It is certain, however, that the preponderance of New Testament images of the church falls on the side of relational (kinship, family, *ethne*) and nurturance imagery. They, not militaristic images, are central to the New Testament's conception of the church and faithful life in Christ if one is to judge centrality by either number of instances or bulk of text involved.

OBSERVATIONS ON BIBLICAL IMAGERY

I offer four observations regarding biblical imagery. Though none can be fully developed here, each merits consideration at length.

The first relates to Paul's leadership style. Significantly, when Paul has the opportunity to play the general and to order people about, he does not do it. He entreats Philemon. To Timothy and Titus he writes, "Do your best to come" (2 Tim 4:9; Titus 3:12),[2] or to do such and such. He instructs the Romans (14:5–8) about the immediacy with which we all stand under the lordship of Christ. Paul has authority, but it is "authority . . . which the Lord gave for building you up" (2 Cor 10:8) and not for other purposes. His letters contain many imperatives, but they carry the impress of instructional rhetoric, not of bare-knuckled exercise of authority. He is no lordling. In this, his practice agrees with his self-description—"we . . . persuade others" (2 Cor 5:11)—and with the restraint enjoined by Peter ("tend the flock of God . . . Do not lord it over those in your charge, but be examples to the flock" [1 Pet 5:2,3]). We are all, Paul and Peter included, subject to King Jesus. *He* exercises authority over his body, the church. There are no (rightful) generals appointed as his stand-ins.

Second, the real war is that of God at war against Satan, while Satan, unable to stand up against God's champion, vents his frustration on God's surrogate and viceroy on earth; namely, us, all of humanity. As followers of Christ we struggle, and our struggles are real. They count. But the real victory is won by Christ, and the triumph that counts is Christ in us, the hope of glory (Col 1:27). Without him our

---

2   Scripture quotations in this chapter follow the New Revised Standard Version.

struggles and accomplishments would be but sideshows. There is much to be said on this topic, but here I can offer only a couple suggestions.

We have been attacked by Satan and have been grievously wounded in the battle—without aid, mortally so. But we are not mere victims caught in the middle in the cosmic conflict between God and Satan. As Christ's followers we "shine like stars in the world" (Phil 2:12–16) and become members of Christ's victory procession through whom God shows forth the fragrance of his grace (2 Cor 2:14–16). We do this by walking in step with the Spirit and not fulfilling the desires of the flesh (Gal 5:16–26), by putting on the mind of Christ (Phil 2:1–11), by being renewed through the transformation of our minds (Rom 12:1,2), by resisting the devil (1 Pet 5:8,9), and by standing firm—clothed in the armor of God—and speaking boldly the gospel of peace (Eph 6:10–20). Our transformation from darkness into light (Eph 5:1–20) and our doing of works of righteousness as God planned for us (Eph 2:10) make us active participants in God's work of casting out the prince of this world system, the prince of the power of the air (more powerful than we are as creatures of the earth, but far below God, to whom belong heaven and the heaven of heavens [Deut 10:14]), and the spirit of disobedience now at work (Eph 2:1–7).

We are colaborers with God, certainly, but we do well not to form too highly exalted an opinion of ourselves or our role. When Satan makes war on the saints, we cannot stand in our own strength. When Satan attacks humankind and we prove unequal to the assault, Christ interposes himself; he steps in and bears the brunt of Satan's attack. In Christ, God accomplishes the deliverance that we could not.

Third, Christ as our and God's champion enters the fray on our behalf and wins the victory (Barker, Lane, and Michaels 1969, 314–16; Lane 1991a, 53–58, 61–65; 1991b, 410–12). Never are we spoken of as winning the victory or carrying the day through our own inherent capabilities. We are made alive in Christ, seated in heavenly places in Christ, made to triumph in Christ, "in whom we have redemption, the forgiveness of sins" (Col 1:14): the constant refrain of the New Testament is "in Christ" (note that these actions are being done on us, in us, to us, and for us; we are their recipients and beneficiaries, not the originators or effective agents of these actions). In the book of Revelation the victory is won by the Lamb. In chapter 19, the saints follow in the train of the all-conquering Christ. Like the storied knights of chivalric days, Christ enters the field, triumphs gloriously, and then invites us to share in his victory banquet.

Fourth, warfare imagery *is* used of the vigilance members of the church should exercise toward Satan and for the fortitude with which believers should bear up under Satan's buffeting (1 Pet 5:8; 2 Tim 2:3). But to my knowledge, militaristic imagery is never used to describe the corporate organizational structure of the church or the entities through which it expresses itself. Nor is military imagery used to depict the way the church or its agencies should carry out their witness to Christ's redemptive love.

WARFARE IMAGERY IN THE BALANCE

Physical exercise, we read in 1 Timothy 4:8, is of some value, though that value pales in comparison to weightier considerations. In what ways might warfare imagery likewise be of positive value?

Advantages of Warfare Imagery

I live in the United States, so in the first place, warfare imagery can be a wake-up call for members of U.S. churches who have never considered that God is at variance, indeed at war, with the evil present in their own society and culture. The church of Jesus Christ is not simply a reflection of society; it has its own inner logic that moves counter to the ways of the world, which "lies under the power of the evil one" (1 John 5:19).

Second, warfare imagery serves as a reminder of whose this war really is, God's, and that insofar as Christ's followers are said metaphorically to be engaged in warfare, it is not against fellow mortals, but against Satan, against our passions, and against all spiritual forces and powers that ensnare into evil and enslave in sin (Eph 6:12). Christ's followers will be assailed by Satan and buffeted by forces of evil; being under attack is a stance that we share in common with all people, whether in the church or not.

Third, reminders of the battle raging around and within us are a call for humble yet resolute resistance—in the face of which, we are assured, Satan will flee (Jas 4:7). Note that we are enjoined to resist the devil, but his flight is not due to some power or virtue inherent in us independent of God. Resistance that causes the devil to flee is joined with submission to God. Resistance to the devil is not simply, with steely willpower, saying no to evil; it is at the same time opening our lives to God, to righteousness, and to God's purposes. This pattern occurs throughout Scripture. In sanctification we are set apart from sin and to God, to righteousness, to holiness, to good works that God has ordained for us (e.g., Eph 2:10; Rom 12:9).

Finally, martial images are a call to undergo training, rigor, discipline, and hardship with fortitude (1 Pet 5:8; 2 Tim 2:3) as ones who bear the name of Christ and who look forward to walking in his victory parade (2 Cor 2:14). The soldier who endures through suffering, we are assured, will also reign with Christ (2 Tim 2:3,12). We are armed spiritually, in Paul's extended metaphor, so that we may be able to withstand the onslaughts of the evil one and be found at the end of the day standing firm (Eph 6:10,11,13). Because the victory belongs to Christ, we have confidence not to quail before the onslaughts of the devil, but to "be steadfast, immovable" and to be "always excelling in the work of the Lord" (1 Cor 15:57,58).

DISADVANTAGES OF WARFARE IMAGERY

If military imagery has legitimate uses, what drawbacks might there be in using warfare rhetoric for speaking of the church's mission? Before addressing that question, let us look briefly at the nature of metaphor.

As mentioned previously, imagery and metaphor in the broad sense are not mere accretions to thought, nor are they merely decorative patches added alongside thought in an appliqué fashion. They are means through which we think and are partly constitutive of understanding (Ricoeur 1977; Sacks 1979; Lakoff and Johnson 1980; Quinn 1991). We are well advised, therefore, to attend closely to the metaphors we use, particularly those selected as focal metaphors, lest we forfeit the multifaceted plenitude of New Testament figures for the church, fixating on just one or a few images out of the abundance employed there.

Metaphor and imagery gain their power by inviting listener and reader to join in the task of constructing meaning. Through them readers and listeners are empowered as partners in the quest for meaning. Partners, yes; but not equal partners, at least at the beginning. By the metaphors they choose, authors/speakers nudge readers/listeners to seek meaning in a particular direction. But good metaphors are lively and volatile. Supersaturated with meaning, they overleap bounds and cannot be restrained to a single predefined path (Ricoeur 1976). In the new landscapes metaphors create, readers and listeners are set free to explore terrain never envisioned by the author. Metaphors also harbor an implicit danger: their very brilliance can be overwhelming, cutting deep channels that powerfully constrain thought and impose blinders that cut off deeper insight.

Which Metaphor?

Metaphor gives a bent or slant, a predisposition, a grid that guides perception and interaction. As complex phenomena, warfare and the military have many different facets that can point in many different directions. If a military model is to be adopted, which aspect is germane? What should be zeroed in upon and what left aside? Should it be the military as a model of discipline, focused effort, strategic planning, hierarchical organization, and ability to impose ultimate claims upon attention, energy, and resources? Or should it be the military that ultimately and absolutely subordinates personnel to a stated goal, imposes top-down authority, deadens initiative, and glories in destructive capability? Is the desired military model the one that manifests a "one size mis-fits all" mentality, that by design builds a morally corrosive ambiance, and that seeks to produce interchangeable and dispensable personnel? Certainly not all facets of the military are equally admirable as models for mission agencies and mission conduct.

POTENTIAL PITFALLS OF WARFARE RHETORIC

Modeling discussion of Christian mission on terms supplied by warfare rhetoric has a number of drawbacks. Some potential pitfalls have already been suggested. Here I mention three in particular: foreshortening of vision, fixation on crisis, and misidentification of the enemy.

Foreshortening of Vision

In the United States, young men and now women are commonly inducted into the army right out of high school or soon thereafter. There are many reasons for this, yet one consideration may possibly outweigh all others: they are essentially still unformed by life. They have not yet encountered the seasoning vicissitudes of life that will make them personally and morally less tractable and less malleable in the hands of drill sergeants and "orders from above" hierarchies.

The urgency of war foreshortens many things. Issues that deserve extended reflection receive clipped answers and peremptory orders. The question for us as Christ's servants is whether our presentations of God's purposes fall into the same trap. Do we give pat answers on motivation, programs, and missionary purposes because extended reflection and discussion might disturb people in the pew, might divert or impede the flow of mission recruits, or just might not sell well? What about training? Does the urgency of the task work against adequate and appropriate training, against taking time for personal spiritual formation, against maturing in Christ, against the seasoning that comes with experience in progressive leadership roles? If so, are we in danger of being mired in a wartime urgency trap? (Other motivations can play a role as well, such as the long-recognized American "activism" in mission and the prototypically American enslavement to instant gratification; that is, the impulse to do everything quickly and with immediate emotional impact.)

Fixation on Crisis

Another form of foreshortening of attention and reflection can come through addiction to crisis. When bombs are bursting and GIs are hugging the bottom of their foxholes, no one questions the presence of crisis. It is not a time for disinterested reflective thought! Questions become basic, and orders have to be followed instantly. But operating in a crisis mode can become addictive and, before long, draining. Students of business single out the ability of business leaders to generate a sense of crisis as crucial if they are to have followers and to move institutions in new directions. But they also speak of the need to move beyond crisis to management and institutionalization of core corporate values. Life by continual crisis becomes enervating, and motivation by crisis works for only a limited time before it becomes organizationally as well as psychologically disruptive and counterproductive.

What of mission organizations? Do our management styles support the personal growth of mission personnel for the long haul, or are they focused on getting whatever quick return is possible, knowing that neither field missionaries nor support personnel will be able to hold up for long? What is the coefficient of so-called burnout for mission organizations (Taylor 1997)?

Misidentification of the Enemy

Warfare rhetoric can be used so broadly that it engenders confusion as to whose the battle is—God's, not ours, and who the conqueror is—Christ, not us. It can also lead to misidentification of whom the battle is against. When Paul does use military imagery, he undercuts it in doing so: we do not live, fight, or wage war according to the standards of this world (2 Cor 10:2–5); our enemies are *not* human persons (Eph 6). We and they, *whoever* among all of humanity they may be, have a common enemy in Satan, that old serpent, the devil, and the powers aligned with him. We need to keep clearly in mind that the battle between God and Satan bears both upon us and upon those to whom we go as messengers of the gospel and heralds of God's grace. As mentioned, people created by God—whether Buddhists, Muslims, Hindus, persons with no religious affiliation, or whoever they may be—are not to be treated as our enemies, but as co-assailees, who are also under assault and who are to be extended what aid it is in our power to give. Further, we are to reach out to them with a generous heart.

What steps are evangelical mission organizations taking to give their personnel new language and new images to replace outmoded and inept formulations? What is being done to insure that missionaries' and church members' hearts and minds are stretched, that new vistas on God's grandeur and his program are being opened up for them, rather than letting their vision be circumscribed by time-worn *shibboleths*?

WARFARE VERSUS FAMILY: ENTAILMENTS
FOR HOW WE THINK ABOUT MISSION

A word of caution is in order at this point: militaristic rhetoric has entailments. If individuals are spoken of as targets for Christian witness or a locale as a missionary beachhead or a populace as the focus of a missionary campaign, they are placed rhetorically in an uncomfortable and unenviable position. Who wants to be caught in the sights of a rifle or to be found on the path of an invading army? A neighbor we can accept, a friend we can love, but who wants to find himself or herself as the target in a theater of mission operations?

Militaristic rhetoric has organizational and theological entailments as well. For example, the language of "the two structures of the church," built as it is on a militaristic image of mission societies, bifurcates mission from church. But mission is an activity *of the church*. Mission is not an activity carried out by some organization other than the church and set up according to principles separate from those that infuse the church. Any language that drives a wedge between church and mission is suspect. The church universal organizes itself into many different forms for many different purposes, but all are expressions of the church and all are obligated to manifest the church's intrinsic character. Whatever the forms it takes and whatever the activities it engages in, the church is called upon to embody and show forth the mind, character, and attitude of Jesus the Christ, its Lord, Savior, and coming King (Phil 2:1–15). This is true both in the church's internal character and relations and in its external contacts and witness. The church is invited by God to be a colaborer in God's missional outreach of love to the world; it therefore is missional by its very nature (Baker 2003).

What of the suggestion that in mission organizations as opposed to congregations, individual workers are expendable in light of the goal, just as individual soldiers are during war? Such language comes from a realm of discourse alien to that of the church. The goal of the church is to present everyone perfect in Christ Jesus (Col 1:28). None of Christ's followers are disposable or expendable. This does not mean that they cannot be corrected, instructed, or disciplined, or that in mission agencies questions of fit, capability, and productivity cannot be addressed. But all must be done in a manner that respects and builds up the individual in question and that upholds New Testament values—presented through multiple images—of familiality, belonging, body connectedness, parenting, and nurturance. Whatever the church does in cultivating, caring for, and disciplining missionary workers has to be in harmony or accord with the character of the church.

Partisans of warfare-oriented rhetoric need to take seriously the diminution and attenuation of warfare rhetoric in the Bible. Certainly the book of Revelation is filled with warfare imagery. The war between God and Satan is what that book is about. But in terms of imagery applied to the church and applied to the life of the believer, there is a progressive reduction. First, there is less talk of war in the New Testament than in the Old Testament. Second, there is a weakening of the sense in which it is used. Warfare passages in the Old Testament are meant fairly literally. Elijah put the priests of Baal to death; following Israelite worship of the golden calf, the Levites strapped on real swords; David forced the Moabite prisoners of war to lie on the ground and killed two out of every three. Nobody reads Paul's passage at the end of Ephesians in that sense at all. His references to armament are obviously figures of speech.

In Acts through Revelation, organic, familial, and nurturing imagery is overwhelmingly dominant. Familial imagery—that is, the language of brothers, sisters, family, household—greatly outweighs warfare imagery. Nurturing imagery conditions everything, if indeed it does not set the prevailing affective tone. Our brothers and our fathers cannot be treated as enemies. Our children cannot be dismissed out of hand or have harsh demands imposed upon them as might be done with mere foot soldiers. The relationship is too near and too dear. What consequences should this have for our rhetorical choices and for the care mission agencies extend to laborers in God's vineyard? Use of warfare rhetoric in missions has consequences. Those consequences lie both outside—among the ostensible objects of evangelistic zeal—and inside, in the way laborers in the missionary force are valued and treated. Warfare rhetoric has its apologists, those who defend its use through both example and advocacy. This preliminary sketch of warfare images and rhetoric in the New Testament and in mission self-presentation brings into view some of the caution flags that should surround such use. May our ears become sensitive to the jarring incongruity of sounding forth gospel proclamation in the language of assault.

REFERENCES

Baker, Dwight P. 2003. The scope of mission. *The Covenant Quarterly* (February): 3–12.

Barker, Glenn W., William L. Lane, and J. Ramsey Michaels. 1969. *The New Testament speaks*. New York: Harper & Row.

Bennett, David W. 1993. *Metaphors of ministry: Biblical images for leaders and followers*. Grand Rapids: Baker.

Boyd, Gregory A. 1997. *God at war: The Bible and spiritual conflict*. Downers Grove, IL: InterVarsity Press.

Driver, John. 1997. *Images of the church in mission*. Scottdale, PA: Herald.

Ellis, John. 1978. *Cavalry: The history of mounted warfare*. New York: G. P. Putnam's Sons.

Froude, James Anthony. 1972. *The Spanish story of the Armada and other essays*. New York: Charles Scribner's Sons. First published 1892.

Jobson, Orville D. 1957. *Conquering Oubangui-Chari for Christ*. Winona Lake, IN: Brethren Missionary Herald Co.

Johnson, Paul. 1991. *Modern times: The world from the twenties to the nineties*. Rev. ed. New York: HarperPerennial.

Kotter, John P. 1996. *Leading change*. Boston: Harvard Business School Press.

———, and James L. Heskett. 1992. *Corporate culture and performance*. New York: Free Press.

Lakoff, George, and Mark Johnson. 1980. *Metaphors we live by*. Chicago: University of Chicago Press.

Lane, William L. 1991a. *Hebrews 1–8*. Dallas: Word Books.

———. 1991b. *Hebrews 9–13*. Dallas: Word Books.

Latourette, Kenneth Scott. 1975. *A history of Christianity*. Vol. 1, *To A.D. 1500*. San Francisco: HarperSanFrancisco.

Maxwell, L. E. 1977. *World missions: Total war*. Three Hills, Canada: Prairie Press.

McGavran, Donald A. 1972. Essential evangelism: An open letter to Dr. Hoekendijk. In *Eye of the storm: The great debate in mission*, ed. Donald A. McGavran, 56–66. Waco, TX: Word Books.

Minear, Paul S. 1961. *Images of the church in the New Testament*. London: Lutterworth.

Neill, Stephen. 1986. *A history of Christian missions*. New York: Penguin Books.

Oliver, Roland. 1952. *The missionary factor in East Africa*. New York: Longmans, Green, and Co.

Piper, John. 1993. *Let the nations be glad! The supremacy of God in missions*. Grand Rapids: Baker Books.

Porter, Andrew. 2004. *Religion versus empire? British Protestant missionaries and overseas expansion, 1700–1914*. Manchester: Manchester University Press.

Quinn, Naomi. 1991. The cultural basis of metaphor. In *Beyond metaphor: The theory of tropes in anthropology*, ed. James W. Fernandez, 56–93. Stanford, CA: Stanford University Press.

Ricoeur, Paul. 1976. *Interpretation theory: Discourse and the surplus of meaning*. Fort Worth: Texas Christian University Press.

———. 1977. *The rule of metaphor: Multi-disciplinary studies of the creation of meaning in language*. Toronto: University of Toronto Press.

Rivera, Luis N. 1992. *A violent evangelism*. Louisville, KY: Westminster / John Knox Press.

Sacks, Sheldon, ed. 1979. *On metaphor*. Chicago: University of Chicago Press.

Samarin, William J. 1989. *The black man's burden: African colonial labor on the Congo and Ubangi Rivers, 1880–1900*. Boulder, CO: Westview.

Shenk, Wilbert R. 1995. *Write the vision: The Church renewed*. Valley Forge, PA: Trinity Press.

Siewert, John A., and Edna G. Valdez, eds. 1997. *Mission handbook: 1998–2000; U.S. and Canadian Christian ministries overseas*. 17th ed. Monrovia, CA: MARC.

Skreslet, Stanley H. 2006. *Picturing Christian witness: New Testament images of disciples in mission*. Grand Rapids: Eerdmans.

Stanley, Brian. 1990. *The Bible and the flag: Protestant missions and British imperialism in the nineteenth and twentieth centuries*. Leicester, England: Apollos.

Taylor, William, ed. 1997. *Too valuable to lose: Exploring the causes and cures of missionary attrition.* Pasadena: William Carey Library.

Trevor-Roper, H. R. 1972. *The crisis of the seventeenth century: Religion, the Reformation, and social change.* New York: Harper & Row.

Tuchman, Barbara W. 1978. *A distant mirror: The calamitous 14th century.* New York: Knopf.

Wagner, C. Peter. 1996. *Confronting the powers: How the New Testament church experienced the power of strategic-level spiritual warfare.* Ventura, CA: Regal Books.

Wallace, Anthony F. C. 1956a. Mazeway resynthesis: A bio-cultural theory of religious inspiration. *Transactions of the New York Academy of Sciences* 18, no. 5: 626–38.

———. 1956b. Revitalization movements. *American Anthropologist* 58, no. 2: 264–81.

Winter, Ralph D. 1974. The two structures of God's redemptive mission. *Missiology: An International Review* 2, no. 1: 121–39.

———, and Steven C. Hawthorne, eds. 2009. *Perspectives on the world Christian movement: A reader.* 4th ed. Pasadena: William Carey Library.

Womack, Stephen. 2000. Recruitment crisis. *Evangelical Missions Quarterly* 36, no. 1: 7–8.

Wright, Louis B. 1970. *Gold, glory, and the gospel.* New York: Atheneum.

Zook, David H. Jr., and Robin Higham. 1966. *A short history of warfare.* New York: Twayne.

CHAPTER 2

SPIRITUAL REALITIES IN THE GOSPELS AND IMPLICATIONS FOR DISCIPLESHIP AMONG ORAL LEARNERS IN NORTHEAST THAILAND

MARK CALDWELL

Grandma Somlee was in the midst of her most vivid nightmare. Crushing pressure upon her chest convinced her that angry spirits had come to squeeze the life breath from her. Just as she felt all must end she saw a white light and heard a voice, which said, calmly, "Do not be afraid. I am coming to you." She had no idea who it was. The next week two Thai believers came to her from the direction of the white light and began to talk. She accepted their message of freedom through Jesus Christ. That night her nightmare returned again but at the peak of her physical pain she cried out, "Jesus, help me!" The pressure and pain was released immediately. When she woke the next day she had no further memory of the medicinal recipes which had formerly employed and enslaved her. She purged her yard of any remnants of the herbal plants much to the ridicule of neighbors. Later she told them, "The spirits were always hungry and never satisfied but God always wants to give. Now I am free." (de Neui, 2003, 137–38)

John Nevius states candidly that when he went to China, he went with an attitude that belief in demons was a horrible superstition and mental illness (1897, 9). However, it did not take long for Nevius to see the reality of the spiritual enemy he was dealing with in the Chinese people he worked among. He eventually sent out a survey asking for the feedback of other Christian workers regarding their encounters with demons and demon possession. He was overwhelmed with the response. As a result, Nevius wrote the book *Demon Possession and Allied Themes* (ibid.). Suffice it to say that Nevius the skeptic became a believer in the reality of the "spiritual forces of evil" (Eph 6:12 ESV).

My experience in working with the Isaan (pronounced *Esaan*) people in northeast Thailand has been similar. When it comes to spiritual realities, the Isaan people often have a "show me" attitude similar to Jesus' interaction with many people in the Gospels (Luke 5:1–11; John 4:40–42; 21:24–29). One of the first questions I ask Isaan believers in Thailand is, what drew them to follow Christ? I can summarize their responses over the last twenty years in three statements: (1) the radical change seen in a friend or family member's Chistian faith; (2) a supernatural healing of themselves or another; (3) their encounter with a supernatural being who spoke to them in a dream or vision.

The latter two encounters were beyond my experience before coming to Thailand. However, as I look at the four New Testament gospels, encounters with supernatural beings were not strange to Jesus or those people with whom he lived (e.g., Matt 4:24; 8:16; 9:32; Mark 3:22; Luke 4:41). Neither was it strange for Jesus and his contemporaries to be involved in supernatural healings, visions, and dreams (e.g., Matt 1:20; 2:12,13; 8:3; Mark 1:41; Luke 1:11,14; 7:10). Jesus prefaced his Great Commission to "go . . . make disciples of all nations" (Matt 28:19 ESV) with "All authority in heaven and on earth has been given to me" (Matt 28:18 ESV). Jesus understood that his disciples would be dependent on God's power as they encountered Satan's opposition to this command (Blomberg, 1992, 5). It is important for those of a folk Buddhist background to know that all powers are subservient to our God. (Folk Buddhist is a term applied to those Isaan/Thai who mix the teachings of Buddhism with other religions and beliefs such as Hinduism, animism, astrology, and materialism.)

Understanding the Isaan culture and worldview, and, as much as possible, working through their cultural norms, symbols, beliefs, and relational values, is foundational to enabling the Isaan to hear, understand, and desire to become disciples of Christ. One of the mission terms often used by those doing cross-cultural ministry is "contextualization." The thought behind much of the contextualization effort is that if we can understand the context and culture of the people we are working amongst and share the biblical truth with them in a way that fits their cultural context, God will work. The weakness of the contextualization effort often is in the assumption that if we can understand and adapt the correct doctrine or truth of the Bible into the local context, people will believe (Hiebert 1994, 84–85). Many oral learners need more than doctrine in written form to believe in a new faith. "Oral learner" is a general term that refers to those whose primary means of learning is through oral communication, rather than written (see Thornton 2013, 2).

Despite an amazing Thai religious mixture (Kitiarsa 2012, 1–2), most of the Isaan people in Thailand call themselves Buddhists. However, most Isaan have very little doctrinal understanding of Buddhism (Komin 1990, 181–82), and Buddhism has been in Thailand for over one thousand years. Buddhism provides an overall philosophy for life and death, but in their daily lives many Isaan are involved with the spirit world (often referred to as animism—an oral tradition present in Thailand long before Buddhism). While helping Isaan people understand the teaching of the Bible is very important, most Isaan people are not interested initially in more information or doctrine about Christianity, particularly in written form. What does attract Isaan interest is someone's experience of God's power in their lives.

Isaan people need to hear (and see presented) that God spoke in Genesis and all kinds of things came into being—before any of it was written down. The large majority of Isaan people read very little (Robert and Robert 2006, 41). Therefore, the primary way to touch their hearts is through their senses and everyday life experience. As John 1:14 states, "And the Word became flesh and dwelt among us, and we have seen his glory, glory as of the only Son from the Father, full of grace and truth" (ESV). Jesus incarnated, or demonstrated, God and his truth by living it out in his daily relationships, ceremonies, and worldview of his Jewish neighbors. Because of their oral, relational culture, it follows that Isaan people need to see God's love and heart for others in those who follow him (the church). While the written Word and its truths must be taught to Isaan disciples, it must be taught so that the Isaan people experience Christ in their relationships, communities, rituals, and arts.

This paper will summarize three key times in Jesus' ministry when he addressed the spiritual realities of being his disciple. Applications from these summaries will be made to the oral learners of northeast Thailand.

SPIRITUAL REALITY OF TEMPTATION AND ITS IMPLICATIONS

It had been another challenging morning of learning the Thai language for my wife and me as new missionaries in Thailand. We returned home in the afternoon from language school and were ready to enjoy some time with our young son. Then a young Thai woman my wife had met previously in our neighborhood came to our door and asked if she could talk with us. We welcomed her into our house and began to listen to her story. After almost thirty years I still remember her story as one that told me I was in for a steep learning curve in understanding Thai people. She said that she had been to Australia to study the year before. While in Australia a Western person approached our neighbor and began to share her Christian faith with our neighbor from a tract. Our Thai neighbor listened politely. After a while the Westerner asked our Thai friend if she wanted to pray a prayer of acceptance of Christ. Our Thai friend humbly followed the Westerner's lead in prayer.

Then our neighbor shocked us with her question: "Now that I am back in Thailand, can I still be a good Buddhist and go to the temple to worship?" As my wife and I talked with her, what became apparent was that the primary reason this lady prayed with the Westerner was to help both of them not "lose face" by causing possible conflict through disagreement. What also became clear was that although our neighbor did not believe she was a Christian and had no intention of following through on her prayer, there was a power in her spoken "prayer" in Australia that she was afraid would interfere with her Thai relationships and Buddhist worship. The important thing to our neighbor was to be able to join her family and friends in the activities of the temple while respecting the spiritual powers around her.

There is a tale of two kingdoms in this young woman's story that is central to the spiritual struggle of any would-be disciple of Jesus. One kingdom is about our neighbor's focus on herself, her family, what she wanted from this life *now*, and her fear of spiritual powers. The second kingdom is the one our neighbor was challenged to join (at least intellectually). In this second kingdom there is one King, who is Creator of the universe and humanity, and who works within us to make us like himself. While it may not be politically correct to speak of spiritual warfare today, there is certainly a battle going on between these two rival kingdoms in Scripture, Isaan, and throughout creation. Most of our Isaan people are more aware and sensitive to the reality of this spiritual struggle than those of us from the West. Examples of this kingdom battle on both a cosmic and more personal basis are seen in Matthew 4:1–11; Mark 1:12–20; and Luke 4:1–13. I will summarize some of the spiritual reality and applications for oral learners from the Gospel accounts: first, of Jesus' wilderness temptation; and second, in the calling of Jesus' first disciples.

Jesus' Wilderness Temptation and Trust in God

Jesus' wilderness temptation is a cosmic conflict of kingdoms that most Isaan folk Buddhists are sensitive to, even if they don't understand who the major players are. It is a story that should be put to song, drama, and memory for the Isaan to hear its truth. The battle is between trust in God as our Creator and provider, versus trust in Satan and/or oneself for what one desires in life. The Gospel writers appear to warn us of impending spiritual conflict that comes when we who were previously bound by sin and Satan publicly pledge allegiance in baptism to Christ as our new Lord (Blomberg 1992, 5). It should also be noted that it is the Holy Spirit who leads Jesus to face his tempter (Matt 4:1), the word of God that Jesus uses to do battle with Satan's temptations (Matt 4:4,7,10), and the angels of God who minister to Jesus after the wilderness temptation (Matt 4:11). Jesus' and Scriptures' promises confirm that God will never leave or forsake us in the midst of the spiritual battles of life (Deut 31:8; Matt 28:20; John 14:17,18).

The spiritual struggle seen in Scripture is not just a battle between good and evil spirits, or between cultural and personal desires.

As Arnold states, "The Bible teaches that there are three forms of evil influence that exert their power over the lives of people to lead them into temptation and away from God. These three enemies are simply described as the world, the flesh, and the devil" (1992; cf. John 12:31; Eph 2:1–3). The "flesh" is defined as the "inner inclination to do evil" (Blomberg 1992, 5). "Flesh" in this sense is what we personally hunger and lust after to satisfy our desires, versus God and his desires for us. "The world" Arnold defines as the

> ungodly aspects of culture, peer pressure, values, traditions, "what is in," "what is uncool," customs, philosophies, and attitudes. The world represents the prevailing worldview assumptions of the day that stand contrary to the biblical understanding of reality and biblical values.

For many Isaan there is also the cultural struggle that says "to be Isaan is to be Buddhist, and to be Christian is to be Western." The contextual quest is how to help the Isaan see they can be Christian without sacrificing their cultural identity. Finally, there is the primary tempter to evil in Matthew 4:1–11—the devil, or Satan. The Isaan people are very aware and afraid of the legion of spirits through whom Satan works, and to some extent the systems and structures used by them for spiritual oppression.

In the three temptations presented in the wilderness narrative of Matthew 4 and Luke 4, Jesus is modeling for his followers how to deal with temptation and tempter. In short, the first temptation is the devil testing a famished Jesus' pride to prove his identity as God's Son by turning stones to bread (Matt 4:3). The second temptation is for Jesus to jump off the temple and tempt God to save him, all to gain the acclaim of the crowds (Matt 4:4–7). The final temptation is to gain the power of a kingdom at the price of falling down in worship before a false god (Matt 4:8–11).

When Jesus answers Satan's temptations with quotes from Deuteronomy, Jesus is saying that he has come to create "a new Israel" (Blomberg 1992, 44). This new people will consist of those who obey God in relationship through faith, love, and God's Spirit within us, rather than disbelieve God in doubt and disobedience of religious law.

Understanding this story is crucial for a new believer whom we are asking to follow Jesus as a disciple. The Isaan people are very aware of malevolent spirits. All three of these temptations—pride, acclaim, and power—are enticing to all people. The temptation for most folk Buddhists is to try to use these spirits for their own gain rather than trust in the power of God to provide, overcome, and walk away from the temptations. The foundation for walking away from these temptations and false gods (beyond the power of God within us) is the understanding that just as Jesus was proclaimed God's beloved (Matt 3:17), so are we (John 3:16; Rom 5:8). Just as Jesus is given God's Spirit for guidance and power to overcome temptation (Matt 4:1), so are we (John 14:16,17,26; Acts 2). When Isaan people understand that we are created in the image of God (Gen 1:27), and God is moving heaven and hell to restore us to right relationship with himself through Jesus, this is good news.

Immediately following Jesus' temptation, he calls his disciples to a new relationship and understanding of God (Mark 1:14–20). Many of Jesus' initial disciples were fishermen who were probably oral learners. Thus, Jesus' challenge of discipling these men should be instructive to us in discipling oral learners today.

Jesus' Call to Discipleship (Mark 1:14–20)

Jesus' call to his first disciples begins by stating that he was "proclaiming the good news of God" (Mark 1:14). It should be noted that Jesus does this orally, and with great simplicity. Simplicity of communication is important if we expect oral learners to grasp and repeat what they've learned with others (versus slick, expensive written material filled with diagrams and principles). Jesus begins defining this good news by stating that the "kingdom of God has come near" (1:15). Thus, Jesus is telling us that there is a King who created and sustains this world, and his kingdom is not simply "near" but "has come" (in the person of Jesus).

Moreover, if we want to be a part of God's kingdom, there are some requirements that we must follow. First, we must "repent" (1:15). Much could be said in defining and illustrating the terms in this passage. Basically the idea with "repent" is doing an about-face from following king me, to following King Jesus. All of this movement from self to

God is grace- and Spirit-driven, with increasing levels of commitment based on response and obedience (Hull 2006, locations 3006–25). After calling for repentence, Jesus calls his would-be disciples to "believe the good news" (1:15). The good news is that we are being offered an opportunity to be restored from sin and death to the relationship we originally had with our Creator in the beginning. Our part in this miracle of grace is trusting in God and his provision, much as Jesus did in his wilderness temptation. Moreover, in following Jesus, the triune God is with us to enable us to overcome Satan, sin, and spirits.

Beyond the call to repent and believe, Jesus also challenges his disciples to "come, follow me" (1:17), allowing Jesus to work through them to draw others to God. The challenge of Jesus here is not just an intellectual one, but it involves a physical obedience. Oral learners are normally people of action, who learn by seeing and doing. Jesus tells them and us that we will learn what it means to be a part of God's kingdom by following him obediently. Repent, believe, and come are all action words that an oral learner can relate to, especially when they understand who the King is who commands them to do this.

Important for oral learners in this passage is the relational context of Jesus' call to them. As was the case with the young Thai woman mentioned earlier, the security and hope of most oral, rural people is in their family and community. Thus, to ask them to commit to a God without the support or understanding of their security network is a major barrier. Jesus was John the Baptist's cousin, and we know John introduced his followers to Jesus and encouraged them to follow Jesus (John 1:35–37; 3:25,36). Further, Jesus invites two sets of brothers to be disciples, at least one of whom was fishing with their father and friends (Mark 1:16–20). Thus, while Jesus asked these men to make radical commitments, he brought their family and community networks in on their decisions. Jesus also visited and healed Peter's mother-in-law in their home (Matt 8:14,15). Jesus was aware of the spiritual reality of family and friends in making spiritual commitments. As a result, Jesus worked to make these people who were important relationally to his disciples aware of what was happening, and hopefully draw them to make spiritual commitments themselves.

The importance of a disciple's family and community is why we want to work to help their family understand and involve them in these spiritual commitments where possible. One ceremony that is a great opportunity to do this in Thailand is baptism.

Jesus' "See and Do" Training

A number of years ago I had the privilege of working with father "Be" in rural, northeast Thailand. Father Be was poor, with a fourth-grade education and a family of seven adult children when I met him. He lived out in the middle of nowhere and wanted help in starting a house church there. As I began to know him better, father Be told me some of his story. He had been one of the village drunks who drank and gambled what little money he had, driving his wife to the point of a nervous breakdown and his children to hunger. However, after his children were grown, father Be's adult daughter and husband had returned home and shared the gospel with her family. Father Be said this was the truth and hope that he had been looking for. He believed, and God began to radically change his life. When he shared his faith in his village, people listened. because they knew that the changes they saw in father Be's life were supernatural.

In contrast to father Be was Pastor See. See was a young, gifted preacher and communicator of the gospel whom I worked with as a new missionary in starting a new church in Bangkok. See had also grown up poor and had moved to Bangkok to seek a better life, where he became a Christian. However, within two years See drove off the members of what had been a promising young church by asking people for money to fund his addiction to gambling. Pastor See later left the ministry.

When we talk about spiritual realities among people—in Isaan or elsewhere—father Be and See are two examples of different responses to discipleship. Chan states that "being a disciple of Jesus Christ means that we learn from Him, fellowship with Him, and obey everything He commands us" (Chan and Beuving 2012, 14). In training the twelve disciples, Jesus himself repeatedly emphasized these three key areas of (1) relationship with God, (2) obedience to Jesus as our teacher (Lawless 2002, 45–49), and (3) learning and growing in faith as a discipler of others (which includes evangelism).

Discipleship that begins with a relationship of repentance and faith, and grows through loving obedience, will lead to disciples who grow as they disciple others. One of Jesus' best examples of training disciples for spiritual realities (with the context of the previously mentioned relationship to God, obedience, and learning) is seen in Jesus' sending out the seventy-two disciples (Luke 10:1–23). The thrust of Jesus' mission to the disciples is to be on the offense in spiritual battle with Satan, demons, and darkness (10:1–3,17,18). As he sent his disciples out, Jesus instructed them that the focus of their message is that "the kingdom of God has come near" (10:9)—a simple, reproducible message. The healings and casting out of demons not only confirmed Jesus' kingdom message, but demonstrated God's power over sin and Satan (Pennington 2012, 199).

Jesus also emphasized the importance of the disciples' relationship with God through his emphasis on God being the "Lord of the harvest" and their need to call upon him in prayer for other workers (10:2). Further, Jesus taught the disciples to depend on God to provide food and housing through their respondents (10:7). Finally, Jesus prepared his disciples for the disappointment of rejection (10:10,11), telling them that it was God's kingdom many of their listeners would reject, not the disciples themselves (10:16). By these words of insight Jesus was working to overcome how Satan would use the despair the disciples might feel from the rejection/opposition of those with whom they shared God's good news.

Later, the disciples returned from their mission rejoicing over the power of God at work in the "submission" of demons (10:17). Jesus' training of the twelve developed further boldness and faith as the disciples began to believe that they could do kingdom ministry. Jesus had a twofold response to the seventy disciples' successful mission. First, he underlined the spiritual battle and defeat of Satan and his powers when God's people declare the kingdom in faith and the power of God (10:18). For Isaan/Thai who often cower before evil spirits, this victory over the demonic is an important message for them to hear. Second, Jesus reminded the disciples that the ultimate source of their joy was not seeing the power of God, but knowing that their own salvation was assured through the grace and power of God. This also is an important message to hear for those who seek personal value in power and success, magic incantations, or obedience to religious law. The response to the disciples' message denied Satan of those who were previously his minions (10:20; Arnold 1992, 84). Luke 10:21 states that Jesus was "full of joy" from the returning disciples' victory. As Larson states, "Up to this point, the battle was between Satan and Jesus. Because of the works of the seventy, Satan experienced a mighty fall" (1983, 182). The struggle against Satan's dominion over this world had now expanded to Jesus' multiplying disciples who were forming a new, powerful community—the beginning of the church.

It is beyond the focus of this paper to speak about discipleship beyond the Gospels, but for our Isaan folk Buddhists I would be remiss if I did not say something about the importance of the church. The reality for many of our Isaan believers is that in a country where less than 0.5 percent are Christians (and most of these are located in the urban areas), many Isaan Christians feel very alone in their Christian faith. Many Isaan people have made a decision to follow Christ without the support of family and community. As mentioned previously, this is very difficult for rural, oral learners who depend upon family and community for their identity and support. Therefore, the invitation to join the church as a new "family" (Eph 3:14,15; Heb 3:6; 10:21–23) is quite important for new oral believers. The church's embracing the new believer in a way that demonstrates to them Jesus' command to love God and neighbor is crucial (while balancing this with love and respect for their natural family).

I was reminded of this recently in a story of a fellow missionary from another part of Thailand. It seems that there was a young Thai woman who believed in Christ, but whose mother forbade her to go to church. The missionary's church was not able to overcome the mother's opposition. However, one of the girl's friends from another church soon began to disciple the young believer and help her mother at her business. In an email to the author dated August 2014, Tim Owens wrote,

> [The friend] would sometimes come home and spend
> Friday night with the new believer, and they would
> study the Bible in the new believer's bedroom. Then in

the morning before the discipler left she would hang out at the family store on the first floor of their shop house . . . and help the mother sell for a while. After a few months of this, the mother was having good conversations with this gal, and the discipler would also bring Christian friends by to the store who were the mother's age. The mother began to anticipate and enjoy their visits. After a while she was open to read the Bible with them and eventually came to faith. Where the Body [church] went, the Head of the Body [Christ] showed up. The mother was getting a look at Jesus through the Body, and she didn't have to join anything or go to another religious meeting to get a look at Him. He came to her. The mother didn't like Christianity initially as a religion that was foreign to her. But she loved Jesus!

As often was the case with Jesus and his disciples, many times people learn more from what we do and how we treat them than what we teach and say. This was particularly the case in what Jesus' disciples learned from Jesus' death and resurrection.

LEARNING THROUGH DEATH AND RESURRECTION

Many years ago a woman was brought into the Baptist hospital in eastern Thailand and soon thereafter died. Her husband soon arrived at the hospital, and when he heard the news of his wife's tragic death, he was heartbroken. The chaplain at the hospital spent time with the husband, trying to console him, give encouragement, and share his Christian faith and hope. The husband responded that if the God of the chaplain would bring his wife back to life, he would believe and become a Christian also. The chaplain prayed for the wife and the husband and went on to visit others in the hospital, thinking he had done all he could do in this situation. Soon some very nervous nurses called the doctor at the hospital and told him they were hearing some strange noises from the hospital morgue. The doctor went and investigated and found to his and the rest of the staff's utter surprise that the noise was coming from where they had recently placed the body of the woman from the accident. They led the healed woman out to the amazed and joyous husband. It was a joyous occasion of thanking God for a miracle. The hospital staff was just as amazed when they went out the following week to visit the husband and wife, and the couple wanted nothing to do with the Western God and religion. The husband was thrilled to have his wife back. According to missionary Jack Kinnison who wrote the author in 2009, the husband had what he wanted and did not want to upset family and neighbors by talking about a new religion.

The disbelief in Jesus by many in the Gospels, despite his miracles, should tell us that there is more involved in faith than experiencing a miracle. Central is seeing the power of God changing a receptive heart to seek a new King and kingdom.

Hiebert notes that animists, because of their focus on everyday life, are more

> interested in issues of power and success than truth
> and logical consistency . . . Moreover, there are four
> human problems that underlie most folk religious be-
> liefs and practices: 1) the desire for meaningful life
> and the problems death raises for the living; 2) the
> desire for the good life, and the threat of calamity;
> 3) the need for guidance and security in the midst of
> daily unknowns; 4) the desire for right in the midst of
> wrong. (Hiebert, Shaw, and Tienou, 1999, 77–79)

Thus, when working with animistic folk Buddhists like the Isaan, our lives and message need to address the problems of death, calamity, uncertainty, and injustice. The ceremony of baptism can be a good picture of many of these problems and how Christ helps us overcome them.

Death, calamity, uncertainty, and injustice would be a good beginning summary of the disciples' experience of Jesus' trial and crucifixion. Satan's power to deceive, destroy (Luke 24:21; e.g., the disciples' hopes and dreams), and kill are front and center in the trial and crucifixion of Jesus. However, crises and trials initiated by spiritual struggle are often critical in the development of disciples and God's kingdom (Bruce 1971, 148). As Boyd states about the crucifixion, "It seems that God used Satan's insatiable lust for more (viz., his desire to capture the Son) to take away what Satan had already acquired (his captives)" (Boyd 1997, 256). This is seen in the life of Peter.

Peter is someone whom many Isaan could identify with—rural, impetuous, and without much formal training. Thus, it should be helpful for an oral learner to look at how Jesus molded Peter as a disciple, particularly as a result of Jesus' death and resurrection. In Jesus' death and resurrection, Peter experienced a death to his own dreams of self-fulfillment and a resurrection to a new dream and life. In the gift of the Holy Spirit, Peter (and we) experienced the presence and power of God within to live out this new life. This is the spiritual reality that any disciple must experience (Matt 16:21–25; Luke 14:25–34).

One of the first pictures we see of Peter's initial character in the Gospels is his recognition of his lack of belief in Jesus when called upon to go back out and fish some more after a night of fishing in which he had caught nothing (Luke 5:1–11). Later, it is impetuous Peter who overcomes his fear of the storm and walks on water in faith toward Jesus—before fear finally gets him wet (Matt 14:28–30). In a dramatic struggle between faith and fear, God reveals Jesus' identity to Peter (Matt 16:16,17). Almost immediately afterwards Jesus condemns Peter as Satan's tempter of Jesus (Matt 16:23). Finally, despite Jesus' prediction that all his disciples would desert him, Peter boldly states that he is willing to die for Jesus. Jesus tells Peter that he will deny Jesus three times, and that is exactly what Peter did—fleeing his accusers in despair (Luke 22:33,34,54–62).

From this picture of Peter we see a bold, religious follower of Jesus who believes Jesus is the long-awaited Jewish Messiah and political king. Peter does all he can to follow Jesus while looking for his place in Jesus' kingdom. But during times of crisis and pressure, Peter allows his fear for self to overrule his faith in God. In short, Peter is a great example of the spiritual struggle of many people who prefer to rely on their own abilities and resources to follow spiritual realities until they face a power or problem that they cannot control.

After Jesus' crucifixion, when Peter was at his lowest emotionally and spiritually, the resurrected Jesus meets Peter while he was fishing. Instead of condemnation and anger at Peter's betrayal, Jesus instead offers Peter forgiveness, relationship, and opportunity to serve (John 21:10–22).

Peter's life and faith are transformed by the love of Christ, the call to follow, and the power of the Holy Spirit. After Pentecost, the Peter who fled in fear before the Roman and Jewish powers is transformed by God's Spirit into a powerful, Spirit-led leader in the church.

Jesus often used metaphors to teach about the kingdom life. One of those metaphors that Jesus used (which relates particularly to rural people's life) to help his disciples understand the power he was offering them is a yoke (Matt 11:25–30). David Platt, in speaking of Jesus' final command to make disciples of the nations (Matt 28:18–20), asks how Jesus could lay such an enormous burden upon us. The answer is found, he says, in understanding this metaphor that "my yoke is easy and my burden is light" (Matt 11:30) (Platt 2013, locations 116–25). Similar to the verse in Matthew 28:18, where Jesus says that God has given him "all authority in heaven and on earth," in Matthew 11:27 Jesus says that "all things have been handed over to me by my Father" (ESV). Thus, Jesus is sharing with his disciples how they can experience God's power and authority in their lives. It should be noted that Jesus is also addressing a Jewish people wearied not only by sin but by Pharisaic law that Satan used to oppress them (i.e., the burden of "heavy labor" that religious law causes [Blomberg 1992, 169] and many Buddhists can relate to). Jesus then tells them to "come to me . . . take my yoke upon you and learn from me" (11:28,29).

Jesus' invitation to "*come* . . . take my yoke" (italics added) is not just an invitation for the disciples to understand or agree with Jesus' teaching. Rather, by being "yoked" to Jesus we first *submit* to his direction of our lives. Second, we *trust in God's Word and promised presence* to overcome the evil one. Third, in *relational obedience* we allow the life of the Spirit to flow into us as the branches do with the vine. Finally, we *receive and go out in Jesus' and the Spirit's power* and authority as his disciples. These are four responses of Jesus' disciples to his call to "follow me" as he showed them the way. Today oral learners can overcome the spiritual realities around them also. As they see this reality modeled and are invited into a church family that invites them to "come . . . trust . . . obey . . . receive and go out in the Spirit's power," disciples are made and God's kingdom comes.

CONCLUSION

This paper has summarized three crucial times in Jesus' ministry when he addressed the spiritual realities of the life of a disciple. Applications from these summaries were made to help oral learners learn and grow as disciples of Christ in the midst of spiritual opposition. Jesus' example in developing oral learners as disciples was through simple, contextualized ministry dependent upon the Holy Spirit to lead, empower, and transform obedient followers.

REFERENCES

Arnold, Clinton E. 1992. *Powers of darkness: Principalities and powers in Paul's letters*. Colorado Springs: InterVarsity Press.

Blomberg, Craig L. 1992. *Matthew*. Logos ed., vol. 22. Nashville: Broadman & Holman.

Boyd, Gregory A. 1997. *God at war*. Downers Grove, IL: InterVarsity Press.

Bruce, A. B. 1971. *The training of the twelve*. Grand Rapids: Kregel.

Chan, Francis, and Mark Beuving. 2012. *Multiply: Disciples making disciples*. Colorado Springs: David C. Cook.

de Neui, Paul H. 2003. Contextualization with Thai folk Buddhists. In *Sharing Jesus in the Buddhist world*, ed. David Lim and Steve Spaulding, 121–46. Pasadena: William Carey Library.

Hiebert, Paul G. 1994. *Anthropological reflections on missiological issues*. Grand Rapids: Baker Books.

———. Daniel R. Shaw, and Tite Tienou. 1999. *Understanding folk religion*. Grand Rapids: Baker Books.

Hull, Bill. 2006. *Jesus Christ, disciplemaker*. Grand Rapids: Baker Books. Kindle edition.

Kitiarsa, Pattana. 2005. Beyond syncretism: Hybridization of popular religion in contemporary Thailand. *Journal of Southeast Asian Studies* 36, no. 3 (October): 461–87.

———. 2012. *Mediums, monks, and amulets: Thai popular Buddhism today*. Chiang Mai: Silkworm Books.

Komin, Suntaree. 1990. *Psychology of the Thai people*. Bangkok: Research Center, National Institute of Development Administration.

Larson, Bruce. 1983. *The communicator's commentary.* Vol. 3. Waco, TX: Word Books.

Lawless, Chuck. 2002. *Discipled warriors: Growing healthy churches that are equipped for spiritual warfare.* Grand Rapids: Kregel.

Nevius, John L. 1897. *Demon possession and allied themes: Phenomena of our own times.* London: George Redway.

Pennington, Jonathan T. 2012. *Reading the Gospels wisely: A narrative and theological introduction.* Grand Rapids: Baker Academic. E-book ed.

Platt, David. 2013. *Follow me: A call to die, a call to live.* Carol Stream, IL: Tyndale House.

Robert, G. Lamar, and Chongchit Sripun Robert. 2006. Cultural and religious perceptions of the Isan people of northeast Thailand. Unpublished study, International Mission Board, Southern Baptist Convention.

Smith, Donald K. 1992. *Creating understanding.* Grand Rapids: Zondervan.

Stein, R. H. 1992. *Luke.* Logos ed., vol. 24. Nashville: Broadman & Holman.

Tambiah, Stanley J. 1970. *Buddhism and the spirit cults in northeast Thailand.* Cambridge: Cambridge University Press.

Thornton, Phil. 2013. Contextual teaching: Changes in content and culture. *Evangelical Missions Quarterly* 49, no. 3 (July). 342–48.

CHAPTER 3

BUDDHIST SPIRITUAL REALITIES: DIVINING AND DISCERNING THE FUTURE

ALEX G. SMITH

During the 2014 midyear World Cup play-offs in Brazil, diviners from around the globe, including Buddhist Asia, attempted to predict the winner by observing the actions of animals like China's panda bear, dogs, and even an octopus in Germany! But nowhere is fortune-telling more avidly active than Mandalay, Myanmar, both along the streets and on the climb to the Buddhist temples at the top of the nearby mountain.

A universal felt need among peoples of all societies throughout the world is the question of comprehending the imponderable, discovering the unknown, and projecting the unpredictable—particularly as it relates to death and guidance for the future. To help folk Buddhists answer these questions, a plethora of diviners, mediums, advisor-counsellors, and soothsayers exist, including Buddhist monks.

Fear of the spirit world and of the future is not uncommon in Buddhist Asia. This is illustrated in the following account from Mongolia, recorded in a missionary's prayer letter. During August 2014, an indigenous Christian, originally from Gobi-Altai, proclaimed the gospel to his people. Formerly, he "grew up as a herder, believing the same things that these people believed" (Stephens and Lin 2014, 1). He encouraged new believers to be baptized. One former Buddhist man, who said he "has given up all fortune-telling" (ibid.), helped prepare a baptismal pool in the tiny shallow stream. This man's father was a Buddhist lama who taught his son the secrets of divining as a shaman. Though the son did not become a formal lama, he practiced the shamanic trade so well, in fact, that his fellow folk herders regarded him to be a lama. The night before the baptisms, the missionaries experienced "evil, scary dreams" (ibid.). Next morning they taught about Creator God, prayed, and encouraged the followers. It had been two years since these Mongolians had believed. They had received no further teaching. Nor did any churches exist in that area yet. That Sunday the former fortune-teller declared "he would not be baptized as he did not want to offend the river god or 'god of the underworld'" (ibid.). Since his wife had not slept well, she too was afraid to be baptized. Another herdsman fearfully declared "his father had drowned in this river" (ibid.). In spite of their prevailing fears, the Mongolian evangelist called the new believers to be baptized. Quite a number of local folk Buddhists sat on the stream's bank as spectators. Suddenly, the wife of the former fortune-teller boldly stepped out into the waters, followed by two other women and one man. This kind of spiritual tension, fear, conflict, and concern for future consequences is commonly typical, particularly across Buddhist Asia.

Buddha primarily ignored the spirit world vividly displayed in Buddhist cosmology. He believed gods, *devas*, spirits, titans, and demons all had to go through the cycle of life (*samsara*) to overcome karma in their processing toward attaining Nirvana. Nevertheless, an 1886 Burmese diagram of Buddhist cosmology included a pavilion for *nats* (guardian spirits, like Thai *chao thi*) and also sun and moon indicating astrological connections. Surrounding the ancient Shwedagon Pagoda are shrines for the *nats*, and auspicious astrological posts for planetary days of the week. Like this example, folk Buddhists all over Asia integrated the spirit world into their Buddhist worldview and perennial practices. This is not unlike decadent Dark Age Europe in the times of Calvin when "impiety so stalked abroad that almost no doctrine of religion was pure from admixture, no ceremony free from error, no part, however minute, of divine worship untarnished by superstition" (Calvin and Sadoleto 1976, 74–75).

On August 18, 2014, GMT BBC World News reported searching afresh for a Burmese Buddhist temple bell lost in the opaque, muddy Irrawaddy River near Yangon, Myanmar. Produced in the fifteenth century, the three-hundred-ton bell is reputed to be the largest cast bell in the world. It sank some four hundred years ago while being transported on a river raft from the famous Shwedagon Pagoda in Yangon. Unfortunately, the huge bell fell off the raft, sinking into the murky depths. Over the years all searches failed to locate it. On BBC, a Burmese shaman, reflecting the views of monks, declared their common opinion that "supernatural forces from the Buddhist spirit world are stopping the discovery of the bell" (BBC America 2014).

Whether in the ancient past or in modern times divination, discernment, and decisive determination identifies and highlights Buddhists' felt need for projecting into the future. While setting forth some general discussion on spiritual realities and powers, this paper will primarily focus on discussing divining and associated means to discern the future.

ANTHROPOLOGICAL AND CULTURAL PERSPECTIVES

From his three-tiered model (religion-magic-science) Paul Hiebert expounded his theory of the excluded middle (1982). This often is a problem for Western Christian missionaries, whose ethnocentric categories do not coincide with those of the spirit-oriented Majority World. Ignoring the central area of magic, they perceive a worldview of expanded science topped by religion. Effective missiologists take into account more of Hiebert's threefold model when working with folk Buddhists. Particularly in this area of magic, the influence of complex spiritual realities affects the planet's Buddhist billion.

In some ways classical Buddhist perspectives, particularly among monks in the *sangha*, are similar to the Western inadequate model. Gods, heavenly beings, and spiritual realities including powers, principalities, and spiritual forces are deemphasized in Buddha's fundamental teaching. Everything is simplified in karma as the cause of all effects amidst total impermanence and emptiness. Thus these invisible spirit realities are ignored or viewed as inconsequential since, even though they may exist, they still face multiple reincarnations until they finally resolve karma to enter Nirvana, a state of nonbeing. Classical Buddhism theoretically espouses a worldview shaped by a small pragmatic science section below with a large block of religion above. However, functionally it endorses the principle of assimilation for its folk followers. Consequently, Buddhism incorporates myriads of spirit beliefs and practices within popular practice.

Since practitioners of mission ought to proclaim Christ in ways that appropriately meet heart needs, they must consider these spirit realities within specific indigenous Buddhist cultures in order to communicate effectively. To ignore spiritual conceptualizations in the target people is to dismiss the primary conditions and strategic means for reaching them. Workers must speak to the heart's core and touch actual felt needs of those they attempt to reach. Therefore, if they wish to succeed in helping their communities, they must understand and connect with their real worldview. The best communication will be through that mental map of spiritual realities. Consequently, it is crucial to observe and understand the differing practices and the multiple practitioners that operate in the world of the spirits, pertaining to any target culture.

In *Magic, Science and Religion* social anthropologist Malinowski affirms that even myth, legends, and folklore are not merely products of decadent past ages. They become renewed as current living forces of fresh experiences and new phenomena. "Magic is the bridge between the golden age of primeval craft and the wonder-working power of today" (1954, 83). Thus such age-long practices as fortune-telling, soothsaying, divining, and similar magical processes employed to project into the future, bring fresh hope to devotees who confidently depend on them. These kinds of foretelling may vary from people to people. However, many of these practices also contain commonalities.

Functional roles for easy access to the unseen world utilize a rainbowed plethora of practitioners such as priests, monks, shamans, soothsayers, magicians, wise men, seers, prophets, witch doctors, spirit mediums including spirit writers, fortune-tellers, crystal or tarot card readers, and such like. They are employed to determine the future and to project prophetic outcomes. Sometimes they identify evil causes for tragedies, failures, defeats, and past sad events. Spirit mediums tend to proliferate trading in predicting the future and in assuring Buddhists concerning what lies ahead. A Thai provincial veterinarian near us wondered about expanding his chicken business. He sought the diviner's help to determine if the government would transfer him to another province within two years. The fortune-teller said he would be moved soon, so he did not expand business. Actually he remained in the province for many years, but the fear of the predicted future clearly affected his decision.

Wikipedia lists a veritable alphabet of terms, with multiple practices used in divination. Among the more unusual are:

Alectromancy: observing a rooster pecking

Bibliomancy: from books, religious texts

Ceromancy: patterns in dripping wax

Extispicy: entrails of animals

Geomancy: markings in the ground

Haruspicy: livers of sacrificed animals

Kau-cim: shaking numbered sticks from a tube

Pyromancy: gazing into fire

Tasseomancy: tea leaves or coffee grounds (2014b)

Differing practices to achieve this divining include prayers made at sacred shrines, ancestral altars, city pillars, and Buddhist *wats* (temples). Spirit mediums also empower amulets, strings, water, cloth, images, and various objects with spiritual forces or powers to help protect, heal, and give advantage over malevolent forces and future enemies. They also infuse these powers into devotees through tattoos and implanted holy defensive devices such as talismans, all aimed at preserving and protecting the lives of the devotees from future attacks.

Divination often becomes crucial when a family is dealing with death of a loved one. Spirit mediums talk with the dead or other spiritual dark forces. Some are possessed with demonic powers, both voluntary and involuntary. These spirit forces help them do abnormal or miraculous things like fire-walking and piercing their bodies with swords and knives without pain. Others consult ancient or ancestral spirits (necromancy) in order to gain guidance on predicting the future. Some even produce and interpret dreams and visions, projecting into times coming ahead. Spirit-walking and calling back the souls or spirits of the endangered or lost are also practiced to extend prospective health and life.

MONGOLIA: EXAMPLES OF DIVINATION

The multiple means of divination in Mongolia illustrate this complexity. In response to my questions concerning Mongolian ways of divining, Bill Stephens, a veteran worker with fluent Mongolian and two decades of experience in both rural and urban contexts, replied with valuable and interesting data. His answer on August 27, 2014 as to who does divining was, "Buddhist lamas, fortune tellers and Islamic mullahs (for the folk Muslim minorities the Kazakh and Khoton)" (Stephens and Lin 2014, 1). The Bible, on which Islam, Judaism, and Christianity were founded, officially proscribed divination and all forms of sorcery. In real life, however, the followers of these religions often secretly, if not openly, participate in these occult practices in Mongolia, as do folk Buddhists worldwide.

Divination is practiced in Mongolia and elsewhere primarily "for purposes of prosperity, health and wealth" (ibid.). Special practitioners divine the future (for the above reasons), the past (why did this person die? or why did this accident happen? etc.), and the present (decisions on whether to move, how to get promotions, how to prosper, how to be healthy, and how to become wealthy).

People consult lamas before making decisions, "to know what will happen." They also do so to locate "lost livestock or lost things." Often they divine through "21 stones" (ibid.). John Hare, founder of the Wild Camel Protection Foundation, illustrates this use of 21 stones. The last paragraph of his article on wild Bactrian camels notes: "One of our team was lost overnight in the Atis Mountains, not a pleasant experience when wolves are howling and the temperature is hitting -15 degrees. Our Mongolian guide reassured us, by divining with 21 stones, he would eventually return safely (which he did)" (Hare 2008).

The blog Under Mongolian Blue Sky ran the article "Mongols and the Dead," which described divining in relation to death in a family:

> I decided to ask my Mongolian teacher about what happens when a person dies in Mongolia, i.e. what are the customs people follow. Mongolians in general are loathe to talk about death . . . He told me that when a person dies they are taken straight away to a lama. However, this isn't just any kind of lama. It's a

particular kind of lama called юм гэдэг хүн (*youm gedeg khoong*). Literally, this means "person who sees things." The family brings the recently departed to the lama who divines the [person's] past lives, etc. The lama then instructs the family when the person is to be buried and how, e.g. in what direction and with what objects . . . Then, while the family waits for the specified time, which would only be an odd numbered day, they gather together to visit with one another, express their condolences and prepare and eat food. It is taboo to say the name of the person who has recently died. (Fink 2006)

Mongolians and other Buddhist peoples in Central Asia also refer to "opening the golden box"—magical receptacle of life, based on a Buddhist *sutra*. Stephens writes, "Lamas do a ceremony that I have not seen and have only heard about called 'opening the golden box,' to determine where a person is after they die" (Stephens and Lin 2014, 1). Interestingly, James Frazer in *The Golden Bough* tells several Tartar, Kalmuk, and Mongol mythical tales about the golden casket or container in which the soul is kept. During mortal combat the hero cannot slay his opponent even after long periods of battle, until he finds out where his soul resides—usually within some receptacle or animal retained in the golden box. When the hero opens the golden casket or box and kills the animals, which contain the enemy's soul, instantly the foe dies (1951, 782–83). C. R. Bawden also describes significant folktales on this Mongolian golden receptacle (2003, 333–40).

Manduhai Buyandelger details the divining process following the death of Bat, the brother of a Mongolian woman named Baasan. Early one morning in October 1998 Bat's body was found in the grasslands between his *ger* and that of a friend whom he visited the day before. Neither police nor doctors could find any reason for his death. The forty-five-year-old had "no heart failure, no wounds, nor internal bleeding." Suspecting Bat's demise may be connected to his initiation as a shaman two months earlier, Baasan sought "the divination services of Buddhist lamas," which all Mongols do during the funeral rites (2013, 235).

> Called the opening of the Golden Box, this practice
> involves retrieving information from a *sutra* titled
> "The Golden Box" and charting the trajectory of the
> person's life and afterlife as given by Burhan Bagsh
> [the Teacher Buddha]. Based on this information, the
> diviner advises survivors of the course of their late
> kinsperson's reincarnation and next life. (ibid., 236)

These written notes discerned from the Golden Box are "expected to be buried with the dead" (ibid).

Shamanistic possession provides another form of Mongolian divining. Many shamans are Buddhist but also utilize unique practices that are more animistic. Stephens describes them.

> Shamans also divine, but they are different. They
> don't use stones or diceor any devices. They become
> possessed by an *ongod* or ancestral spirit. Yet in or-
> der to become possessed they wear special clothes,
> perhapsof deerskins, and beat a special drum with a
> special stick. Sometimes they drink vodka too. (Ste-
> phens and Lin 2014, 1)

Shamans enter ecstasy and trance states. Deemer writes that shamans are "mystics that secret away in the mountains, migrating with herds of reindeer, falling into trances, channeling spirits, predicting the future—changing the future" (2009). The shaman may be male or female. Primarily they are mediums between two worlds, the observable physical world below and the invisible spiritual world above. Using drums is typical of shamans, as is telepathy found in other Buddhist and tribal mediums.

Mongolians follow Tibetan Buddhism. Tibetan Buddhist monks combine monotonous chanting of musical incantations or verse, drum beating, *dungchen* horn blowing, gongs, and *tingsha* cymbals to invoke or dispel the spirits in liturgies, ceremonies, or rituals. The combined sound effect is to condition the hearers. A Tibetan form of divination also uses human bones and skulls—*yama* (whole, decorated skulls) or *kapala* (skull caps). The use of these sacred skulls include taking a curse off a family, offering food and wine to the gods, guiding a misled soul to the right path, to help reach enlightenment, and ritualizing for empowerment. (Fuge 2012, 2)

Stephens mentions another unique way of divining. "People also cast *shagai* or sheep or goat ankle bones" to divine (Stephens and Lin 2014, 1). *Shagai* are the talus or knucklebones. The diviner casts four *shagai*. Positions of each determine the future. Some ordinary people also use them for playing various games, not unlike reading horoscopes. *Shagai* is a popular means of telling fortunes in Mongolia.

"Dice are also used by fortune tellers" (ibid.). Fortune-telling is predicting information about a person's life and/or future. In principle it is similar to divination with this difference: divination is used for predictions usually related to religious rituals or invoking deities or spirits. Fortune-telling, at least in the West, is less formal or serious. It is more a form of popular culture, in which belief in occult operations are often not taken overly seriously. However, for peoples in the East, fortune-telling becomes a more serious endeavor and pursuit.

We could discuss many other ways of divining in Asia among Buddhists from various nations, but space demands a termination of cultural exploration here. Let us now consider biblical matters on this issue.

BIBLICAL ANALYSIS OF DIVINING, DISCERNING, AND DETERMINING

God promised Abraham and his descendants that if they followed him with all their hearts he would personally lead and direct them into the future. Despite experiencing God's miraculous deliverance from Egypt and his faithful preservation and provision throughout forty years in the desert wilderness, Israel frequently rebelled. They forgot his victorious conquests over the corrupted nations in the Levant. They habitually rejected God's reign, reverting to desecrated worship of graven images, idols, and the false gods of the surrounding Gentile nations. They committed gross immorality in spiritual, social, and physical adulteries, including temple prostitution in holy high places and in the temple of the Lord.

Consequently, God's judgment fell on Israel, dramatically affecting their future. He withdrew his promised presence in the Shekinah glory, allowed foreign forces to route Israel's armies, gave the Ark of the Covenant into enemy hands, and permitted foreign nations to control his promised land. These enemies destroyed his holy temple and desecrated his holy city of Jerusalem. They took his holy nation into captivity and left his land in desolation. Behind Israel's rebellion and the enemy's actions were evil, powerful realities—both human and spiritual—principalities, authorities, and powers, such as the prince of Persia (Dan 10:12,13). Archangels like Michael and Gabriel countered them. Significantly, these confrontations related to Israel's future (Dan 10:14). Battles in the heavenlies affected future events on earth. Nevertheless, God's promises for Israel's eventual future remained firm.

The Bible contains both positive and negative causes for predictions, whether past or future. Miraculous means of guidance like the pillar of fire at night, the cloud by day, Moses' fiery bush, Aaron's rod, were recognized and followed. Special equipment like teraphim, ephods, and Urim and Thummim were used religiously along with special prayers for discerning projected outcomes. Practitioners utilized these unique items to find the will of God for future victory or to reveal causes for past problems and failures. Israel's prophets, priests, and princes divined the future for Israel. Some were genuinely God inspired, others false practitioners. Discerning decisions for future action followed God's prescribed methods using various instruments.

Teraphim had two uses: household gods (Gen 31:34) and idols of cultic ritual in temples (American-Israeli Cooperative Enterprise 2012, 1–2). They were possibly "a survival of primitive ancestor worship," which became "later a sort of Manes oracle" (Jewish Encyclopedia 1906). "Teraphim were employed in divination in the period of the Judges (17:5; 18:17) and like the divining ephod were later condemned by Josiah (2 Kings 23:24). Samuel equated Saul's rebellion with iniquity, divination and idolatry (1 Sam 15:23)" (ibid.). Teraphim's most important function was divination, "chiefly for oracular purposes," probably in connection with "casting the sacred lot" (ibid.).

"Ephod" had two meanings: (1) a garment used by the high priest, and (2) an image (ibid.). Gideon took the Midianites' golden earrings to make an ephod (Judg 8:24–27). Judges 8:27 "clearly describes an ephod as an object employed in divination" and "the sacred oracle," suggesting "a portable image before which the lots were cast" (Jewish Encyclopedia 1906).

Urim and Thummim were a "priestly device for obtaining oracles, . . . one of three legitimate means of obtaining oracles in early Israel" (American-Israeli Cooperative Enterprise 2012, 1). Urim, dreams, and prophets were three ways the LORD may have answerered (1 Sam 28:6). Urim and Thummim became extinct after the fall of Jerusalem or early exile. Possibly they were a kind of lot (stones or sticks), like casting of lots (1 Sam 10:20; Isa 34:17) (American-Israeli Cooperative Enterprise 2012, 2). They were objects connected with the breastplate of the high priest (breastplate of judgment) and used as a kind of divine oracle. Two may have represented "revelation and truth" or "lights and perfections" (Jewish Encyclopedia 1906). Numbers 27:21 indicated "Joshua and his successors could speak to the Lord only through the mediation of the high priest and by means of the Urim and Thummmim" (ibid.). General consensus holds that this involved some form of casting lots (cleromancy) to determine matters (Wikipedia 2014a).

Casting lots was used frequently in the Old Testament to discern God's direction, choice, and will. Aaron cast lots using two goats, representing Jehovah and the scapegoat respectively (Lev 16:8). Achan was revealed as the source of mortal sin, probably by using some form of lots (Josh 7:14–18). The land was divided by casting lots before the Lord (Josh 18:6). By the sailors casting lots, Jonah was identified as responsible for the violent storm (Jonah 1:7). Haman cast lots to determine the future day to destroy the Jews in Shushan (Esth 3:7). The New Testament records fulfilled prophecy by Roman soldiers casting lots for Jesus' garment (Ps 22:18; John 19:24). After noting Scripture and praying, the apostles drew lots to choose a replacement for Judas Iscariot (Acts 1:15–26).

From that point on, the New Testament commonly transitions to using dependence on prayer rather than on lots. The Gospels and Acts still feature prophetic utterances, dreams, visions, appearances, and words of angels. But increasingly the direction of the Holy Spirit through consequent inner conviction, along with sanctified rational common sense, seems to have mostly become the mode of discerning the future (Acts 16:10).

Satan projected the future to tempt Adam and Eve. "You will be like God" (Gen 3:5). He used the same approach to tempt Christ. "All these things I will give You if . . ." (Matt 4:9 NKJV). Adam rejected God's word; Christ remembered God's word. Focus on the future stretches from Eden to Armageddon, from Genesis to Revelation. A similar concern for discerning the future affects Buddhists.

BUDDHIST BELIEFS AND PRACTICES OBSERVED

Chinese professor Zhou Qi started a research project in 2009 on divination in Buddhist theory and practice. In her rare analysis of prediction in Chinese Buddhism she proposes to "demonstrate how Buddhism in China explains and practices prediction." She affirms, "It is widely recognized that the main theories of Buddhism oppose anything like prediction or augury, although there are some Buddhist classics which do mention or give some explanation about prediction." She notes that Buddhist discipline forbids practitioners and believers to predict or augur, while in reality these "have always been present." The Buddhist doctrinal system is based on "the karma theory, the logic of which determines that the Buddhist theories generally oppose augury or prediction." Nevertheless, "doctrines do exist which not only try to explain the unknown but also give predictions and even presuppositions about the future." She argues astutely that inherent in the two fundamental Buddhist theories of *pratitya-samutpada* (dependent origination) and karma is the law of causation. So both, while denying prediction or augury, "are doing the prediction itself" (Qi 2012).

Several foretelling events surrounded the birth of Siddhartha Gautama, who later became known as the Buddha or Enlightened One. His mother, Queen Maya, had taken a vow of chastity. Later she had a dream in which a white elephant entered her side causing her to conceive miraculously. The famous Hindu seer Asita had predicted thirty-two signs (*lakshanas*) or distinguishing marks that would identify the Buddha at birth. Some of these were somewhat fanciful such as symbols of the *cakra* wheel on the soles of Buddha's feet and light radiating from the pores of his skin. Likewise, some physical features were extraordinary, like forty teeth, webbed fingers and toes, and a golden body. At the name-giving ceremony for Siddhartha, seven Brahmin priests raised two fingers, inferring that he would be both a great king and a Buddha. One priest named Kondanna disagreed and raised only one finger, thus strongly predicting that the child would only be a Buddha, a religious teacher; never a king.

Following his enlightenment at age thirty-five, Buddha seemed to ignore divining since all life and elements were immaterial, irrelevant, illusionary, impermanent, and ever changing. He proposed and taught that self-insight alone, along with attaining Nirvana, was the whole goal and answer to karma in overcoming past suffering and multiple existences, and above all, escaping or being liberated from future existences and life (Dhammananda 2002, 24). Generally therefore, divining the future was futile, and relying on projecting what lay ahead was irrelevant, because all was the product of one's own karma. Karma for the future could not be predicted as it was predicated upon the good or bad works and the positive or negative actions a person intentionally took.

At Bodh Gaya, where Siddhartha Gautama was enlightened during the full moon, he perceived significant insights on three successive nights. The first night Buddha saw 100,000 of his previous existences or rebirths, all the product of karma; the second, the four stages in the cycle of life through which all sentient beings passed according to their karma: birth, sickness, old age, and death; the third, the Four Noble Truths including the Eightfold Path, by which one could be freed in the future from ignorance, emptiness, and the inevitable cycle of life. No other provision was foretold.

One interesting later prediction of Buddha on the future of Buddhism is noted in the Vinaya Pitaka (2:253); namely, if women were admitted to join the monkhood (*sangha*), then Buddhism would be shortened to only five hundred years (Buddha Dharma Education Association and BuddhaNet 2008) instead of five thousand. This proved to be invalid.

Another major prediction of Buddha projected a Maitreya Buddha to follow him in the future after the passing of many *kulpa*, when the dharma was totally forgotten. Maitreya, currently in Tusita heaven, is the only Bodhisattva recognized throughout both Theravada and Mahayana traditions (Manjushri Buddhist Community 2013).

Some modern Japanese interpreters of the Sutra of the Lotus Flower of the Wonderful Law see a prediction in Shakyamuni Buddha's claim, "You are buddhas," as future fulfillment of becoming buddhas. This *sutra* also noted future devils and their devilish deeds (Kosei-kai 2009, 1–2). Ehi Passiko explains that in Anguttara Nikaya 7:66(2) of the Tripitaka, Buddha predicted the end of the world, with some elaborate details, including the appearance of seven suns around the earth—a cause for global warming and eventually total disintegration of the earth and our world system. This "will happen in an unimaginable long period of time in the future" (Passiko 2009, 3).

> The world will end due to the impermanence of the nature, impermanence of the compounded things, the aging of things . . . No Gods, no devas, no satan, no higher beings and no human will ever be able to end the world system. The world is ended by itself, by natural causes, namely aging and death. (ibid.)

Though Buddhism has no teaching on biblical apocalypse, tradition states that Buddha taught the Kalachakra Tantra, which predicts future holy wars in 2424 from Shambala, a human realm, ending just before the golden age of Kalachakra begins. The Shambala warriors' conflict is with Muslims and others. Some scholars claim this is only symbolic, though texts clearly indicate a form of Buddhist jihad (Berzin 2001).

Overall formal classical Buddhism has little focus on discerning or affecting the future, except for overcoming karma with intentional meritorious deeds and, as Dhammananda writes, through the transfer of merit to others following Buddha's prescribed manner (2002, 393–97). Yet Buddha predicted future states of the world. One morning before awakening, King Pasenadi of Kosala, a contemporary of Buddha, had sixteen frightening dreams or omens. He went to ask Buddha about the meanings of them. From them Buddha predicted future conditions in the world and for the future of Buddhism. Buddha foretold that many showed the declension of humanity morally and religiously. Some indicated the fall of monks into immoral and commercial laxities (Veerananto 2008).

For the most part classical Buddhism has little emphasis on divining or projecting the future. Folk Buddhist practices filled the void of this excluded middle or, more accurately, the excluded whole in classical Buddhism. Terwiel affirms, "Even those aspects of religion that are obviously at the very heart of the Buddhist tradition are interpreted by both the farmer and the rural monk in their own characteristically magico-animistic manner" (2012, 262).

Recognizing this, modern Buddhist writer Sri Dhammananda significantly added a concluding chapter 17 on "Divination and Dreams" in his fourth edition of *What Buddhists Believe* (2002, 398–418). He affirms, "Buddhism does not condemn astrology . . . There is a direct link between the life of an individual human being and the vast workings of the cosmos" (ibid., 402). The zodiac "accounts for the birth of unusual people during certain months" (ibid., 400). Horoscopes "show the karmic force a person carries calculated from the time of birth" (ibid., 401). He notes three energies—cosmic, karmic, and mental—interacting concurrently (ibid., 402). So a skillful astrologer understanding these forces "can reasonably accurately chart the course of one's life, based on the moment of the person's birth." But "only a Buddha can predict anything with perfect accuracy" (ibid., 403). He concludes, "Buddhism teaches that through the intellect a person can arrange his or her life in harmony with the planets, and also cultivate inherent talents and manipulate them for his or her personal betterment" (ibid., 405).

Dhammananda recognizes other forms of predicting. "Buddhism does not refute belief in deities, spirits, astrology and fortune-telling." However, "a person must overcome all problems and difficulties by his or her own efforts and not through the medium of deities, spirits, astrology or fortune-telling" (ibid., 406). "The Buddhist attitude towards consulting mediums is non-committal." Though this is "not a Buddhist practice . . . there is no reason for Buddhists to object to such practices" (ibid., 409). He noted that Nagasena, Buddhist scholar in Kashmir around 150 BC, detailed six causes for dreams, including the intervention of supernatural forces, the influence of future events, and prophetic dreams. Nagasena stated the last category "are the only important ones" (ibid., 411).

From my observations folk Buddhists use many avenues to obtain guidance for their uncertain future. They consult with *bhikku* (monks), shamans, soothsayers, magicians, fortune-tellers, wise men, seers, prophets, spirit mediums, and various kinds of spirit/witch doctors to determine and project the future. They also seek help from the ancestors and make offerings to them to appease their spirits (hungry ghosts—*preta*), especially in times of peril, trial, testing, tragedy, disaster, or danger. Buddhists utilize interpretations of dreams, visions, appearances of demon apparitions, advice from practitioners, the cast of the die, magical numbers, or objects, and even the natural sound of certain animals like the tokay gecko (*Gekko gecko*), a foreboding omen.

Such a conglomerate world of divining, magic, and uncertainty identifies and indicates a deep felt need of Buddhists concerning ominous futures. Thus missiologists need to take this seriously into consideration, particularly in the early stages of evangelization, church planting, and discipling.

MISSIOLOGICAL THINKING AND APPLICATIONS

Where such a dynamic felt need is prevalent, the urgent necessity to develop good and adequate functional substitutes pertains. Therefore, Christian equivalent alternatives to local roles and practices of divining should be researched and applied, especially to help seekers and first-generation converts transition from involvement with demonic spirit practices. It was easier for God to take Israel out of Egypt than to take Egypt out of the Israelites. Like ancestral worship, these kinds of culturally ingrained "life and breath" habits tend to be automatically and persistently perpetuated even after becoming Christ believers, *unless* effective substitutes for those cultural functions are implemented in the church's ministry.

Here the application of Arnold Van Gennep's rites of passage is relevant. He proposed three interrelated steps: separation, transition, and incorporation (1960). Thus, as conversion transfers people from the old state to a new state, a transition is required. Functional substitutes provide that transition. Problems arise when no provisions for this transition are taught or implemented. Where inherent felt needs of converts are not addressed or met, Christians may secretly practice old ways underground, giving rise to real syncretism. As a new missionary I was invited by one Christian family to dedicate a new shack built for a newly married daughter. I complied but afterwards noticed that prior to my arrival, candles and incense had been burned on the steps of this new home as offerings to the protective spirits. Secret syncretism! In another remote village, a Buddhist rice merchant and his family believed. A house church began in their home. For several years I noticed they did not grow vibrantly in the faith. I found the cause was that the wife felt she could not give up her images kept in the bedroom. Once she did, the church blossomed.

By studying the role of divining in Buddhist cultures, we understand its cultural function of predicting. Then we can adopt a model or role that is culturally relevant to help transfer allegiance from human agents to God, who controls the future. The goal is to transfer and transform fear to confidence, uncertainly to assurance, and anxiety to trust. True, Christians do not know the future and cannot fully predict it. As believers we know by faith and assurance in the Holy Spirit that our futures are in the Lord's hands. We trust the Bible. Nevertheless it is neither unbiblical nor unchristian to find means to help allay the fears of Jesus' people coming out of Buddhism who still have a deep concern and fear for their future.

Significantly, in *From Times Square to Timbuktu*, Granberg-Michaelson dedicates five chapters to "excellent strategic and theological reflection." His third of four principles suggests that "theology must always be local and contextual, but our most important place for interaction is in the themes of power and suffering" (2013, 1). That clearly fits the spiritual realities model for folk Buddhists.

Fear of the spirit world and suffering because of karma and the inescapable cycle of life (*samsara*) are the bane of Buddhists. The uncertainty of the future adds fuel to fear. They often leave it to luck or fate! Therefore, first of all, workers should train seekers and believers to truly know that the Lord is sovereign and living today. The future is in his hands. So teach them to trust Creator God, depend on Christ through prayer in his name, and maintain unswerving faith in this all-powerful God. This instruction is essential, especially in regards to the future. Humans have no real control over the future, except to place it and themselves fully in God's hands. To live through the unknown and uncertain, the fearful and unexpected, the insecure and frightening in our contemporary, scary world calls for a faith that constantly affirms God is, God controls, and God is dependable even when Satan assails us. Talk about God's care of the future for Moses, Joseph, Daniel, Paul, and Jesus. Sharing lessons and living illustrations of how believers from Buddhist backgrounds overcame burdens of the present and fears for the future help instill "faith in God." That may be the most important experience church planters can bequeath seekers and new believers among Buddhists (Mark 11:22–26).

Christians, especially those from the West, must also grapple with the divining spirit world of Buddhists in their endeavor to reach them. Workers must comprehend that worldview and humbly adapt roles that bridge their own cultural void of hidden middle issues. Denying them is detrimental to communication. Acknowledging them as spiritual realities helps build bridges for contact, while adapting their function enhances contact and communication.

Furthermore, teach Buddhist seekers to trust the power of a loving and living God to control the future. Be a model of this before them. Instruct them to experience his unfailing compassion for humanity and to rely on his abundant grace and mercy towards those who call upon him. Also remember his longsuffering with them. Instruct them about Creator God's protection, divine provision, and general providence to all peoples, whether they trust or deny him. God's purposes are primarily for salvation of those lost without hope and for redemption of the repentant, not retribution. Telling testimonies of how God helped overcome crises or provided resources in time of need strengthen faith in those fearing the future. Emphasize memorizing Scriptures like Psalm 23 and Matthew chapters 5–6. This encourages the life of faith. Strong churches crafted from communities with fragile, uncertain perspectives about the future are established through clear changes of worldview and founded on solid Bible-based theology. This transitional change demands a reorientation to trust Almighty God, not to be dependent only on self as Buddha taught. That is a quantum leap for Buddhist-background believers.

I will never forget visiting a couple in Hirosaki, Japan, who owned and ran a small restaurant. They were converts from Buddhism. Their restaurant took much of their time, including Sunday, which usually was a busy and most profitable day. As new Christians they were concerned to attend church and to keep Sunday in a more biblical way. So they decided to honor and trust God and to close the restaurant on Sundays. The other restaurant owners nearby and many of their friends and family told them they were crazy and that in a few months they would be bankrupt and would lose their business. However, by faith and obedience the couple held their vow to God. Surprisingly, their business blossomed greatly during the week and was most prosperous. Several of their nearby Buddhist restaurant owners went out of business within a few months of reproving the couple. God was faithful against all fears of future failure. Their business only got bigger for honoring God.

A further way to overcome fear and frustration of temporal necessities and future exigencies is to develop local churches to be functional community centers, both to help local believers be ministering and to serve others in the surrounding Buddhist area. As the monastery functions as a center for community activities, so should the church be serving in the midst of the community. That is another form of functional substitute. Buddhists may view this as Christians making merit. But genuine unselfish service is the outflow of gratitude to God for providing salvation, not in order to gain redemption. The form may be similar, but the functional motive of true loving compassion and action is different. Nearly forty verses in the Gospels and Epistles propose actions to help "one another" (Smith 1977, 25–26).

Be examples teaching that family values come from prayerful devotions through family togetherness. Families that pray together help each other through times when future crises arise. Families that face tough times together, by God's grace get through them, becoming stronger. Fundamental principles of parenting and raising a family, nurturing children, finding a mate, applying for employment, and the value of education for children and parents are all additional topics for churches seeking to be involved in the consulting needs of the surrounding community. This means that while pastors, elders, and professionals in the congregation may primarily be coaches and trainers of the lay people of the church, it is the whole church that is at work in the community. That is the goal. All believers should be imbedded in their local communities. One church I know had a policy that every new member joining the church had to commit to serve in a designated ministry of the church. Thus all members old and new had practical involvement in church and community. They could change assignments each year, if desired. The leaders of the church were more like mentors and supervisors, but all were involved in the surrounding community.

Another common fear of rural and inner-city Buddhists is having adequate finances to live on. Many live day to day, hand to mouth. Many fall into deep debt to unscrupulous moneylenders. When they have money, they tend to spend it without thought for what tomorrow may hold. Qualified members in churches can counsel families or hold classes to instruct and train community members on how to handle finances properly, including living within their means, keeping some savings aside for emergencies, setting budgets realistically, doing basic accounting, and how to develop cooperatives and credit unions. Possibly even establishing rotating community pool-funds, whereby all the community families, including Christians, participate in providing regular contributions. Then each member shares by turn in accessing the funds for specific needs or projects. Similarly, church members can give training in public health, basic preventive medicine, cleanliness, and healthy living and nutritious eating habits. Effective communication in these lessons can be enhanced through storytelling, using local parables, folklore, or legends, as well as using Christian-oriented indigenous poetry, music, drama, and dance.

It is crucial to understand the cultural forms and deep felt needs of the people in order to serve them and their families truly, particularly in times of unexpected crisis, loss, frustration, and hopelessness. Therefore the church and its laypeople and leaders should carefully consider adapting vital roles that complement key needs and expectations of folk Buddhists in their penchant for divining the future.

Finally, serious thought to develop adequate functional substitutes for key roles like divining (as wise counselling) and fortune-telling (compassionate advising on future concerns) may prove to be better ways of connecting with folk Buddhists. Meeting the dynamics behind their needs for indigenous fortune-tellers or diviners clearly calls for wise selection and implementation of specific roles. Romans, Corinthians, Ephesians, and 1 Peter list almost twenty spiritual gifts. Members should be encouraged to use their biblical gifts of discernment, faith, prophecy, counsel, knowledge, exhortation, helps, and prayer for the sake of the community. With experience, such applied gifts will be honed and sharpened efficiently. Pastors and elders usually see their roles more focused on preaching, administration, and teaching. By adding an engendered role of wise counsellor using compassion, and confronting problems in acceptably indigenous ways, they could function much like the native diviner. With empathy, understanding, loving consideration, prayerful comfort, and insightful advice such counsellor-advisors could excel and even exceed the prowess of fortune-tellers.

One area needing more attention concerns death in the family. More involvement of pastors in this role similar to the diviner as well as comforter is culturally required among Buddhists. Church leaders and members, too, need to be more aware of what is happening in their communities. They must be more ready to visit and advise them and to be available and open to those divine interruptions that just happen to come along. They ought to be more involved with the local peoples, businesses, and community leaders. Early morning visits to coffee shops in Buddhist Asia find local clearinghouses for the latest news and gossip. Getting to know and befriend temple abbots and monks is another avenue of awareness. Praying for them and sometimes with them creates respect and bonding, which is worth the effort.

CONCLUSION

Among the different sects of Buddhism exists a large variety of means to predict or divine the future, with variegated methods to discern it. Much of this relates to guidance through magical means or spirit forces and human discernment. Frequently, deciding on future actions is dependent on the outcome of advice, specific directions, and various ways the future or fortune is forecast through specialized practitioners.

God is the ultimate solution to divining the future and dealing with the diverse myriads of spiritual forces plaguing Buddhists' nagging questions about projecting predictions. God alone points them to peace and satisfying direction in life, not found by their own devices, proposals, programs, or self-efforts. Practitioners of mission need to scratch where it itches; that is, apply the good news to the real concerns of Buddhists, not just insensitively or ignorantly preach good pet sermons. They need to consider the realities of conditioning spiritual forces in order to communicate effectively within specific indigenous

Buddhist cultures. To ignore the excluded middle of spiritual realities in the target people is to dismiss the primary conditions and strategic means of reaching them. We must speak to the heart's core and meet actual felt needs of those we attempt to reach. Both Western practitioners and local church leaders should take into consideration these hidden spiritual realities. Therefore, if they wish to succeed in influencing their Buddhist communities, they must understand their worldview. The best communication will be through that mental map of spiritual realities—a world of mixed magic, intense divining, and control from multitudes of spirits. This includes understanding and ministering to all three areas of Hiebert's model, but particularly the middle "magic" section.

Teaching on the character of the living Creator God and his relationship to people on earth, including his providing, protecting, preserving, and preparing for the future is crucial to help overcome Buddhist self-dependence. It shifts in favor of trusting a personal, loving God. Instilling a trust in God for the future, no matter what it holds is a precious, transforming gift to new and old followers of Jesus alike.

Getting the local church to function in serving as a community center to the wider surrounding populace is a strategy that communicates and engenders practical help and valuable witness. Training families, teaching public health and preventive medicine, and assisting them to manage finances, helps prevent some future crises or at least gives families tools to deal with them better. The church as God's local representative is to influence its community and infuse it with the presence and power of Christ. Using functional substitutes, relevant to roles of divining and fortune-telling among folk Buddhists, helps bridge gaps for communicating and builds confidence with local families. Some new roles for church leaders and lay people to meet the deep needs of fortune-telling and divining are needed. Particular gifts like discerning of spirits and counseling, genuine friendly help in empathy, comfort, and encouragement, and other roles can be enhanced for this purpose. Pastors, elders, and some members ought to add the roles of wise counsellor and compassionate advisor, appropriately meeting cultural dimensions of the diviner and fortune-teller. This requires more involvement personally with families and communities in view of potential future crises they face, especially in the death of relatives. While the Bible indicates various means of divining and discerning the future, most of those means are now extinct or unused in the church. For the most part faith, prayer, and dependence on God have superseded them. But in folk Buddhist cultures a plethora of divining means are still employed. Church leaders need to build bridges across this void to transition over the cultural gully by adapting and enhancing their roles of advisor, counsellor, discerner, prophet, and friend. By so doing many fearful and uncertain Buddhist families in their communities may be drawn closer to the kingdom of God. Likely a good number of family networks will hopefully enter it, to the praise of God's glory.

REFERENCES

American-Israeli Cooperative Enterprise. 2012. Jewish Virtual Library. http://www.jewishvirtuallibrary.org (page discontinued).

Bawden, C. R. 2003. *Mongolian traditional literature: An anthology.* London: Kegan Paul. BBC America. 2014. GMT BBC World News, August 18, 2014.

Berzin, Alexander. 2001. Holy wars in Buddhism and Islam: The myth of Shambhala. http://bibliotecapleyades.net/mistic/holywars_buddhism_islam.htm (accessed June 12, 2014).

Buddha Dharma Education Association, and BuddhaNet. 2008. Women in Buddhism: Questions and Answers; Question 15. http://www.buddhanet.net/e-learning/history/wbq15.htm (accessed November 3, 2014).

Buyandelger, Manduhai. 2013. *Tragic spirits: Shamanism, memory, and gender in contemporary Mongolia.* Chicago: University of Chicago Press.

Calvin, John, and Jacopo Sadoleto. 1976. *A Reformation debate.* Ed. John C. Olin. Grand Rapids: Baker.

Deemer, Andy. 2009. Chasing the shaman in Mongolia. Asia Obscura (blog). May 29. http://asiaobscura.com/2009/05/what-the-fortune-teller-told-me-mongolia-2.html (accessed September 13, 2014).

Dhammananda, K. Sri. 1998. *What Buddhists believe.* Kuala Lumpur: Buddhist Missionary Society.

———. 2002. *What Buddhists believe.* 4th ed. Kuala Lumpur: Buddhist Missionary Society.

Fink, Lisa. 2006. Mongols and the dead. Under Mongolian Blue Sky (blog). November 13. http://hellomongolia.typepad.com/ hello_mongolia/2006/11/mongols_and_the.html (accessed August 28, 2014).

Frazer, James George. 1951. *The golden bough: A study in magic and religion.* New York: Macmillan.

Fuge, Lauren. 2012. Tibetan skulls. Science in a Can (blog). October 12. http://sciencesoup.tumblr.com/post/33392691662/tibetan -skulls-human-bones (accessed September 14, 2014; page discontinued).

Granberg-Michaelson, Wesley. 2013. *From Times Square to Timbuktu: The post-Christian West meets the non-Western Church.* Grand Rapids: Eerdmans.

Hare, John. 2008. Wild Bactrian camel: On the brink of extinction. Wildlife Extra. http://www.wildlifeextra.com/go/world/ bactrian-camel.html (accessed August 27, 2014).

Hiebert, Paul. 1982. The Flaw of the Excluded Middle. *Missiology* 10, no. 1: 35–47.

Jewish Encyclopedia. 1906. http://www.jewishencyclopedia.com (accessed February 18, 2014).

Kosei-kai, Rissho. 2009. Prediction. In *Buddhism for today: A modern interpretation of the threefold lotus sutra.* (http://www.rkworld. org/publications/buddhism fortoday_B6.aspx (accessed June 12, 2014; page discontinued).

Malinowski, Bronislaw. 1954. *Magic, science and religion.* New York: Doubleday Anchor Books.

Manjushri Buddhist Community. 2013. Maitreya. Buddha and Bodhisattva Directory. http://www.manjushri.com/Buddha-List/Maitreya.html (accessed June 12, 2014).

Passiko, Ehi. 2009. End of the world as predicted by the Buddha Gotama. November 22. http://www.facebook.com/notes/ehi-passiko/end-of-the-world-as-predicted-by-the-buddha- (accessed June 12, 2014; page discontinued).

Qi, Zhou. 2012. Divination in Buddhist theory and practice. International Consortium for Research in the Humanities. http://www.ikgf.uni-erlangen.de/research/research-projects/ritual-and-religion/divination-in-buddhist-theory-and-practice.shtml (accessed September 11, 2014).

Smith, Alex G. 1977. *Strategy to multiply rural churches: A central Thailand case study*. Bangkok: OMF Publishers.

Stephens, Bill, and Kwai Lin. 2014. Prayer letter. August.

Terwiel, Barend. 2012. *Monks and magic*. 4th ed. Copenhagen: World Institute of Asian Studies.

Van Gennep, Arnold. 1960. *The rites of passage*. Chicago: University of Chicago Press.

Veerananto, Phra Khru Palat Veeranon. 2008. 16 predictions of the Buddha. http://www.meditationthailand.com/16predictions.htm (accessed June 12, 2014).

Wikipedia. 2014a. Cleromancy. http://en.wikipedia.org/wiki/Cleromancy (accessed February 18, 2014).

———. 2014b. Fortune-telling. http://en.wikipedia.org/wiki/Fortune-telling (accessed August 28, 2014).

CHAPTER 4

TRANSFORMING POWER ENCOUNTERS INTO PEOPLE MOVEMENTS IN THE BUDDHIST WORLD AND BEYOND

DAVID S. LIM

What's wrong with God's harvest in the Buddhist world? Yes, there has been some church growth in various places in the Buddhist world over the last several years, mostly through deliverance ministries. Yes, experiences of miraculous power encounters (PEs) have led a number of individuals to faith in Christ in Buddhist contexts. But in this sector of the world Christian growth has been slower than population growth. Donald McGavran described the supreme goal of missionary effort as "Christ-ward movements of people" (2005, 91), yet signs and wonders have not resulted in major "people movements" (PMs). The high visibility and dramatic effect of PEs in public gatherings have resulted in individual and family conversions, but have left no particular conversion impact in predominantly Buddhist countries.

How can we form Christ-centered communities (CCCs) through PMs in cultures that believe in supernatural forces? In most Buddhist contexts, dealing with spiritual realities remains one of the biggest challenges in evangelizing populations and transforming communities. I believe that my experience among predominantly folk Buddhist ethnic Chinese Filipinos holds relevance for ministries among members of any culture with supernatural beliefs and practices. My suggestions on how to form CCCs through PMs are based on studies of examples from the Muslim world (Garrison 2014; Schattner 2014), the Han and post-Mao rural Chinese (Deng 2005; Lyall 1954; Tang 2005), and Christianized folk religionists in India, Myanmar, and Indonesia.

Why can't Christians more effectively develop Christ-centered communities in Buddhist cultures dealing with supernatural realities? This paper presents three practices that will help move ministry beyond the dramatic towards the goal of Christ-ward movements of people. These are based on my trinitarian missiology of sharing Jesus as the way (missiology), the truth (Christology), and the life (ecclesiology) (Lim 2003). These three practices are (1) a missiology of redefined friendship evangelism (FE) for allegiance encounter, (2) a Christology of theological contextualization (TC) for truth encounter, and (3) an ecclesiology of transformational spirituality (TS) for love encounter.

A MISSIOLOGY OF REDEFINED FRIENDSHIP EVANGELISM

First of all, friendship evangelism must be redefined. It must be friendly with a new communal focus that includes the missionary in the process. Not individualistic such as in Law One of *The Four Spiritual Laws*, "God loves you and has a wonderful plan for your life," but also "God loves your people and has a wonderful plan for your community." Evangelizing must be relational, inviting people together as friends to join us in a spiritual journey, not as salespeople prompting a decision to close a deal. A missiology of redefined friendship evangelism includes three components: study local worldviews, highlight commonalities, and avoid conflictive differences.

Study the Local Worldviews

There is a need to understand the wide range of beliefs of our Buddhist friends. Listen carefully to shared views (including religious ones) and nonjudgmentally, with "gentleness and respect" (1 Pet 3:15), even if we disagree. Corrections for all of us will come later, as together we prayerfully reflect on the Scriptures during our friendship journey with the guidance of the Holy Spirit (John 16:12–15).

In Chinese contexts there is a need to understand the three main worldview concerns of the cosmic realm, the present invisible realm, and the human realm. Chinese believe the universe is permeated with the cosmic breath or life force called *qi*, usually described as *yin* and *yang*. Everything that exists results from the interplay of these two forces. Humans are a small part of this cosmic reality, and as such must seek to live in harmony with it and with the infinite number of gods, deities, spirits, and ancestors that make up the invisible realm. Tan (1996, 65) classifies many of the nonhuman beings in this Chinese pantheon in the following chart:

ORGANIC	MECHANICAL	
Jade emperor (Tien)	*Ming yun, qi*	
Gods and goddesses	*Yin* and *yang*	
		Other worlds
		This world
Earth gods:	Five elements:	
Sages	Magic	
Mythological figures	*Feng shui*	
Spirits and ghosts	Divination	
Ancestors	Palmistry	
Animal spirits (totem)	Luck	
		Empirical world
People	Acupuncture	
Animals	Matter	

Figure 1: Folk Chinese Worldview

Hiebert, Shaw, and Tienou (1999) describe three levels of reality in the primal worldview: the bottom level is the empirical world as experienced through the senses; the top level includes cosmic realms beyond human experience. In between, one finds the unseen "middle level." These three levels emerge out of the intersection of this world (earth, universe) and other worlds (heaven, hell), of the seen (empirical) and the unseen (transempirical). Hiebert also points out that the "boundaries between the categories are often fuzzy" and the "organic and mechanical analogies form a horizontal continuum with many shades between the poles" (ibid., 50). Applying this model to the Chinese worldview that has adopted a Buddhist as well as folk Filipino Christian worldview, the Filipino-Chinese Christian worldview looks like this (Uayan 2005, 70):

Organic	Mechanical
God the Father, Jesus, Tien Chu, Buddhist / Taoist gods and goddesses	*Ming yun* / Fate or fortune *Yin* and *yang* Other worlds
	This world
Kuan Yin / Ma-Tzu, Virgin Mary, angels, Satan, devils, ghosts Earth spirits, dwarves sages / Saints Mythological figures, ancestors, animal spirits (totem)	Priests / pastors / faith healers *Feng shui* masters Five elements, *feng shui* Magic, divination Palmistry/horoscope good luck charms
	Empirical world
People Animals and plants	Chinese medicine/doctors Matter

Figure 2: Folk Filipino-Chinese Worldview

Take note that the spirits consistently belong to the middle level, separate from the upper level. Spirits (including ghosts and ancestors) exist and have to be accorded their due. They can provide help, but they can also create problems. If the living experience misfortune, it may be due to neglect of the spirits. Meeting these needs depends on a complex understanding of the status of the particular spirit and the believer. There is no single answer (Chamberlain 1987, 47).

Syncretism is present in all religions, but the high value of harmony in Chinese cultures accommodates greater integration than more exclusivist religions such as Christianity and Islam. Chinese religion intermingles ancient traditions such as divination and ancestor veneration with the "greater traditions" of Confucianism, Daoism, and Buddhism. Textual Buddhism has assimilated with folk beliefs and practices to become an indigenous Chinese Buddhism meaningful to insiders and confusing to others.

Highlight Commonalities with the Buddhist Worldview
Friendship evangelism entails an attitudinal change in relating to Buddhism and other faiths. Unlike the Christian exclusivist outlook, an appreciative approach highlights commonalities for relevance,

contextualized witness, and deepening understanding. We should emphasize what unites, not what divides. Christians and Buddhists can view each other as seekers of the truth. Christians can embrace Buddhist values and beliefs that do not contradict Scripture. In the Buddhist worldview the face of Christ can be found revealing some aspects of the mystery of God (Richardson 1981; Sanneh 2003; Singh 1926). In fact, there are many commonalities in the Christian and Buddhist worldviews, particularly in cosmology, demonology, exorcism, and in the ways power encounters are viewed (Yong 2003, 102–10).

Commonalities in Cosmology
Both Buddhists and Christians believe there is more to reality than the material world, and both believe that the supernatural world is intrinsically interrelated with the material realm. Buddhists believe that the demonic is often, if not always, the source of evil, suffering, and *dukkha*. Christians see the hand of Satan in causing injustice. Evil therefore is to be resisted and in extreme cases exorcised. The roots of the idea of the demonic in Buddhism trace back to the Indian religious context from which the religion originated, where the illusory nature of phenomenal experience is posited against the eternal reality of Brahman. The gods of the Vedic religion were transmuted over time and emerged as a pantheon of Buddhist supernatural beings. Early on, the Vedic deity of sensual love and worldly enjoyment, Kama ("desire"), and Yama ("restraint" or "death"), were absorbed by Buddhism. What emerged was the notion of a supernatural being, first as a sympathetic onlooker to the laws of karma, evolving then into the chief of departed souls (god of death), and finally into the "king of the law" who judges and dispenses punishment. Thus developed the premier Buddhist symbol of the demonic—Mara—as that of tempter who arouses desires that lead to death. The identity of Mara clearly blends with the Christian view of Satan. Buddhism has concepts that are similar to the Christian understanding of the cosmological dualistic conflict between good and evil in the universe with eternal consequences!

Commonalities in Demonology
There are similarities, too, in what Christians and Buddhists believe about the demonic, particularly in their views of exorcism. The way for-

ward for Buddhists to overcome Mara and evil is through the Buddha and his dharma. The Buddha and Mara are opposing forces played out in the human realm. The Buddhist religious consciousness is colored by the dynamics of the confrontation between the forces of Mara leading to bondage on the one hand and that of the Buddha leading to liberation on the other. Commonalities with Christian demonology can be seen in Theravada traditions of exorcism in Sri Lanka, and the Mahayana in Tibetan China.

The centrality of the Pali scriptures to Sinhalese Theravada Buddhism accounts in part for the basic features of its demonology and its rites of exorcism. In a complex, multitiered cosmos, human health and prosperity are most immediately implicated by the activity of various deities and *devas*. When afflicted, Sinhalese seek out various healers including holy men, Buddhist monks, astrologers, oracles, priests, traditional medicine men, and exorcists. If the problem is diagnosed as originating from demonic sources, rituals of exorcism are performed.

Similar doctrinal and ritual structures can be found in Tibetan Buddhism (De Nebesky-Wojkowitz 1956; Fisher 1978; Lopez 1997), Chinese Mahayana religion (Ching 1993; Yip 1999), and Korean and Japanese traditions (Kiyota 1987; Fukuda 2012). Demonic figures are especially wrathful and terrifying, including vampires, witches, zombies, goblins, and other malignant spiritual beings. Tibetans turn to lamas, Buddhist monks, priests, and other specialists for help with their afflictions and misfortunes. Both Buddhists and Christians believe similarly that the demonic world is real and the demons can be confronted, engaged, and vanquished through rituals of exorcism.

Commonalities in Exorcism

What transpires during exorcisms? Again, there are some ritual similarities in the ways in which Buddhists and Christians perform rituals to engage with the demonic. In both traditions, a supreme power is recognized: that of Jesus by the Holy Spirit, and that of Buddha through the dharma and the *sangha*. The invocation of their respective names are central; the identification of the offending spirits is done. Mantra-like repetitions of various phrases of prayer and exorcism formulas are used. Visualization is frequently exercised, and the clap and other physical gestures are employed. Christians emphasize baptism (in water for non-Pentecostals and in the Spirit for Pentecostals) and a moral life of discipleship in the way of Jesus as an ongoing antidote, while Buddhists also emphasize the importance of righteous living according to Buddha's precepts in walking the Eightfold Path. Perhaps Christians can affirm appreciatively that successful attempts at exorcism through Buddhist monks and rituals are also God's "common grace" at work among those who are oppressed by the demonic? All victories against any form of evil can ultimately come from God alone.

Commonalities in Viewing Power Encounters

Five categories of Buddhist views of PEs compare with Christian responses to the questions, "How do we understand the demonic, and what do we do about it?" The discernible overlap in views and practices indicate that the following should be considered as potential starting points for redefining friendship evangelism in community. First, in the realist view, demons are actual beings that cause sickness, misfortune, and tragedy to the living. Often demonic entities are understood as unfulfilled ancestral spirits who, because of unfortunate circumstances surrounding death, have not been adequately laid to rest and therefore return to haunt their descendants. If the offending spirit is identified as an ancestor of the family, appropriate measures are taken to appease the disturbed spirit. If the offending spirit is identified as a stranger, exorcism is in order. Most Christians share this popular view of spiritual realities in this world.

The next three views are interrelated and pertain more to the Buddhist intelligentsia, although some lay Buddhists may espouse varying versions of each. They are the views of the nondualist, the psychological, and the skillful means. A Christian response to these three will be discussed below. In the nondualist view the fluid movement between the various realms of heavens, earth, and hells correlates with the conviction that heaven is in some sense equivalent to hell and that *samsara* is Nirvana, and vice-versa. The result is that ultimately there is no ontological divide between the divine and the demonic. As such, demons, along with all other things, are codependently originated phenomena. This means that demons are not essentially morally wicked, malevolent, or evil, but rather that each is an aspect of consciousness that is finally nondual.

The psychological view sees the demonic as projections of the mind. This was realized by the twelfth-century Tibetan Buddhist monk, Milarepa, who sought to understand why traditional exorcism techniques sometimes did not work. Milarepa eventually dispelled his "tormentors" by way of recognizing them for what they were: projections of his own mind, ultimately of the same nature of luminosity and emptiness. However, given the view of Buddhist nondualism, experiences of the demonic are just as real as a tiger or a samurai. Both the conscious and the ritual response are equally important since each is a reaction not only to the demonic but also to oneself and the total situation.

The view of skillful means builds on the Buddhist doctrine of *upaya*, the notion that different persons at different times and places are aided by different techniques in their quest for enlightenment. In this view, the Buddha himself can be manifest in both divinely glorious and demonically hideous forms at different moments; even Mara can help. Sinhalese ritual exposes false identities of the demonic while unveiling the true reality of the Buddha. Demons are considered manifestations of the wheel of *samsara* and serve to inspire living human beings to attain better rebirths and ultimately to escape rebirth altogether. Both groups of sentient beings need to treat each other appropriately in order to further their own goals of deliverance or liberation.

There are Christians who have adopted any of these three nondualist views, particularly those who accept and endorse New Age understanding and highlight Christian monastic mystical traditions. They appreciate the Buddhist experience of nonduality and practice integrating the mind and body through yoga and other practices, believing that through positive meditation the evil and demonic will fade into oblivion as ultimately illusion. Thus contemplation should be the source of action and beliefs in the pursuit of peace of mind. And if indeed one's consciousness reaches "nothingness," there need be no fear for the ultimate "blank" is actually divine (or God), not Satan, Mara, or the demonic. There are many Christians in various health professions who believe that the so-called "demonic" can be dealt with mainly through "inner healing" and clinical psychiatry.

This fits into another postmodern view introduced by Wheatley and Kellner-Rogers (1992, 1996) called new science, derived mainly from quantum physics. It follows Albert Einstein's theory of general relativity, which states the formula $E=mc^2$, meaning that energy and matter are essentially one. The Big Bang produced not only a vast amount of positive energy in the form of mass and energy but simultaneously produced an equal amount of negative energy in the form of space (space stores the negative energy in the form of gravity). If we add up all the mass and energy in the universe and subtract the negative energy of space it equals zero; the balance sheet of the universe is reconciled. Advocates of new science have recently become more convinced that the whole physical reality actually emerged out of consciousness or mind. The universe emerged out of an underlying quantum field, the underlying sea of potential, which is infinite, omnipresent, and omnipotent. The universe is much more like a great thought than the "great machine" metaphor of the Newtonian paradigm. We may know *noetically*, as William James coined it, to describe the process of direct knowing without sensory input. This intuitive way of knowing fits into the mystic tradition of Christians and the common experience of Buddhists.

The fifth view approaches the question of what the demonic means from a sociocultural and sociopolitical perspective. Here suggestions of cultural anthropologists regarding the demonic in Burmese society pertain beyond the confines of Buddhism:

> *Nats* [the Burmese departed dead] are associated with
> . . . every structural level of traditional Burmese so-
> ciety, beginning with the individual, and proceeding
> through the ascending levels of household, kinsmen,
> village, district, region and nation. Taken, then, as a
> political relationship, the relationship between *nat*
> and people is one between lord and subjects, which,
> for traditional Burma . . . is a despotic relationship
> . . . Being despotic they evoke the same sentiments
> evoked by government. These sentiments can be easily
> expressed. Since they cause trouble, avoid them; if they

cannot be avoided, placate them; if their assistance is desired, bribe (propitiate) them. (Spiro 1978, 131,138)
The reality of the demonic correlates with the oppressive socioeconomic and political conditions in which Buddhists exist worldwide. This does not mean that the demonic are purely symbolic or imaginary realities. Considered in this framework, rituals of exorcism function to reorder Buddhist social life and relationships. To say that this is a reductionist interpretation of Buddhist demonology misses the point. The issue in the light of nondual Buddhism is not whether or not demons exist, but how they exist, what their functions are, and how they can and should be dealt with.

Many Christians today also believe in this secularized version of PEs in the Bible and in history. This view has been elaborated best by Walter Wink (1984, 1986, 1992, 1998a, 1998b), who sees that we are confronting "powers and principalities" in social structures, and they are created, fallen, and redeemable. In this view, God is within everything (panentheism), which implies that all creatures (humans and institutions) are potential revealers of God. Most liberation theologians share the same view that the powers are not disembodied spirits but "incarnated" in institutions, structures, and systems. These powers (personal or impersonal) are in demonized people, pigs (Mark 5), and political systems (Rev 12–13). They become idolatrous and demonic when they pursue vocations other than those which God created them for and make their own interests the highest good. Through the gift of spiritual discernment, the church should call them to repentance (Eph 3:10). It is possible, therefore, for Christians to interpret PEs as sociopolitical confrontation just like this fifth view in Buddhism.

Disregard Conflictive Differences

Of course there are differences between Christianity and Buddhism, sometimes glaring ones. Yet FE implies that raising unnecessary difficulties for evangelism should be discouraged. Public criticism of politics or religion should be avoided. There is no use arguing, since winning an argument usually means losing a friend. Let our approach be marked with "gentleness and respect" (1 Pet 3:15; see also Col 4:5,6).

There should be only one criterion for an "allegiance encounter" in evangelism: "Christ and him crucified" (1 Cor 1:18–2:5). He is the fulfillment of the best of all religious searching and consciousness. Much of what constitutes religion is *praeparatio evangelica*, seeds of God's truth from which all other truths are derived and developed. As Paul told the Lystrans, "[God] has not left himself without testimony" among all nations since God had answered their prayers to the pantheon of gods in their Greek and Roman mythologies (Acts 14:17). He appreciated the Athenians' religiosity rather than rebuking their idolatry (Acts 17:22–23). In this dialogic and appreciative approach, we also show that we are willing to learn from other traditions, while also inviting them to listen to ours.

For most converts of PEs and witnesses to PEs, their first allegiance will naturally be to *"Christus victor"* (the victorious Christ), in whose name they experienced his all-powerful victory over deities and spirits in their local worldview. Such faith in Jesus is enough for salvation and baptism. There is no need to completely understand the uniqueness of Jesus as Lord and Savior. Such truths will come through prayerful reading and study of Scriptures and by the guidance of the Holy Spirit. Saving faith is simply to turn one's allegiance from "other gods" to the God they got to know in the PE (1 Thess 1:9). Saving faith is just to repent and believe in Jesus.

After coming to faith in Christ, the Holy Spirit will guide new believers into "all the truth" (John 16:13–15), even as all Christ followers are being guided. Together we can study the biblical texts (Acts 17:11). New believers can learn of Christ and his teachings now and unlearn all that is unbiblical in their worldviews later in the discipling process. Salvation is through a simple faith to follow Jesus, so all can come just as they are in their socioreligious context with no requirement for immediate worldview change. If this were not so, who of us could claim to be saved, since our worldviews are not yet completely biblical either (1 Cor 13:8)? Most of us expect too much from new believers, usually that they not only believe in Jesus, but that they also follow all the right beliefs and practices (read: our denominational traditions) from the very start. Our objective should be to pursue growth together not as aggressive taskmasters but as supportive friends, partners on the journey.

A CHRISTOLOGY OF
THEOLOGICAL CONTEXTUALIZATION

The second challenge for forming Christ-centered communities through people movements is to promote a Christology of theological contextualization (TC). This means furthering the appreciative approach of FE in "truth encounter" by connecting with the continuity of God's initiatives already present in cultural and religious backgrounds (1 Cor 7:18,19). This empathetic approach promotes indigenous Buddhist theologies and catalyzes more ineffectual PMs to form CCCs. When related to spiritual realities and PEs, a positive accommodation of the popular Buddhist cultural worldview avoids creating an "excluded middle" in varied contextualized theologies of PEs. This involves three related actions: initiation of community organizing, acceptance of various new theologies, and prevention of heresy and syncretism.

Initiation of Community Organizing

In order to promote a Christology of theological contextualization in CCCs, we should first determine who will lead the theologizing. People movements require indigenous leadership, chosen by the people themselves (Deut 17:14,15). Upon entry into the community, God will direct us to the "person of peace" (the local welcoming host, Luke 10:6). We should also befriend other community leaders, including the religious. There will come an opportunity for a power encounter that God has prepared. It is at that teachable moment that those involved, with permission of the healed, can catalyze a community organizing process. This is when the community defines a felt need and then chooses a few among themselves to address it. This new "people's (or community) organization" and the "person of peace" will constitute the core group to be evangelized and discipled to lead the PM and TC in their community and region.

Since God's objective is to disciple entire peoples to Christlikeness in their sociocultural context, we must practice holistic discipleship with community and even religious leaders. This includes befriending local healers, shamans, and Buddhist monks and nuns. In most animist societies decisions are made as a group usually led by the chief or elders of the community (Tippett 1973, 123–24). These are the key players in

theologizing, educating, and eventually changing the worldview of the populace. We should honor these leaders by participating in the activities of our new community, including the religious festivals. As we join in civic and socioreligious affairs, we cooperate in establishing God's *shalom* together and will experience how God will form a CCC in that place.

In contrast with the prevalent "extraction evangelism" of Christian missions, this is movement from within that encourages converts to stay in their families and communities so that they can share their faith with their network (Lim 2010). The focus is on conversions of adults, preferably leaders of households, clans, and even entire peoples. Most missions have focused on the marginalized and youth. These often have been put under unnecessary stress and persecution because of our rejectionist and separatist stance. Not being major decision makers, these young converts are considered rebels and traitors when they refuse to follow family traditions. There is much wisdom in the early church's practice of converting (and immediately baptizing) heads of households and whole families, thereby ensuring a solid communal network for reaching others and avoiding unnecessary persecution of individual young converts.

By definition communal conversions require community involvement. The worker needs to earn the right to be heard by the community. Successful missions have been done through works of mercy like health care, education, and community development work. In fact, any professional skill will do but must be done faithfully as a Christ follower without falsehood from the start. This is the advantage of the Christian expatriate: even without power encounter, genuine community service cannot help but be visible, and access to leaders will be unavoidable. However, unless combined with a sensitivity to focus on befriending leaders to Christ and urging them to take leadership in building the CCC, there will be very minimal possibility of having mass conversions or PMs.

Because of the strong family ties and ethnic solidarity in mos Buddhist cultures, change cannot be imposed from outside. Expatr ates must yield leadership to new believers to decide which beliefs ar practices to adopt or modify and which ones to discard. The "man (woman) of peace" must remain an insider, and the local leaders shou

be encouraged to use old forms and reinvest them with new meaning and value. Such changes must be done as soon as possible. "When good functional substitutes have been proposed and accepted at the time of the primary religious change . . . these have stood the test of time and proved effective" (Tippett 1987, 185). PMs can happen only when they are truly self-governing and self-theologizing. They can happen only through insiders.

Acceptance of Various New Theologies

At this stage the incipient CCC is empowered to do self-theologizing. Outsiders must release control and accept all kinds of theologies of PEs, including what may appear as unfamiliar understandings of signs and wonders, exorcisms, or other strategies. Time and energy should not be wasted perfecting and correcting theologies, cosmologies, and demonologies. Instead, trust the Holy Spirit to guide Christ followers over time into all truth (John 16:13–15). God delights in creativity and diversity. Without judgment or legalism (1 Cor 1–4; Rom 14:1–15:7) celebrate this God-given freedom of conscience. Let us learn together as each group discovers anew the formulations of the faith in light of the Scriptures and local expression. This inclusivist stance radically differs from the general exclusivistic denominationalism and separatist ethos of mainstream missions today.

Pentecostals and neo-Pentecostals have shown evidence how even those from secularized and nonreligious cultures in the West can develop their own theologies on PEs biblically and creatively. Perhaps one of the most developed is that of Charles Kraft. In his cosmology and demonology he has classified the types of spirits and shown that in each category there are spirits assigned by Satan and competing spirits (angels) assigned by God. On God's side are angels and archangels (Dan 10:13,21), and on Satan's side are counterfeit, competing "wicked spiritual forces in the heavenly world" (Eph 6:12 GNT) like principalities (*archai*), authorities (*exousiai*), world rulers (*kosmokartores*), and spiritual forces (*pneumatika*) of this dark age.

Dealing with Ground-level Spiritual Realities

The Gospels show that early in his ministry Jesus spent much time and energy healing the sick and casting out demons. But since most of us

find our personal record for power encounters not as good as Jesus' record, a variety of theologies have evolved to rationalize this. Traditional evangelical (non-Pentecostal) theologies of PEs have tended to limit Satan's activity largely to tempting people to sin. The antidote, therefore, was to learn more about the kinds of temptation employed and how to combat them. This meant looking to the Bible for what to pray in order to overcome. If a person seemed unable to resist, he or she was advised to pray and study the Bible more fervently. If a person seemed to be having emotional difficulties, he or she was advised to see a Christian counselor or simply to forget the past. The latter advice was often based on a misinterpretation of Philippians 3:13, "forgetting what is behind."

Neil Anderson's "truth encounter" theology focuses on dealing with self-image. This works well with those who are able to take cognitive control of their emotional wounds and hear the truth of who they are. Anderson observed what we all see: Satan's primary attack on Christians is in the areas of self-image. Satan doesn't want us to discover our new Christ-centered identity. Freedom is gained through learning and assimilating basic scriptural truths concerning who we are in Christ. Anderson assumes that when such truths are believed, emotions get healed, and if there are any demons, they leave (1990, 166–69).

Another truth-oriented theology of PEs is Ed Smith's "theophostic" perspective whereby healing is attained through uncovering the lies we have believed and then allowing Jesus to come and speak truth to us, thus healing the wounds caused by the lies. Though this approach appears to be quite cognitive, theophostic practitioners encourage people to feel deeply the emotions associated with the beliefs and to let Jesus heal wounds at all levels. This takes people well beyond Anderson's approach and may help visualize even deeper levels of previously unrecognized struggle.

Deliverance-based theologies are those that assume that demons are the major problem and that casting them out is the way to get people healed. They note that Jesus seemed to do nothing to the possessed other than to free them from their demons, so they go after the demons and try to drive them out. This has tended to be the approach of Pentecostals and neo-Pentecostals. It often results in a violent physical manifestation such as vomiting or other disagreeable reactions, sometimes even causing injury to the person in the process of obtaining freedom. Ernest Rockstad's method of calling the demons into the healer, what he labels, "pouring the demons through," is one example. Doris Wagner's use of a questionnaire to discover in prayer which demons are present and calling them out one by one is another.

Inner healing–based theologies and ministries focus almost exclusively on dealing with emotional and/or spiritual "garbage," as John and Paula Sandford do, or, after dealing with the garbage, go on to tackle any demonic "rats" that might be attached to the garbage, as Kraft does. The Sandfords do not completely neglect demons but seem to deal with them only if they make their presence obvious. Kraft's approach is to look for them (and usually find them) if the amount of garbage the person has been carrying seems to predict that there may be rats attached. He has observed that demon strength is linked to the amount and type of garbage in the person's life, thus recommending dealing first with the garbage and then with the demons. Kraft testifies that with this approach they almost never have any violence, vomiting, or other disagreeable occurrences.

Dealing with Cosmic-level Spiritual Realities

Those emphasizing cosmic-level spiritual engagement are authors and practitioners of the so-called "Third Wave," such as Peter Wagner (1996), Bob Beckett, George Otis Jr., John Dawson (1989), Cindy Jacobs, and Ed Silvoso. These evangelists and pastors have gone global, successfully winning people to Christ by employing the principles of cosmic-level spiritual "warfare."

Cosmic-level engagement parallels approaches described removing cosmic-level rats through dealing with cosmic-level garbage such as locations dedications to spiritual powers or disunity and competition among spiritual leaders. Kraft believes cosmic-level spirits have authority over ground-level spirits but gain and maintain their rights only through human permission. Satan is not interested in territory or institutions for their own sake but in the people and powers over such things granted by people to whom God gave original authority.

In Luke 4:6,7, Satan boasted that he could give Jesus all power over the kingdoms of the earth because "it has all been handed over to me, and I can give it to anyone I choose . . . if you worship me" (GNT).

This approach includes fostering unity among local pastors to repent of critical and competitive attitudes and then move to increased intercessory activity aimed at specific geographical areas or spiritual problems. The language used is to "break" satanic power by claiming authority over it in Jesus' name. Also included is the practice of spiritual mapping—researching both God's and the enemy's activities historically and in the present in the target area. The findings from this research become the focus of intercession and repentance and what is termed *identificational repentance*. This involves the present generation accepting responsibility for the sins of its predecessors and repenting on their behalf as did Ezra (Ezra 9), Nehemiah (Neh 1), and Daniel (Dan 9).

There will also usually be prayer walks, involving the intercessors in walking around and praying over the territory to be taken, thus claiming it for Christ. These will sometimes be held on mountaintops overlooking the area to be captured. Beckett is fond of claiming areas by driving stakes into the ground that have been empowered through prayer. Silvoso employs a combination of techniques designed to take whole cities for God. Dawson (1989) is strong on discovering and focusing on the "redemptive gift" of a city, meaning God's reason for the founding of the city.

With all the emphasis on technique, it needs to be underlined that those involved in cosmic-level spiritual engagement are primarily concerned about evangelism based on sound theology. The aim of these techniques is to break the power of the evil one over people and territory for the specific purpose of winning the lost and enabling people to grow in Christ. Few Christians will agree with all of the above theologies and practices of PEs. A Christology of theological contextualization expects, invites, and welcomes a multitude of contextual theologies emerging from all self-theologizing CCCs as they discover truths from the Scriptures for themselves.

CCCs developing from the Buddhist world show that although they retain the God-honoring core of the community's primal worldview, they now relate to it with confidence in Christ, no longer in fear of spirits (1 Cor 8; 10; 1 Tim 4:4,5). Along with believing in the one Creator God and thanking him for his wonderful creation, we can sanctify all things and overcome evil with the word of God and prayer (Eph 6:17,18). These are the weapons to demolish "strongholds" so that we can "take captive every thought to make it obedient to Christ" (2 Cor 10:4,5).

Christ-centered theological contextualization is best expressed in 1 Corinthians 9:19–23, becoming "all things to all people." If local converts remain in their socioreligious identities (7:18,19), they may not only be able to win others but also to be true to the multicultural essence of biblical faith. Will converts have to surrender their identity and culture to follow a "foreign Jesus"? Does the conversion demanded by the gospel include changing a socioreligious identity? Or will "vernacular translations" of Scripture open the door for Christ to enter fully into new cultures? Walls perceptively notes, "Christian faith must go on being translated, must continuously enter into vernacular culture and interact with it, or it withers and fades" (1997, 152).

Prevention of Heresy and Syncretism

There should be no fear of heresy as long as one believes in the supremacy and uniqueness of Christ and no fear of syncretism as long as allegiance from idolatrous and occult practices is turned to Christ. All the rest of cultural forms can be adopted and used for Christ-centered ends to fulfill indigenous functions and convey Christ-oriented meanings, as it was done in the Bible: anointing oil (Jas 5:14), Paul's aprons and handkerchiefs (Acts 19:12), Peter's shadow (Acts 5:15), and Jesus' garment (Luke 8:44) (Fukuda 2012, 147). Such critical appreciation of what is already there is not lowering the gospel to the lowest denominator, but raising it up to the highest possible revelation!

CCCs should develop not just their own theology but also their own spirituality—to express and live out the faith in light of prayerful reflection of Scripture. As they become more other-centered and ministry-oriented, they will be freed from the fear of the demonic and of syncretism. The main principle of TC is to adopt the existent socioreligious culture as much as possible (1 Cor 7:18,19). It is to integrate Christian faith with the ethnic and religiocultural identity of the people, with indigenous church leadership from the beginning. Missiologists have called these the four characteristics of indigenous churches: self-governing, self-propagating, self-supporting, and self-theologizing. Failure to do so has resulted in the transplanting of foreign churches, and not the planting of indigenous churches. Such "cultural dislocations" invite real syncretism, even Christo-paganism or "split-level Christianity."

Chinese religion, which permeates the society, is inseparable from Chinese culture. Religion in China was so woven into the broad fabric of family and social life that there was not even a special word for it until modern times. Chan and Hunter stress that "religion is part of culture and the cycles of daily life [in Asia]" (1994, 54), thus, conversion should not "deculturize" a convert. Any change in religious beliefs and practices will immediately signal to family and community a change of cultural identity. If converts try to adopt the evangelist's culture, their attempt should be firmly and gently resisted. Otherwise they cannot function as "persons of peace," and will lose their privilege to lead a PM to form CCCs among their own people. We must allow young believers to follow their family tradition (Gen 18:2; 27:29; 33:3; Phil 2:10), including bowing down in worship (Fukuda 2012, 219–30), offering incense (Mal 1:11), eating food offered to idols (1 Cor 8; 10), and making tablets or scrolls (1 Cor 15:29). Out of love, they must never cause their families, clans, and communities to stumble over socioreligious practices (1 Cor 8:9–13; 10:32,33).

Many evangelicals have a rejectionist "theology of culture," having forgotten that most of their own socioreligious expressions have been "baptized" into Christian usage by their previously pagan ancestors. They deny and reject for others what their faith ancestors have done. Instead they should follow Bavinck's view of *possessio* ("taking possession") of "heathen forms of life," and make them new; and in the case of PEs, retaining and enlisting its practices in the service of Jesus Christ is "perfectly proper" (1960, 178). Tippett observes,

> In the process of incorporating converts into their new fellowship group or congregation, indigenous forms, rites, festivals, and so forth, which can be given a new Christian value content, have greater likelihood

of finding permanent acceptance than foreign forms and rituals. (1987, 185)

The expression of these new Christ-centered theological contextualizations will most certainly differ from mainstream Westernized Christianity. There is no singular universal form of Christianity suitable for all believers at all times. But discerning the local response to the gospel within each culture is the hard work of contextual theologizing. Caught in the tension of Scripture, the majority church tradition, and the local culture, each believing community must choose the way to follow Christ and obey God's word in context. We must believe that the Holy Spirit will use the Word to illumine and direct each group of believer to be God's kingdom of priests in Christ, as they reflect on Scripture together. Sometimes outsiders are privileged to enter into that conversation as partners on the journey, learning new theology along the way. Even if they never write a textbook, local believers will proclaim daily theological decisions by how they live out the faith. Some errors may arise, but the believing community around them will keep them in check.

AN ECCLESIOLOGY OF TRANSFORMATIONAL SPIRITUALITY

Corollary to friendship evangelism (allegiance encounter) and theological contextualization (truth encounter), CCCs should also be empowered to develop an ecclesiology of transformational spirituality (love encounters), in three basic ways: focus on biblical spirituality, develop missional spirituality, and retain simple structures.

Focus on Biblical Spirituality

To develop transformational spirituality, new converts from popular Buddhist backgrounds should be discipled to focus on prayer and obedience in response to what they learn in their Bible reflection. As they grow in faith and love for Jesus Christ, the Holy Spirit will surely guide them to become less concerned about religious ritual practices to appease spirits and demons. Rather they will grow "into Christ" (Eph 4:15), liberated from sin (Col 3:5) to become more generous, more caring towards and sharing with their neighbors, which is the *agape* law of Christ (Isa 1:10–18; 58:1–12; Amos 5:21–24; Mic 6:6–8; Rom 13:8–10; Gal 5:13–23; 6:1,2), which takes away all fear (1 John 4:18).

The best way for Christ followers to demonstrate God's power is to love our neighbors through our "good works." This is what biblical spirituality is all about: to glorify God as God's light in the world through our good works (Matt 5:16), which is the summary of the Torah in the Great Commandment (Matt 22:37–39) and in the Golden Rule to do to others what we want to be done to us (7:12), which is the positive and higher version of Confucius' dictum, "Don't do to others what you don't want to be done to you." This is perfected in Jesus' new commandment, which raises the standard to the highest level, loving one another as he loved us (John 13:34,35), self-sacrificially!

Faith in Christ results in good works (Matt 7:21–23; Jas 2:14–26) through community service. The present-day church growth practice of counting attenders of religious services is misdirected. We should be counting how many Christ followers are actually loving their neighbors and doing good in their community, just like Jesus did and taught (Matt 25:31–46; Luke 10:25–37; Acts 10:38).

All Christ followers should devote time, energy, resources, and skills to community service, from our homes, offices, and any community. If needed and capable, we can build community ministry centers, and also turn our existing church buildings into such. There is really no need to build more religious buildings for conducting more religious services, for any meeting turns into a church (= Christ-centered worship/liturgy) when it includes prayer and Bible reflection/sharing (Matt 18:19,20; John 4:21–24; 1 Tim 4:4,5), as those gathered urge each other to "love and good works" (2 Tim 3:16,17; Heb 10:24,25 ESV). If Christ followers will be known as people who love, care, and share, it will be most likely that a PM will spread to form CCCs quite organically or naturally, just like what happened in the 1980s and 1990s in China, and perhaps in all PMs.

Develop Missional Religiosity

Such love should translate into a spirituality that values a missional lifestyle of simplicity, self-sacrifice, and appreciation of all peoples and their cultures, starting with one's own. Hence, love will transform the primal worldview and its practices from "glory to glory" in CCCs. The theologies, liturgies, and orthopraxes that will evolve will contribute to the enrichment of the glorious unity-in-diversity of the Christian faith. Historically, Christianity has been able to turn pagan and secular traditions into Christ-centeredness (though imperfectly with much difficulty), so there should be no lack of confidence that she can take on the whole Chinese religious and other folk Buddhist worldviews and practices, too. The Chinese and folk religionists can be spiritually formed and give relevant witness to their compatriots by developing their distinctly contextual forms of worship, catechesis, and festivals.

There had been a significant model of missional religiosity (MR) among the Chinese: *Tao Fong Shan* ("The Mount Where the Wind of *Tao* [or *logos*] Blows") in Hong Kong. Its buildings use Chinese temple architecture, and its Christian community has sought to live out and demonstrate the most sensitive and contextual integration of the Christian faith and Chinese culture, including ancestral veneration. It was founded by the Norwegian Lutheran missionary Karl Reichelt (1877–1952), who arrived in China in 1903 troubled to observe the poor relationship between Christians, especially Western missionaries, and the general population. He made a sustained firsthand study of the life and practices of the best of Confucianism, Buddhism, and Taoism in China. He set up a Christian "monastery" in Hong Kong in 1927, which introduced "the universal, the cosmic, the all-embracing Savior Jesus Christ" to all those who visited this "monastery." Converts were baptized, but instead of letting them join the existing churches, he encouraged these "friends of the *Tao*" to spread out and evangelize in the temples and monasteries. Reichelt wrote, "Although not joining the external church, such enter the yearly increasing number of unknown and unregistered Christ-followers" (Kung 1993). Although it had a plan to multiply into a movement, it had a complex structure that made it difficult to replicate.

Yet Reichelt's approach "from above" almost succeeded as a PM by focusing on the socioreligious elite. There may still be some "top down by insiders" opportunities today, like in Singapore where 40 percent of the university graduates are Christians (Chia 1999, 33). My school, the Asian School of Development and Cross-cultural Studies and some sister schools in the International Council of Higher Education are also aiming to do this through empowering nationals in Asia and elsewhere to gain academic credentials to form CCCs through catalyzing PMs "from the top down *and* from the inside out."

Yet the preferred MR should be "bottom up" through the people movements or disciple multiplication movements that are growing among rural folk Buddhists in China (Deng 2005; Oblau 2005; Tang 2005), Japan, and Myanmar today. MR for folk religious cultures means freedom from fear of ancestors, nature spirits, fate, and/or gods, which is the source of so much superstition. A transformed socioreligious culture will reflect more and more the simple faith of the Torah, even made simpler with no more blood sacrifices after they have been fulfilled in Christ on the Cross. It will develop "simple religiosity" so that it can be missional: easy to replicate across borders and cultures in our globalized, pluralist world.

Such simple religiosity consists of both evangelism and sociopolitical action, with signs and wonders (Mic 6:6–8; Matt 28:18–20; Luke 4:18,19; Rom 15:18,19; 1 Pet 2:9,10). Such was the spirituality of Jesus Christ and the apostles as they made disciples and modeled servant leadership by just equipping new believers to live according to God's will (Mark 10:42–45; 2 Tim 2:1,2; 1 Pet 5:1–3). Following the pattern of how Jesus discipled his first disciples (Mark 3:13–15), each Christ believer just needs to be equipped with three MR skills: (a) hearing God through prayerful meditation (quiet time such as *lectio divina*) to turn his Word (*logos*) into a word (*rhema*) to be obeyed; (b) making their own disciples and being discipled through participating in a "house church" with fellow believers in sharing life and Bible reflections together, whereby each one learns how to do personal devotions; and (c) doing FE to share what they learn of God and his will with their networks of nonbelieving relatives and friends, including doing PEs.

These disciple makers can be produced through being discipled by other disciple makers who seek to equip all believers (Eph 4:11–16) in small groups, usually in their residences and workplaces, for a season. The best disciple-making strategy combines with community development and C-5 (high contextualization) strategies, which is sometimes labeled an insider movement. As Christ-centered individuals and families will be "incarnated" in the structures of their communities, they will naturally rise to servant leadership roles as they love and serve their neighbors in practical ways. As they facilitate the holistic development of their neighborhood, they transform their proximate communities "from the inside out" as they share their blessings as servant-partners with other communities in establishing *shalom* wherever they live and work.

Retain Simple Structures

The third component of TS is for disciple multiplication movements to develop and maintain simple structures in house church networks. Maintaining simple structures will help prevent "split-level Christianity" with two sets of local healers. In animistic societies, the Christ believers develop "double belonging" because traditional healers are easily accessible when people need medical care. In house church networks, each Christ follower is trained and empowered to use their respective spiritual gifts in loving people, including those who need healing and deliverance ministry, right in their community.

This was how the early church literally turned the Roman Empire upside down within a few years (Acts 17:6). They did not ordain a clergy class, nor construct (or even rent) a religious building nor hold regular religious services, except to "break bread" weekly in their homes. It was the teaching and practice of the Apostle Paul (perhaps the best model of a cross-cultural missionary) not to plant a growing "local church," but an indigenous people movement in house church networks that are formed by converts who did not have to be dislocated from their families and communities (1 Cor 7:17–24). With consistent contextualization (1 Cor 9:19–23), he just needed to disciple a few persons of peace to make their own disciples from house to house and from city to city.

This New Testament practice of simply setting up CCCs is not different from that of Old Testament Israel, which shows God's design of a "simple faith" structure for a discipled or transformed people:

- They did not set up local shrines or temples in each village or town.
- There were no weekly Sabbath worship services. Synagogues as multipurpose community centers came later in 200 BC for teaching Diaspora Jews.

- There were no weekly nor monthly collections of "tithes and offerings" for church maintenance. First Corinthians 16:1–4 shows weekly collections in the early church were mainly for meeting local needs, especially of widows and orphans (Acts 6:1; Jas 1:27).
- There were no "full-time" clergy. The Levitical priests were provided not just with cities, but also with pasturelands (Josh 21). They were not exempt from being stewards of God's resources, thus they were shepherds and cowboys to provide livestock products for their community (2 Thess 3:6–13). This was how they learned to be expert butchers for animal sacrifices in the temple.
- The OT Jews were required to celebrate communally as a people in the national temple only three times a year: Passover, Pentecost, and Tabernacles (Deut 16:16; etc.).
- Teaching and obedience of the "way of God's righteousness" was in homes (Deut 6:1–11).

PMs fulfill God's goal best as his people are organized as CCCs filled with tiny "churches" that meet in "homes." It is not "churchless Christianity" nor "religionless Christianity," but "simple Christianity." Its mission is to reproduce simple groups of Christ worshipers without elaborate religiosity. This fulfills God's covenants with Abraham that through him all families on earth will be blessed (Gen 12:3; Gal 3:14,29), and with Israel that she will be a kingdom of priests (Ex 19:6; 1 Pet 2:9,10).

Thousands of CCCs were formed through PMs in the rural villages of central and southeast China in the post-Mao era as the house church networks learned to practice the "priesthood of all believers" without the structures of Christendom or denominations. Many of these PMs remain missional through the Back to Jerusalem movements, but many have lost their momentum as they became part of Christendom again, especially with the return of ordination, seminaries, church buildings, and imported discipleship materials. In Asia, and perhaps in the world, most house church networks are neo-Pentecostal in theology, so we may rightly consider them the "Fourth Wave" and perhaps the "Last Wave" of the Holy Spirit. And interestingly, if all the house church networks in Asia were one denomination, they would constitute the largest denomination in Asia today.

CONCLUSION

So, what should go right in the harvest in order to multiply CCCs through PMs in the Buddhist world and beyond? After PEs, Christ-centeredness must be contextualized in spirit-oriented and power-oriented communities that will transform Chinese, Buddhist, and similar cultures from within through insider movements. After PEs, there need to be the right allegiance encounters through a missiology of redefined friendship evangelism, and there need to be local truth encounters through a Christology of theological contextualization love encounters through an ecclesiology of transformational spirituality. With the rise of new religious movements, mostly with Buddhist and primal worldviews in our postmodern, globalized world, this approach may be the most relevant and effective mission strategy globally in the twenty-first century, too.

The eternal destiny of more than 2 billion folk Buddhist and folk religionists is at stake. Without this shift, we condemn them to reject Christ through a Christianity that is perceived to be foreign and irrelevant to their spirit world and devoid of power to transform their communities from the inside out. For those who hesitate, for the sake of the gospel and by God's mercies, at least prayerfully support those who are trying to take these nine recommended steps to transform power encounters into people movements.

REFERENCES

Anderson, Neil. 1990. *The bondage breaker*. Mandaluyong, Philippines: OMF Literature.

Bavinck, J. H. 1960. *An introduction to the science of missions*. Philadelphia: Presbyterian & Reformed.

Boyd, James. 1975. *Satan and mara: Christian and Buddhist symbols of evil*. Leiden: Brill.

Chamberlain, Jonathan. 1987. *Chinese gods*. Subang Jaya, Malaysia: Pelanduk.

Chan, Kim Kwong, and A. Hunter. 1994. Religion and society in mainland China in the 1990s. *Issues and Studies* 30, no. 8: 54–75.

Chia, Anita. 1999. A biblical theology on power manifestation: A Singaporean quest. *Asian Journal of Pentecostal Studies* 2, no. 1: 19–33.

Ching, Julia. 1993. *Chinese religions*. Maryknoll, NY: Orbis Books.

Dawson, John. 1989. *Taking our cities for God: How to break spiritual strongholds*. Lake Mary, FL: Creation House.

De Nebesky-Wojkowitz, Rene. 1956. *Oracles and demons of Tibet*. The Hague: Mouton.

Deng, Zhaoming. 2005. Indigenous Chinese Pentecostal denominations. In *Asian and Pentecostal: The charismatic face of Christianity in Asia*, ed. A. Anderson and E. Tang, 437–66. Oxford: Regnum.

Fisher, James, ed. 1978. *Himalayan anthropology: The Indo-Tibetan interface*. The Hague: Mouton.

Fukuda, Mitsuo. 2012. *Developing a contextualized church as a bridge to Christianity in Japan*. Gloucester: Wide Margin.

Garrison, David. 2014. *A wind in the house of Islam*. Monument, CO: WIGTake Resources.

Hiebert, Paul, R. D. Shaw, and Tite Tienou. 1999. *Understanding folk religion*. Grand Rapids: Baker.

Kiyota, Minoru, ed. 1987. *Japanese Buddhism*. Tokyo: Buddhist Books International.

Kraft, Charles. 1979. *Christianity in culture*. Maryknoll, NY: Orbis Books.

———. 2002. Contemporary trends in the treatment of spiritual conflicts. In *Deliver us from evil*, eds. A. Scott Moreau, Tokunboh Adeyemo, David G. Burnett, Bryant L. Myers, Hwa Yung, 177–202. Monrovia, CA: MARC.

———, ed. 2005. *Appropriate Christianity*. Pasadena: William Carey Library.

Kung, Timothy. 1993. Evangelizing Buddhists. *International Journal of Frontier Mission* 10, no. 3 (July): 118–23.

Lim, David. 2003. Towards a radical contextualization paradigm in evangelizing Buddhists. In *Sharing Jesus in the Buddhist world*, ed. David Lim and Steve Spaulding, 71–94. Pasadena: William Carey Library.

———. 2010. Catalyzing "insider movements" in Buddhist contexts. In *Family and faith in Asia: The missional impact of extended networks*, ed. Paul de Neui, 31–46. Pasadena: William Carey Library.

Lopez, Donald, Jr., ed. 1997. *Religions of Tibet in practice*. Princeton, NJ: Princeton University Press.

Lyall, Leslie. 1954. *Flame of God: John Sung and revival in the Far East*. London: OMF.

McGavran, Donald. 2005. *The bridges of God*. Reprint, Eugene, OR: Wipf & Stock.

Oblau, Gotthard. 2005. Pentecostal by default? Contemporary Christianity in China. In *Asian and Pentecostal: The charismatic face of Christianity in Asia*, ed. A. Anderson and E. Tang, 411–36. Oxford: Regnum.

Richardson, Don. 1981. *Eternity in their hearts*. Ventura, CA: Regal.

Sanneh, Lamin. 2003. *Whose religion is Christianity?* Grand Rapids: Eerdmans.

Schattner, Frank. 2014. *The wheel model: Catalyzing sustainable church planting movements*. Rocklin, CA: William Jessup University.

Singh, Sadhu Sundar. 1926. *The spirit world*. Madras: Christian Literature Society.

Spiro, Mulford. 1978. *Burmese supernaturalism*. Expanded ed. Philadelphia: Institute of the Study of Human Issues.

Tan, Chiu Eng. 1996. The cosmos, humans and gods: A comparison of non-Christians and Christians on Chinese beliefs in metro-Manila. PhD diss., Trinity International University.

Tang, Edmond. 2005. "Yellers" and healers: Pentecostalism and the study of grassroots Christianity in China. In *Asian and Pentecostal: The charismatic face of Christianity in Asia*, ed. A. Anderson and E. Tang, 467–86. Oxford: Regnum.

Tippett, Alan. 1973. *Verdict theology in missionary theology*. Pasadena: William Carey Library.

———. 1987. *Introduction to missiology.* Pasadena: William Carey Library.

Uayan, Jean. 2005. Chap Chay Lo Mi: Disentangling the Chinese-Filipino worldview. In *Naming the unknown God,* ed. E. Acoba, 65–77. Mandaluyong, Philippines: OMF Literature.

Wagner, Peter. 1996. *Confronting the powers: How the New Testament church experienced the power of strategic-level spiritual warfare.* Ventura, CA: Regal.

Walls, Andrew. 1997. Old Athens and new Jerusalem: Some signposts for Christian scholarship in the early history of mission studies. *International Bulletin of Mission Research* 21 (October): 146–53.

Wheatley, Margaret. 1992. *Leadership and the new science.* San Francisco: Berrett-Koehler.

———, and Myron Kellner-Rogers. 1996. *A simpler way.* San Francisco: Berrett-Koehler.

Wink, Walter. 1984. *Naming the powers.* Philadelphia: Fortress.

———. 1986. *Unmasking the powers.* Philadelphia: Fortress.

———. 1992. *Engaging the powers.* Philadelphia: Fortress.

———. 1998a. *The powers that be.* New York: Doubleday.

———. 1998b. *When the powers fall.* Philadelphia: Fortress.

Yip, Ching-Wah Francis. 1999. Protestant Christianity and popular religion in China. *Ching Feng* 42, no. 3–4 (July–December): 130–56.

Yong, Amos. 2003. *The Holy Spirit and the non-Christian faiths: Towards a pneumatological theology of religions.* Grand Rapids: Baker Academic.

PART II

CULTURAL PRACTICES

For God does speak—now one way,
now another—though no one perceives it.
Job 33:14

I was found by those who did not
seek me; I revealed myself to those
who did not ask for me.
Romans 10:20

We fix our eyes not on what is seen,
but on what is unseen, since what is seen
is temporary, but what is unseen is eternal.
2 Corinthians 4:18

CHAPTER 5

HOW BUDDHIST SPIRITUALITY INFLUENCES AND SHAPES ASIAN CULTURAL PRACTICES: MISSIOLOGICAL IMPLICATIONS

SHERYL TAKAGI SILZER

People in every culture view the world from their own perspective and unconsciously believe that other cultures can be understood similarly, even though they often do not understand what their own cultural perspective is. This common misunderstanding leads to miscommunication and can even reshape the gospel message into a culturally limited message.

In my work as a multicultural trainer and consultant for the past twenty years, I have observed that when people discover their cultural self-identity, they realize that they are living by a cultural perspective of the gospel message that does not always lead to godly living or represent the true gospel message. People who have been Christians for a number of years, and have been doing things in the same way for a long time, typically believe that their way of doing things is biblical. Their familiar habits justify judging other ways of doing things as wrong and as not biblical. By holding on to cultural ways of doing things, many cross-cultural workers may become frustrated when their efforts do not produce the results they desire.

This chapter identifies some of the cultural differences between Western (North American and European) and Eastern (Asian) cultures in order to help cross-cultural workers examine the extent to which their ministry efforts are culturally shaped and to enable them to see how enhancing their understanding of Buddhist spirituality can lead to more culturally sensitive ways of presenting the gospel message to Asian Buddhists.

CULTURAL DIFFERENCES BETWEEN
THE EAST AND THE WEST

In Scripture (Ps 103:12) the East and the West are referred to as opposites; differences are clearly seen in regards to cultural practices. The cultural ideal of a person in the West is an individual whose identity is in making personal decisions; the cultural ideal of a person in the East is a member of a family, community, or group who relies on the family or group to make decisions. Ho notes,

> In the West, there is growing awareness of the tension between two conceptions: The first, rooted in individualism, is that of the autonomous self; the second, more relationally and socially concerned, is that of the self conceived in terms of engagement with others.
> (Ho et al. 2001, 393)

This difference has been described as Individualism versus Collectivism. Individualistic cultures view the world from the individual's perspective, while Collective cultures view the world from the perspective of the relationships within the family, community, or group. An Individualist's life revolves around what he or she does, says, and thinks; the Collectivist's life revolves around what the group does, says, and thinks (cf. Hofstede 2001, 209–54).

This basic difference can be observed in a number of cultural practices such as social interactions, communication styles, friendship styles, visiting, eating, working, resting, and cleaning (outlined in detail in Silzer 2011). The Individualist focuses on the physical aspects of life, separating the physical from relational or spiritual aspects; the Collectivist focuses on relationships and integrates the spiritual and the physical.

Western culture is influenced by Plato's dualism of the material versus the spiritual realm. Plato viewed the spiritual realm as permanent and unchanging (Hiebert 1999, 2). Plato's philosophy was further expanded by Cartesian dualism, which separates the physical from the spiritual or mental (Dilley 2004, 135). Eastern cultures are influenced by Buddhism and reject any form of dualism of the physical and spiritual. Buddhism also rejects the dichotomy of good and evil and of right and wrong. Instead, Buddhists believe in an awakening to what is beyond good and evil (Abe 1996, 145). Compared with Western cultures that highlight thinking, beliefs, and truth, Buddhism does not actively discuss its beliefs. According to Yong (2013, 12), Buddhism is more a religion that acts on its beliefs.

Different thinking patterns arise from how cultures perceive the world. Western cultures tend to view the world in physical terms of how people can control nature; Asian cultures view the world in terms of people's relations to nature (Stewart and Bennett 2005, 115–16). Maynard (1997, 21–22) states that this difference is also reflected in language. English is an action-oriented language characterized by direct communication styles focusing on the person doing the action; Asian languages are more descriptive and are characterized by indirect communication styles focusing instead on a description of the person through topic-comment language structure. In the topic the person who does something is identified, while in the comment the relational cues of the context are given.

Two main social dimensions can describe all cultures: how people are differentiated or Structure (Lingenfelter 1996 and Douglas 1982 refer to this as Grid) and how people consider themselves similar or Community (Lingenfelter 1996 and Douglas 1982 refer to this as Group). These two dimensions form four basic cultural types—Individuating, Institutionalizing, Hierarching, and Interrelating (Silzer 2011, 28). Western cultures are a combination of Individuating and Institutionalizing; Eastern cultures are a combination of Hierarching and Interrelating. The main difference between the East and the West is the community perspective of life versus the individual perspective of life. That is, how much time and energy is spent with others and how much social responsibility group members take for one another. This difference is also referred to as Individualistic vs. Collectivistic.

In Weak Community cultures (i.e., the West), individuals can choose whom they want to spend time with and how much time they want to spend with others. People in Strong Community cultures (i.e., the East) do not generally have a choice of who they spend time with or how much time they spend together. Such decisions are all determined by the community. People in Weak Community make decisions about what kind of social responsibility they want to take for others;

people in Strong Community make decisions on how to take social responsibility for other people in the group (Kim 2001, 29).

In Weak Community an individual takes care of his or her own needs, whether emotional, physical, or spiritual; in Strong Community the members of the community take care of each other's needs (emotional, physical, and spiritual) through an established system of reciprocity (Lebra 1979, 195). This system maintains group harmony, an important ideal for Strong Community (Marcus and Kitayama 1991, 224).

People in Strong Community cultures, as in Asia, have a sense of identify and belonging to the group and are born with a debt to the community, not just to their parents and not only just to their community, but also to their country or the region where they were born. This sense of indebtedness requires a system of reciprocity that includes sharing tangible and intangible resources (Chan 2000, 121). However, this system creates an ongoing indebtedness that can never be repaid. Exchanges can also be described as social credit or gaining face (Zhang, Cao, and Grigoriou 2011, 131). That is, what a person does for someone else (e.g., a favor or help in time of need) needs to be reciprocated at a later time (Su, Mitchell, and Sirgy 2007, 301). A person can build up social credit by sharing resources with group members and will expect to receive resources at a later date (Douglas 1992, 146). The items that are exchanged are not necessarily equal in value. For example, loyalty can be given in return for protection. The concepts of honor and shame are closely connected with relationships (Wu 2013b). In a Strong Community society, sharing is also a sign of the closeness of the relationship. When a person travels, he or she returns with a gift. When someone has done a favor, he or she can expect a repayment in the future (Prasol 2010, 80).

Western culture, on the other hand, is Individualistic, with Weak Community (no long-term relationships that include reciprocity to reinforce the relationship). People in Weak Community groups and Individualists prefer making their own decisions and choosing their own areas of responsibility. They also prefer equal treatment.

The cultural practices of the West and the East are opposite in many ways, and it is easy for people from the West to misunderstand people from the East and vice versa. In order to understand Buddhist spirituality, it is necessary to understand how Buddhism views the person or the self, how Buddhist beliefs reinforce that view of the person, and how these ideas influence Asian cultural practices.

HOW BUDDHISTS VIEW THE PERSON OR SELF

Similar to Strong Community cultures, the Buddhist view of the person is not as an isolated individual but as part of all creation. People and everything else in creation are considered to be interwoven and interdependent (Verhoeven 2010, 95). In fact, in Buddhist thought people do not have an independent existence (Lancaster 1993, 516), and what happens to one person affects the others (Bean 2010, 18, 24). As such, the relationship of individuals within Buddhism has a broader perspective of life that encompasses not only present relationships but also past and future relationships. What one person does affects others, and what one person does is done for the benefit of others. Buddha reflects a Strong Community view; he was not only interested in helping individuals achieve enlightenment, he also wanted to make the world a better place by addressing the corrupt social order of his day (Iyer 1973, 235).

Unlike the Western view of the self as a person who can define himself or herself in relation to what they think, feel, and decide, the Buddhist or Eastern view of the self is much more community oriented. That is, what people say, think, feel, and decide is in relation to what the group says, thinks, feels, and decides. The Eastern individual does not have an identity apart from the group.

Buddhists believe that the person is composed of five aggregates (*khandas*) that flow together, are interdependent, and give identity to a person along with a temporal existence. These aggregates are: their material composition (*rūpa*), sense impressions (*vedanā*), perception (*saññā*), mental formations (*saṅkhāra*), and consciousness (*viññāṇa*). After death these five *khandas* are rearranged to form the reborn person (Gosling 2013, 908, 913).

These five aggregates develop a connection with all of creation, and a person cannot be understood outside of their environment/context (physical, social, and spiritual). However, suffering occurs because these aggregates are not permanent (unchanging); they are impermanent (changing) (Tse-fu Kuan 2009, 156). The word for suffering comes from the Sanskrit *dukkha*, which can be translated as "bad space or difficult situation" (Peacock 2008, 210). Suffering can be physical or mental, but it also includes being alone or even the feeling of being alone.

Although many believe that Buddha denied the existence of a person or a self, he actually did not. Instead, Buddha believed that it is the person who is attached to desires or greed (*tanha*) who experiences suffering (Verhoeven 2010, 100). However, a person can follow the Eightfold Path in order to overcome their suffering (Howard 2008, 27), and at the same time they become a person without a self or a "no-self" (Lindahl 2012, 233).

The goal of Buddhism is to free people from suffering by explaining its causes (Bhagat 1976, 160). The state of being free from suffering is called Nirvana or the space/place where there is no greed, hatred, or ignorance (Faden 2011, 42). This is the state whereby the person has awakened to the truth of "no self" or the self without its desires and attachments (Verhoeven 2010, 107). Nirvana is a pure and "self-luminous" awareness of the self (Fink 2013, 120). It is also in the here and now. "Nirvana is a condition where the self no longer rules . . . Nirvana is . . . the end of suffering not of existence" (Verhoeven 2010, 105).

> There are three kinds of suffering: physical suffering (pain, privation, and discomfort), mental suffering (the discrepancy between our illusion and reality, the disappointments), and realization that clinging to one's personality or individuality is suffering. (Lama Anagarika Govinda 1961, 69)

Buddhism teaches that the way people attach themselves to everyday events in life can bring suffering (birth, aging, sickness, death, sorrow, lamentation, pain, grief, despair, displeasure, separation from pleasure, not getting what one wants).

> The Noble Truth of suffering (dukkha) is this: Birth is suffering; aging is suffering; sickness is suffering; death is suffering; sorrow, lamentation, pain, grief and despair are suffering; association with the unpleasant [persons or objects] is suffering; dissociation from the pleasant [persons or objects] is suffering; not

to get what one wants is suffering—in brief, the five aggregates [five groups of clinging that form the object of attachment, the notions of I, mine, and self] are suffering. (Rahula 1976, 93)

The basic beliefs of Buddhism (known as the Four Noble Truths) address the impermanence of life. The first Noble Truth is that there is suffering (*dukkha*, worries and anxieties) throughout life (birth, illness, death, being separated from a loved one, etc.). This suffering needs to be embraced and understood. The second Noble Truth is that the cause of this suffering (worries and anxieties) comes from conflicting desires, a thirst for things that cannot quench it, or the wrong desire structure. The third Noble Truth is that the wrong desire structure can be replaced by the right desire structure. The fourth Noble Truth provides the way to replace the wrong desire structure through the Eightfold Path of Truth that can lead to nirvana (quietude, a calm and tranquil state) (Kishimoto 1967, 115).

According to Buddhist thought, a person's past and present actions constitute their karma (Humphreys 1994, 12). That is, a person's past actions and deeds determine who/what they are today (a person, an insect, or another living being); their present actions and deeds either lead them toward or away from Nirvana.

Buddhists believe that by following the Eightfold Path a person's right actions can replace a wrong desire structure with the right desire structure. The Eightfold Path is divided into three sections. The first section is Wisdom (*panna*), which comes from right understanding and right aspiration. The second section is Morality (*sila*), which comes from right speech, right action, and right livelihood. The third section is Concentration (*samadhi*), which comes from right effort, right mindfulness, and right concentration (Tsering 2005, locations 161–76). Wisdom (*prajna*) replaces delusion (*moha*), moral righteousness (*sila*) replaces self-love (*rage*), and purification of the mind (*samadhi*) replaces hatred (*dosa*). Replacing the wrong structure is the path to purification (Swearer 1998; Krishan 1983, 205). Good actions are considered to be purifying in that they can minimize the effect of bad deeds. These actions are not only purifying, they are also meritorious; that is, they produce merit that can lead to Nirvana.

In Buddhist thought there are a number of different kinds of actions or good works that gain merit: e.g., supporting the monks, familiarizing oneself with the religion, and being a leading lay follower (Adamek 2005, 136). A person can also share material things, behave in a moral way, and train their mind to gain merit. Other examples of meritorious actions include having polite and modest conduct, doing service for the common good, involving others in good deeds, rejoicing in the good deeds of others, explaining Buddhist teachings to others, and correcting others' view to the right (Buddhist) views.

Other actions/deeds that gain merit are commissioning the construction of Buddhist images (bells, *stupas*, shrines), copying and reciting scripture, purchasing land for the construction of Buddhist temples, donating calligraphy, praying for the monks, making murals with inscriptions, and constructing visual images of Buddha in natural material as well as media form—photos in magazines, drawings, written articles and books, radio programs, flower offerings, etc. "Good works" is basically giving or sharing of resources and is the main means to ensure a better rebirth, and participation in community moves people towards Nirvana (Walsh 2007, 355).

Buddhist teaching presents a number of guidelines for giving. Gifts should be given to a worthy recipient (monk or nun) and with a liberal spirit, not speculating on the benefits. Giving should be done in a ritual and respectful way, and with a pure motive. A spiritual tie between what is given and the merit received enhances karma for the giver and can lead to Nirvana or salvation.

Doing good deeds or actions is believed to have a cumulative effect as a means of earning merit. The more a person gives/shares, the more they have. A person can also share his or her merit with others. This contributes to his or her salvation (increased karma) as well as rescuing or helping others. The Buddhist thought of karma, action, and deeds can be seen as being very similar to the practice of "good works" in the Asian church (Adamek 2005, 143).

The Buddhist view of the person and the basic beliefs of Buddhism reinforce Asian cultural practices that come out of Strong Community values. The next section will discuss this connection in more detail.

THE INFLUENCE OF BUDDHIST
SPIRITUALITY ON ASIAN CULTURE

Buddhism reinforces the Strong Community view of the person in three ways: the definition of the self within community, the importance of relationships within the community, and the integration of material and spiritual benefits of reciprocity or earning merit through reciprocity.

The first way that Buddhist spirituality influences Asian culture is the definition of the self within a community and not as an individual. The Asian self is a person who is not alone or does not feel alone. The five parts of the person (material composition, sense impression, perception, mental formations, and consciousness) are also interrelated with others as well as all of creation. This definition of the person makes Asians conscious about the other people in their group—what they do and say, how they look, and how they use their resources.

The second way Buddhist spirituality influences Asian culture is through the importance of relationships within the community. Because the goal of Buddhism is to free people from suffering that they experience in life—birth, illness, death, loneliness—family members are there to go through those experiences together so the person does not have to be alone. The family provides everything for its family members—physical/material, social, and spiritual. At the same time, the suffering a person experiences is a result of belonging to a family or group (birth, illness, separation, death, etc.). If a person were alone, they would not have as many sources of suffering, although being alone would be suffering in itself (Lama Anagarika Govinda 1961, 69).

The importance of relationships within the community is also seen in the concept of face and honor and shame, where everything about one's family is important: where they were born, who they are related to, etc. It is important to behave oneself in such a way as to maintain the reputation or face of one's family. Face is a concept that affects every part of Asian social life (Ho 1976, 867) and includes one's "appearance and look, as indicator of emotion and character, as focus of interaction and relationship, and as locus of dignity and prestige" (Yu 2009, 151). Face is so important that it is relevant to any social interaction. Ho states that face is the respectability and/or deference that a person can claim for him/herself from others, by virtue of the relative position he occupies in the social network and the degree to which he is judged to have functioned adequately in the position as well as acceptably in his social conduct. (1976, 883)

Face has also been described as a social, interpersonal commodity that as a resource can be "threatened, enhanced, maintained, and bargained over" (Oetzel, Garcia, and Ting-Toomey 2008, 384). Asians, as members of a strong group or community and influenced by Buddhist spirituality, are concerned about how others view them, and this concern motivates them to behave in a manner that is acceptable to the others. By taking care of others, one also takes care of oneself (Persons 2008, 2).

The third way that Buddhist spirituality influences Asian culture is through the integration of material and spiritual benefits or earning merit through good works. In Chinese the word for relationships or networks of family and friends is *guan xi* (关系). This term highlights the purpose of relationships as the sharing of resources. "The term indicates carefully constructed and maintained relations between persons which carry mutual obligations and benefits" (Qi 2013, 309). Sharing resources is the main means by which Strong Community cultures support, maintain, and foster relationships. When a person shares a resource, it is automatically expected that the recipient will reciprocate in some way in the future. The basis of this sharing is modeled in the family through the Confucian virtue of filial piety, in which a child is born indebted to his parents for the care they will provide for the child during his upbringing. Children are expected to reciprocate when their parents grow old and are not as capable of caring for themselves (Jordan 1998, 267).

The integration of the material and spiritual as seen in the sharing expected of relationships also extends to the Buddhist concept of good works. These actions can be done either for oneself or on behalf of others to enable them to participate in your good works. Karma, the accumulation of good deeds or merit shared with others, enables the person who shares as well as others to increase their own karma in order to achieve a better life in the next reincarnation. Doing good deeds or actions also has a cumulative effect as a means of earning merit. The more a person gives/shares, the more they have. A person can also share his or her merit with others. Sharing is believed to contribute to a person's salvation (increased karma), as well as rescuing or helping others (Adamek 2005, 136, 143).

Next we will look at the missiological implications of the three ways that Buddhist spirituality influences Asian culture.

MISSIOLOGICAL IMPLICATIONS

A major challenge for global mission work today is helping mission workers recognize and overcome the ways their own cultural perspectives negatively affect their ministry.

In rethinking how to present the gospel in a more culturally accepted way to Buddhists, we must first consider the definition of the person or self. The interdependent Eastern person perceives the world very differently from the independent Western person. The Asian views the world as integrated physically and spiritually, but the Western person views the world as a dichotomy of the physical and the spiritual. The integrated person is considered to be composed of the five aggregates (see above); they are not just one person but are connected to other people as well as to nature. This difference requires the Western Christian to adjust the presentation of the gospel message to be more understandable to the Easterner.

For example, Western Christians, being individualistic, tend to focus on individuals rather than on their family or community. Although it is difficult for an individualist to focus on a family or an entire group of people, this may be the wiser option in working with Buddhists. Furthermore, a presentation of the gospel based on a benefit for an individual rather than for the family might be interpreted as selfish and as being antithetical to Buddhist spirituality. Verses such as Acts 16:31 ("Believe in the Lord Jesus, and you will be saved—you and your household") speak to the collective nature of believing.

Secondly, due to the importance of relationships in Asian culture, there are several things a Westerner should consider. One is that a Buddhist should be viewed as part of a group rather than as an individual.

When a Westerner develops a friendship with one person, he or she must think of that person as part of a group and focus on the social context of the person rather than just on personal characteristics. It is very difficult for a Buddhist to consider becoming an adherent to another belief system, because that would threaten not only every aspect of their life and their relationships but also their identity, which has developed over generations. If a Buddhist becomes a believer, he or she may also need to make a break with their family, and there needs to be another Strong Community group that will welcome new believers. In fact Buddhists who become believers may need to replace not only the care and concern that they have received from their family and community but also their identity.

Another thing to address in relationships is the Western dichotomist point of view where work is separated from relationships and where judgments are made regarding something being right or wrong. The better focus might be what is good/right for the person rather than what is wrong. Westerners tend to prioritize work over relationships and prefer planning ahead and developing a strategy rather than developing relationships. When things do not go as planned, as happens with relationships, Westerners may find unexpected surprises that they do not know how to address. Westerners can replace the right-and-wrong approach to ministry with an approach that can encompass the truth from both sides or the "both and" approach (Wu 2013a, 5). Dichotomist thinking tends to separate the action from the person; the integrated Easterner prefers being able to see how spirituality is integrated into everyday life and living, particularly in relationships. The Easterner feels more comfortable developing a relationship before hearing about different beliefs. When the Westerner can demonstrate a good relationship as well as explain their beliefs, the gospel will make more sense to the Easterner.

In gaining more understanding of Buddhist relationships, Westerners also need to understand the importance of "face" and how it is related to Asian identity and the family/group context. Instead of immediately judging why a person responds in the way that they do, consider their family context and how the response maintains or upholds their family reputation. Consider also how doing something for one person now may be a means of gaining social capital or an opportunity for witness later. Individualistic actions can lead the Easterner to distrust Westerners and to discount any message or relationship that Westerners may seek to develop.

The third way that Buddhist spirituality influences Asian culture is through the integration of material and spiritual benefits or earning merit through good works. With the goal of Buddhism being to alleviate the suffering people experience in everyday life (birth, illness, separation, death, etc.), the Westerner can recognize the importance of these daily events and look for ways to help. The Westerner can think of joining in the everyday concerns of Asians as demonstrating their beliefs through their actions. If the Asian Buddhist can also recognize God's truth in the life of believers in dealing with everyday life events, they may be drawn to those people who demonstrate the gospel message. Yong suggests that due to the relational focus of Buddhist cultures, ministry to Buddhists should focus not so much on beliefs as on the whole identity of people and their lives. Ministry should attend to the narratives of their lives and be willing to enter into their journeys as well as to share one's own journey, thus letting actions speak louder than words (Yong 2013, 15–18). Song (1999, 6–7) suggests that outreach to Buddhists should be more about experiencing God's grace in the world than involving people in numerous activities in order to convert them.

As the Westerner reaches out to the Buddhist, keep in mind that the Buddhist will also want to reciprocate. The ongoing nature of reciprocity is also difficult for Westerners to understand, as we have been socialized to take care of our own needs. When we worked in Asia, we made sure we had everything we needed as good Individualists. However, the people complained that they wanted to help us but we did not have a need for their help. Rather than recognizing a need we have and immediately filling it, we need to allow others to recognize our need and offer their help. As there are appropriate as well as inappropriate ways of reciprocating, check with people to find out what is and what is not appropriate. Sharing requires much wisdom, as there can be negative consequences if whatever is shared is not reciprocated appropriately (e.g., either too much or too little). In Eastern cultures, reciprocity can be passed on to one's children and their children. Although various people in the community can be consulted about the reciprocating process, it is also a good practice to rely on God's wisdom in making decisions about reciprocity. The Buddhist will also understand 1 Timothy 5:8: "Anyone who does not provide for their relatives, and especially for their own household, has denied the faith and is worse than an unbeliever." Buddhists will also understand the numerous passages that speak about how we should relate to one another.

Western Christians who focus on ethics/morality may find that their message is indistinguishable from the Buddhist understanding of meritorious deeds. The Easterner may, in fact, have a clearer connection between works and spiritual benefits (helping one another along the path away from the wrong desire structure to the right desire structure and the end of suffering). The Westerner's explanation of a future benefit of morality (avoidance of undesirable punishment) may not make sense to the Easterner. The major challenge will be wanting to explain how biblical good works (Eph 2:8,9) are different from Buddhist good works. However, it might be better to allow biblical good works to be demonstrated by your actions rather than looking for ways to explain it.

After considering the above three areas of difference between the East and the West, it is vital to revisit our theological understanding of how God views us from the perspective of being made in his image (see Silzer 2011, 9–19). This theological basis will not only enable us to understand the differences but will also provide insights on how God wants to relate to the other.

God made all people, Easterners and Westerners, in his image to be like him for who we are and not for what we do. We may have different perspectives on the way things should be done because of our cultural upbringing, but we are all the same before God.

If we do not believe, or cannot accept, that we are unconditionally loved by God because we are made in his image, it will be difficult for us to accept or to relate well to people from another culture. We may tend to judge other ways of doing things as wrong, creating a barrier in our relationships. When we understand how much we are in need of Christ's redemptive work on the Cross, we can embrace others as similarly in need of God's love. This understanding will also open our minds to how our cultural practices can prevent us from reflecting God's image. All human cultures have both positive and negative elements, reflecting God's image in some ways and fostering false beliefs in other ways.

Although initially there was only one language, multiple languages came into existence after the Fall when people tried to be like God and built a tower to make a name for themselves (Gen 11) (see Smith and Carvill 2000, 7–8). From the beginning, God's desire was to unite people from every language and culture through the person and work of Christ. This complete unity will take place in heaven around the throne when people from every nation, language, and tribe will praise and worship God together (Rev 5:7; 7:9). However, God also desires people to experience this unity now (Eph 4:3).

In order to move towards the unity that God desires, we each need to understand who God is and what it means to be made in the image of God. For the purposes of this paper, we view God in light of the Trinity—our Father, the Son, and the Holy Spirit. As our Father, God takes responsibility for us as his children (Isa 64:8; 2 Cor 6:18), similar to a human father. The Father is our authority figure and decision maker. Christ, his Son—who is the Word, the Truth, and the Way (John 1:1; 14:6)—sets the example for us through living the truth in his earthly life and through his obedience in becoming human so he could die for our sins (Phil 2:5–11). God the Holy Spirit guides us and teaches us the things we need to say and do (Luke 12:12; John 14:26; 1 Cor 2:13). The Spirit enables us to demonstrate the fruit of the Spirit (Gal 5:22,23) in our relationships with one another.

Saucy (1993, 22–23) presents three main views of what it means to be made in the image of God—the substantive, the functional, and the relational views. These three views represent God: (1) as authority (2 Cor 6:18), responsible for decision making (e.g., giving the Law); (2) as responsible for creation (Col 1:16) and truth (John 14:6); and (3) as responsible for community (1 Cor 12:13). When we reflect the image of God in these three ways, God, rather than we, receives the glory.

The substantive view of the image of God views the image as something that uniquely distinguishes people from the rest of creation, such as the freedom of choice or our will (Hoekema 1994, 68–73). God created us to be like him in our ability to choose between good and evil. Through our will we can choose to depend on God or to rely on our own wisdom (Prov 3:5,6).

The functional view of the image of God views the image as taking responsibility for creation (Gen 1:28; Col 1:16,17). This aspect has been referred to as taking dominion or responsibility, as God gave Adam and Eve dominion to rule over and care for the earth and all the creatures of the earth (Gen 1:26–30). God entrusted to us the care of creation as his representatives (Hoekema 1994, 67).

The relational view of the image of God views the image of God in terms of human relationships with God, with others, and with creation (ibid., 75–82). Human relationships form the body of Christ (1 Cor 12:13), in which each person has a particular role and function like the parts of a body that function in unity according to the gifts God has given (1 Cor 12:7). Each person has a gift that enables the whole body to function properly (1 Cor 12:12). Therefore, everyone should have equal concern for one another (1 Cor 12:25) and should honor or treat members that are weaker or considered less honorable with special care (1 Cor 12:22–24). One member cannot say that they do not belong (1 Cor 12:15), and another member cannot say that they do not need other members of the body (1 Cor 12:21). Relationships also reflect the fruit of the Spirit (Gal 5:22,23).

We can reflect the image of God in our ministry by recognizing that different cultural types have different ways of making decisions, taking responsibility, and relating to one another. Our way may not be the only way, and other ways may in fact reflect God more easily. We can also remember that there will be people from every tribe, nation, and people in heaven (Rev 7:9), including people from the East as well as the West. Our challenge now is to work together in a God-honoring way in which others can see the image of God reflected in our relationships, not only with East/West coworkers, but also in our united effort to reach others with the gospel message.

CONCLUSION

We have briefly examined the cultural differences between the East and the West in terms of the difference between Strong and Weak Community. In Strong Community cultures, such as those in the East, the person is viewed as part of a whole, while in Weak Community cultures, like the United States, the person is viewed individually and not as a part of others. When we compare the cultural description of the East with Buddhist spirituality, we discover many similarities that make it difficult to separate Asian culture from Buddhist beliefs. The missiological implications suggest that both East and West need to consider the extent to which their ways of presenting the gospel are cultural and therefore not fully understood by the other. Revisiting what it means to be made in the image of God provides a basis to continue this discussion.

REFERENCES

Abe, Masao. 1996. *Zen and comparative religions*. Honolulu: University of Hawaii Press.

Adamek, Wendi L. 2005. Impossibility of the given: Representation of merit and emptiness in Medieval Chinese Buddhism. *History of Religions* 45, no. 2: 135–80.

Bean, Andrea. 2010. In light of Anatman: Toward a feminist no-self. *Journal of Theta Alpha Kappa* 34, no. 1 (Spring): 18–31.

Bhagat, M. G. 1976. *Ancient Indian asceticism*. New Delhi: Munshiram Manoharlal.

Chan, Sin Yee. 2000. Gender and relationship roles in the Analects and the Mencius. *Asian Philosophy* 10, no. 2: 115–32.

Dilley, Frank B. 2004. Taking consciousness seriously: In defense of Cartesian dualism. *International Journal for Philosophy of Religion* 55: 135–53.

Douglas, Mary Tew. 1982. Cultural bias. In *In the active voice*. 183–254. London: Routledge, Kegan and Paul.

———. 1992. The origins of culture. In *Risk and blame: Essays in cultural theory*. London: Routledge.

Faden, Gerhard. 2011. No-self, Dôgen, the Senika doctrine, and Western views of soul. *Buddhist-Christian Studies* 31: 41–54.

Fink, Charles Kedric. 2013. Consciousness as presence: An exploration of the illusion of the self. *Buddhist Studies Review* 30, no. 1: 113–28.

Gosling, David L. 2013. Embodiment and rebirth in the Buddhist and Hindu tradition. *Zylon* 48, no. 4 (December): 908–15.

Hiebert, Paul G. 1999. *The missiological implications of epistomological shifts: Affirming truth in a modern/postmodern world.* Harrisburg, PA: Trinity Press International.

Ho, David Yau-Fai. 1976. On the concept of face. *American Journal of Sociology* 81: 867–84.

——, Shui-fun Fiona Chan, Si-qing Peng, and Aik Kwang Ng. 2001. The dialogical self: Converging East-West constructions. *Culture and Psychology* 7, no. 3: 393–408.

Hoekema, Andrew. 1994. *Created in God's image.* Grand Rapids: Eerdmans.

Hofstede, Geerdt. 2001. *Culture's consequences: Comparing values, behaviours, institutions, and organizations across nations.* Thousand Oaks, CA: Sage.

Howard, Veena Rani. 2008. Listening to the Buddha's Noble Truths: A method to alleviate social suffering. *Pacific World*, 3rd series, no. 10 (Fall): 23–43.

Humphreys, Christmas. 1994. *Karma and rebirth.* Surrey, England: Curzon.

Iyer, R. N. 1973. *The moral and political thought of Mahatma Gandhi.* New York: Oxford University Press.

Jordan, David K. 1998. Filial piety in Taiwanese popular thought. In *Confucianism and the family,* ed. Walter H. Slote and George A. DeVos, 267–84. Albany: State University of New York Press.

Kim, Eun Y. 2001. *The yin and yang of American culture: A paradox.* Yarmouth, ME: Intercultural Press.

Kishimoto, Hideo. 1967. Some Japanese cultural traits and religions. In *The Japanese mind: Essentials of Japanese philosophy and culture,* ed. Charles A. Moore, 110–21. Honolulu: University of Hawaii Press.

Krishan, Y. 1983. Karma Vipaka. *Numen.* Vol. 30, fasc. 2, 199–214.

Lama Anagarika Govinda. 1961. *Psychological attitude of early Buddhist philosophy and its systematic representation according to Abidhamma tradition.* London: Rider.

Lancaster, Brian L. 1993. Self or no self: Converging perspectives from neuropsychology and mysticism. *Zygon* 8, no. 4 (December): 507–26.

Lebra, Takie Sugiyama. 1979. Reciprocity and the asymmetric principle: An analytical reappraisal of the Japanese concept of on. In *Japanese culture and behaviour: Selected readings*, ed. Takie Sugiyama Lebra and William P. Lebra, 192–207. Honolulu: University of Hawaii Press.

Lindahl, Jared. 2012. Self transformation according to Buddhist stages of path literature. *Pacific World*, 3rd series, no. 14: 231–27.

Lingenfelter, Sherwood G. 1996. *Agents of transformation: A guide for effective cross-cultural ministry.* Grand Rapids: Baker Books.

Marcus, Hazel Rose, and Shinobu Kitayama. 1991. Culture and the self: Implications for cognition, emotion, and motivation. *Psychological Review* 98, no. 2: 224–53.

Maynard, Senko K. 1997. *Japanese communication: Language and thought in context.* Honolulu: University of Hawaii Press.

Oetzel, John, Adolfo Garcia, and Stella Ting-Toomey, eds. 2008. An analysis of the relationships among face concerns and facework behaviours in perceived conflict situations: A four-culture investigation. *International Journal of Conflict Management* 19, no. 4: 382–403.

Peacock, John. 2008. Suffering in mind: The aetiology of suffering in early Buddhism. *Contemporary Buddhism* 9, no. 2 (November): 209–26.

Persons, Larry Scott. 2008. Face dynamics, social power, and virtue among Thai leaders. PhD diss., Fuller School of World Mission.

Prasol, Alexander. 2010. *Modern Japan: Origins of the mind; Japanese mentality and tradition in contemporary life.* Hackensack, NJ: World Scientific.

Qi, Xiaoying. 2013. Guanxi, social capital theory and beyond: Toward a globalized social science. *British Journal of Sociology* 64, no. 2: 308–24.

Rahula. 1976. Setting in motion the wheel of truth (Dhammacakkappavattana-sutta). In *What the Buddha taught: Revised and expanded texts from Suttas and Darmmapada.* New York: Grove.

Saucy, Robert. 1993. Theology of human nature. In *Christian perspectives on being human: A multidisciplinary approach to integration*, ed. James Porter Moreland and David M. Ciocchi. Grand Rapids: Baker.

Silzer, Sheryl Takagi. 2011. *Biblical multicultural teams: Applying biblical truth to cultural differences.* Pasadena: William Carey International University Press.

Smith, David I., and Barbara Carvill. 2000. *The gift of the stranger: Faith, hospitality, and foreign language learning.* Grand Rapids: Eerdmans.

Song, Choan-Seng. 1999. *The believing heart: An invitation to story theology.* Minneapolis: Fortress.

Stewart, Edward C., and Milton J. Bennett. 2005. *American cultural patterns: A cross-cultural perspective.* Yarmouth, ME: Intercultural Press.

Su, Chenting, Ronald K. Mitchell, and M. Joseph Sirgy. 2007. Enabling guanxi management in China: A hierarchical stakeholder model of effective guanxi. *Journal of Business Ethics* 71: 301–19.

Swearer, Donald. 1998. Buddhist virtue, voluntary poverty, and extreme benevolence. *Journal of Religious Ethics* 26, no. 1 (Spring): 71–103.

Tse-fu Kuan. 2009. *Rethinking non-self: A new perspective form Ekottarika-āgama.* London: Equinox.

Tsering, Geshe Tashi. 2005. *The Four Noble Truths: The foundation of Buddhist thought.* Vol. 1, *Wisdom.* Kindle edition.

Verhoeven, Martin. 2010. Buddhist ideas about no-self and the person. *Religion East and West* 10: 93–112.

Walsh, Michael J. 2007. The economics of salvation: Toward a theory of exchange in Chinese Buddhism. *Journal of the American Academy of Religion* 75, no. 2 (June): 353–82.

Wu, Jackson. 2013a. Contextualizing the gospel in any culture: A model from the biblical text for a global context. *Global Missiology* 3, no. 10 (April): 1–40.

———. 2013b. *Saving God's face: A Chinese contextualization of honor and shame.* EMS Dissertation Series. Pasadena: William Carey International University Press.

Yong, Amos. 2013. A heart strangely warmed on the middle way: The Wesleyan witness in a pluralistic world. *Wesleyan Theological Journal* 48, no. 1 (Spring): 7–27.

Yu, Ning. 2009. What does our face mean to us? In *From body to meaning in culture: Papers on semantic cognitive studies of Chinese.* 151–86. Amsterdam: John Benjamins.

Zhang, Xin-an, Qing Cao, and Nicolas Grigoriou. 2011. Consciousness of social face: The development and validation of a scale measuring desire to gain face versus fear of losing face. *Journal of Social Psychology* 151, no. 2: 129–49.

CHAPTER 6

THE IMPACT OF BUDDHISM ON ANCESTOR VENERATION IN VIETNAM: HARMLESS CROSS-CULTURAL ASSIMILATION OR DARK SPIRITUAL INFLUENCE?

TIN NGUYEN

The tradition of ancestor veneration existed in Vietnam before Buddhism entered the land around the time of Christ. Vietnamese society was built on relational networks in ancient times and continues to depend upon them today. In this culture, family bonds have often been considered to be the most sacred of treasures. In this formerly war-torn country, mothers had hopelessly held the remains of their dead children in their arms. Children had lived through the loss of parents who had died before they reached old age. This kind of trauma was a common and nationwide experience. The tradition of veneration of the dead has been a way for Vietnamese to express their respect, affection, and longing for those who have passed away. Over thousands of years this tradition has grown to become a way of life. Under the influences of both spontaneous development of indigenous animistic beliefs and of foreign religions, the tradition has become in many cases much more powerful than even a propositional religion. The reason for this is because ancestor veneration transcends history and permeates all aspects and levels of the society.

The tradition of ancestor veneration has posed one of the biggest and most enduring challenges to the undiluted proclamation of the gospel in Vietnam from the very beginning of mission activity there. It is not a trivial matter to declare the tradition to be idol worship and then to ban it completely. Nor is it biblically faithful to welcome the tradition uncritically. So what must the church do in this sensitive situation?

This chapter is structured as follows. First, it presents the history of ancestor veneration against the Vietnamese cultural backdrop, especially highlighting the Buddhist spiritual influence on the tradition. Second, it presents and evaluates the approaches taken by the Vietnamese Catholic Church and by its Protestant counterpart. Finally, it proposes a strategy for interacting with the tradition of ancestor veneration that is both biblically defensible and culturally relevant.

A HISTORY OF THE TRADITION OF ANCESTOR VENERATION IN VIETNAM

Ancestor veneration is one of the most ancient traditions of Vietnam. No one really knows exactly when it began. It is customary for Vietnamese to pay their respects to their ancestors and ascribe to these forebearers all the good things they enjoy today. One popular Vietnamese saying expresses this idea as, "When you drink the water, remember the source" ("*Uong Nuoc Nho Nguon*") (Dang 2012, 5).

Growing up, Vietnamese are taught that there are two worlds: the world of the living and the world of the dead, sometimes called the underworld. The existence of this underworld is comforting to the living in the sense that at death their loved ones have not disappeared forever but only passed to another world. Hence, the dead continue to exist and are still part of the family. The indigenous concept of family spans many generations and encompasses both the dead and the living. Family relationships transcend the boundary of the two worlds.

The tradition of ancestor veneration was reinforced when Confucianism entered Vietnam from China around the second century before Christ, when the first Chinese domination of Vietnam started (Tran 1919, 41). Harmony is one of the core beliefs of Confucianism (Truong 2010, location 738). People are instructed to live in harmony with other people and with nature. In a Confucian society, the virtue of filial piety is promoted. Filial piety calls for respect for one's parents and ancestors. The two concepts of Confucian harmony and filial piety coalesce into a resilient demand for harmony among family members across generations in both worlds. For that reason, honoring ancestors and maintaining harmony in the family are important Vietnamese virtues (ibid., location 791).

All of the knowledge and rituals regarding ancestor veneration is orally passed from generation to generation without written records. Ancestor veneration is primarily observed by means of rituals. It is customary that a family altar is erected at the most prominent place in the house of an unbeliever's house. There are many occasions throughout the year that the tradition is observed. These occasions include death anniversaries of family members, Lunar New Year, the weddings of descendants, and harvests. These events provide a good opportunity for extended family members to strengthen their family bonds.

Figure 3: Paper money offered at family and territorial deity altar.
Source: author's collection.

Acts of veneration include, but are not limited to, bowing before ancestor pictures, visiting ancestor graves, and offering food and burning incense at the family altar. Taking good care of ancestor graves is a sign of respect for the dead, which usually brings praises from family and friends. It is believed that ancestors will bless the descendants who take care of their graves. On the other hand, leaving ancestor graves unattended commonly results in criticism and even condemnation from the community, which cannot be ignored in a communal society such as Vietnam. The tradition of ancestor veneration permeates the daily life of the Vietnamese people. It is considered a natural extension of the respect to living elderly people in the family.

HOW VIETNAMESE PEOPLE VIEW ANCESTOR VENERATION

To the majority of non-Christian Vietnamese, the distinction between veneration and worship is hard to make and, more importantly, unnecessary. In Vietnam as well as in other East Asian countries where monotheism is a foreign concept, it is natural for people to bow before a statue or a picture of somebody they respect, living or deceased. If that is considered worship, so be it. What is the big deal anyway? It might be a concern for those who subscribe to a monotheistic viewpoint such as Christianity. Many ancestor worshipers would say that they venerate their ancestors out of respect and gratitude. Having said that, the practice of ancestor veneration can be filled with pragmatism. People are taught that when they venerate their ancestors they will receive blessings, generally defined in terms of longevity, prosperity, and peace. On the other hand, curses such as bad luck, sickness, and even death will likely come upon them if they do not venerate ancestors.

In an evangelical perspective, one will move from the domain of respect to the sphere of worship when prayers and offerings are involved. When the object of worship is not God, it is idolatry. In this light, the practice of Vietnamese ancestor veneration is clearly idolatrous, because the ancestor worshipers consider their dead ancestors deities who can be appeased and pleased, bless and curse. When praying to the dead ancestors, the ancestor worshipers believe in their power. When offering things to the dead ancestors, they believe that the dead ancestors can somehow accept the offering and bless them.

Superstition plays a prominent role in ancestor veneration. In light of the fact that the underworld is never fully understood by mortals, people practice the traditions the way they see fit. One natural way is to extrapolate what happens in the living world to the underworld. For example, ancestor worshipers believe the dead still need to be fed and cared for. That is the reason why they offer food and personal things that are usually made of paper and can be burned at offering rites. Affluent Vietnamese spend a great deal of money on paper currency, paper automobiles, and paper furniture. As technology advances, paper laptops, paper flat-screen televisions, and even paper iPads are offered as well.

Vietnamese believe that the underworld is the permanent residence for the dead until reincarnation takes place. However, as the living culturally go home during the Lunar New Year, the dead also return home to spend time with their families. This is just an extrapolation of a Vietnamese New Year tradition. Therefore, to welcome the Lunar New Year, Vietnamese cleanse their houses to receive ancestors. When the New Year celebration comes to an end, they send off their ancestors back to the underworld.

Fear dominates the practice of ancestor veneration. While love, respect, and blessings are often mentioned as the motivation for the tradition, fear for punishment is ubiquitous. People are convinced that if they do not venerate their ancestors, bad things will surely happen to them and their family. They believe that the dead are somehow more powerful than the living. They can bless, curse, or even harm the living. One way to appease ancestors is to pay respect to them by offering food and visiting their graves. It is interesting to observe that even those who faithfully follow all of the required rituals of ancestor veneration still encounter unpleasant things in life. They dare not question the efficacy of ancestor veneration, but instead attribute instances of bad luck to karma—another elusive concept of Eastern religions. The law of karma would explain the occurrence of unpleasant things as consequences of bad deeds in previous lives. In short, bad luck is basically one's own fault. As soon as death, illness, unemployment, and other bad things happen, Vietnamese people are quick to place the blame for them on a lack of a sufficient amount of ancestor veneration in the family. The concept of transfer of credits or curses is popular among Vietnamese ancestor worshipers. They believe if a family member does not venerate ancestors, the entire family or even the extended family is somehow cursed. However, they also believe that one can do extra to make up for the laxity in devotion to the ancestors of other family members.

BUDDHIST INFLUENCE ON
VIETNAMESE ANCESTOR VENERATION

The original tradition of ancestor veneration in Vietnam had nothing to do with Buddhism. Even today, many Vietnamese people would adamantly claim to be nonreligious, or *luong* in Vietnamese, while they in fact practice ancestor worship. As far as such people are concerned, ancestor veneration is not a religion. Moreover, they do not consider themselves to be Buddhists. According to the Pew Research Center, 45 percent of the population are in various indigenous religions (figure 4). The majority of them are ancestor worshipers who are heavily influenced by Buddhist philosophy.

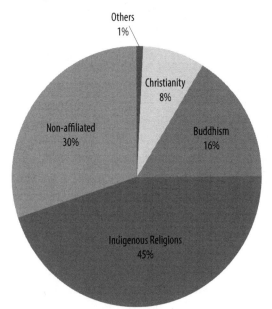

Figure 4: *Religious distribution in Vietnam.*
Source: *www.pewforum.org/uploadedFiles/Topics/Religious_*
Affiliation/globalReligion-full.pdf (page discontinued).

For over two thousand years since it entered Vietnam, Buddhism has deeply influenced and remarkably changed the way Vietnamese people venerate ancestors. While the process of assimilation might have begun unintentionally, there are today deliberate and well-reasoned outreach strategies developed by Vietnamese Buddhist organizations to lure ancestor worshipers into Buddhism. Ancestor veneration under the influence of Buddhism has become more institutionalized in Buddhist forms. At the same time, Buddhism has adapted itself to Vietnamese indigenous beliefs. There are reasons, both objective and subjective, why Buddhism has been able to make such inroads into the indigenous tradition of ancestor veneration in Vietnam.

First, the way of Buddha in Vietnam is promoted as a means of self-discovery. Buddhism is not propositional and centered on objective truths, but rather it is experiential and relativistic. It encourages personal quests for truth, however that truth may be defined. Strengthening the fusion of Buddhism with the Vietnamese tradition of ancestor veneration is the fact that the variety of Buddhism that entered Vietnam from China is Mahayana. This is a syncretistic and locally adaptable sect. Unlike Theravada—the other major sect of Buddhism, which is more atheistic and monastic in nature—Mahayana, whose mandate is to bring enlightenment to all human beings, sees no issues with the tradition of ancestor veneration. Over the course of history, Buddhism in Vietnam became heavily ritual oriented (Dang 2012, 449–51). At Buddhist events, in addition to praying to Buddha and other Buddhist deities, Vietnamese Buddhists are also encouraged to pray to their ancestors. Effectively, ancestor veneration and Buddhist worship have virtually merged. This allows Vietnamese ancestor worshipers to become Buddhists effortlessly.

Buddhist scholars have wailed about the commercialism of contemporary Mahayanan pagodas, where Buddhist monks offer places for people to keep the ashes of deceased relatives. This has become a significant source of revenue for many Buddhist pagodas. It also draws people to the locations, first to visit the ashes and second to pay tribute to the pagodas. This is just one strategic effort to bring Buddhism into the practice of ancestor veneration.

Second, the way that Buddhism presents itself to Vietnamese people impacts how it is perceived. Historically speaking, the concept of established religion has had a bad connotation in Vietnam. It reminds people of Western invasions and the century-long dominations that followed, and of the wars that cost millions of lives and ravaged their beautiful country. All three great religions from China—Taoism, Confucianism, and Buddhism—have advertised themselves as philosophies that suggested ways of life as opposed to propositional religions that professed objective truths. People adopting the Chinese religions have had the freedom to pick and choose what they like to form their own spiritual path. Ancestor veneration fits well into these Chinese philosophies, because it also considers itself a way of life and not a religion. In return, Buddhism is ready to offer ways to venerate ancestors. Therefore, assimilation is bound to happen, or at least it is likely to happen.

Third, while it might have started out as an unprompted way to pay respects to ancestors within the family, ancestor veneration in Vietnam has expanded to include national heroes and international figures. The respect for Confucius has long crossed the border of China and entered many neighboring Asian countries. His wise sayings and philosophy have been embraced by Vietnamese and other peoples as their own. Many Asian cultures and societies bear indelible marks of Confucian philosophy. When Buddhism entered Vietnam, having listened to Buddha's teaching, Vietnamese people quickly embraced his perspective and venerated him, because he was a good man with many wise sayings to learn from.

Fourth, to counter the spread of Christianity, there are efforts within the Buddhist population (with the support of the government) to turn Buddhism into an inseparable component of Vietnamese culture. As a result, it may enjoy the unquestioned acceptance of the mass population. Annual Buddhist events have become Vietnamese national holidays. During such festivals, high-profile government officials visit prestigious pagodas to burn incense before the images of the Buddha and previous incarnations like Guanyin as well as national heroes.

Fifth, Buddhism has provided Vietnamese ancestor veneration with an institutionalized spiritual foundation. It would not be an overstatement to say that Buddhism has heightened the level of superstition and the degree of fear that already dominate the landscape of ancestor veneration. Already soaked with superstition and fear, ancestor worshipers are now equipped with a mechanism not only to examine their motives and actions but also to connect with their loved ones in the underworld. Being a service religion, which seeks to satisfy the needs of its devotees, Vietnamese Buddhism openly supports all rituals pertaining to ancestor veneration. Buddhist monks offer to conduct funerals for ancestor worshipers at virtually no charge. They are willing to come to private residences to pray for the deceased so that they may avoid reincarnation. A vague understanding about the underworld is now reinforced with the teaching of karma and reincarnation. Buddha and other Buddhist deities are now the object of prayers for the otherwise abstract prayers of ancestor worshipers. Before the coming of Buddhism, rituals of ancestor veneration were simple and spontaneous. With the presence of Buddhism, there is now chanting, preaching of Buddha's teaching, and other Buddhist rituals.

In summary, with over two thousand years of influence, Buddhism has made Vietnamese ancestor veneration a Buddhist-friendly religion without the awareness of the ancestor worshipers. The two religions, or philosophies, or ways of life, whatever you prefer to call them, are assimilated into a folk religion specific to the Vietnamese. In an effort to bring ancestor worshipers back to a healthy respect to ancestors and a knowledge of God, the church needs to appreciate the laudable aspects of ancestor veneration and use them to build bridges to lead ancestor worshipers to Jesus, who commands respect for parents and ancestors. In Matthew 15:1–9, when the Pharisees and the scribes accused Jesus' disciples of disobeying the ancestors, Jesus reaffirmed God's command for hornoring parents and succinctly exposed the accusers as the ones who disobeyed God and dishonored parents.

Before I conclude with suggestions on how to interact with ancestor worshipers, I now review the historical approaches the Vietnamese Catholic Church and her Protestant counterpart have taken in dealing with ancestor veneration.

THE VIETNAMESE CATHOLIC APPROACH TO ANCESTOR VENERATION

When the Catholic Church established its position in Vietnam in the first decades of the seventeenth century, she had to deal with the indigenous tradition of ancestor veneration. The central question at issue was always, "Is ancestor veneration merely a healthy act of honoring ancestors or is it a form of idolatry and therefore smacking of superstition?" The answer to this question would help the church establish her view on the tradition as well as her outreach strategy toward ancestor worshipers. On the other hand, the tradition could be a barrier for mission. Believers were eager to know how to venerate their beloved ancestors without violating the first commandment. At the same time, nonbelievers would love to know how to become Christians without forsaking their families.

Throughout the history of mission in Asia, different stakeholders at different times have answered that crucial question differently. History has taken many turns as a result of those answers. The Chinese Rites Controversy, which lasted nearly three centuries and involved many of the Pope's decrees, with each one annulling the previous one, illustrates the intricacy of the issue.

When the early Catholic missionaries arrived in China in the sixteenth century, they had to make a judgment about the Chinese ancestor and Confucius rites (Minamiki 1985, 10). Were they religious and idolatrous in nature or just cultural and social? Jesuit missionaries were the first to plow the mission field of China under the exclusive assignment of Pope Gregory XIII (Phan 2003, 112). Under the influence of the accommodationist policy championed by Alessandro Valignano (Phan 2005, 113), they accepted the rites of ancestor and Confucius veneration as legitimate. Later on, when the Dominican, Franciscan, and Augustinian missionaries, who embraced a missionary approach different from the Jesuits' accommodationist policy, entered China, they objected to the Jesuits' acceptance of Chinese rites. On the basis of the new findings, the Catholic Church condemned the Chinese rites of ancestor and Confucius veneration in 1645 (Phan 2003, 113). The Chinese Rites Controversy officially started and quickly expanded to Japan and other East Asian countries.

In 1656, after the Jesuits made another attempt to defend their case, the Catholic Church reversed its position on Chinese rites of ancestor and Confucius veneration. The church considered the rites civil and not religious. In 1704, Pope Clement XI condemned the Chinese rites as idolatry. In 1716 the same pope decreed that missionaries who did not observe his instructions would suffer the penalty of excommunication (ibid., 114–15). Understandably, the condemnation of the Chinese rites met with strong opposition from the Chinese emperor.

Even though the controversy happened within the borders of China, it concluded in Japan. When Japanese Catholics demanded a clarification of the government-issued decree that they had to pay homage to Confucius, the government replied that "they [the required acts of veneration] did not have any religious character" (Minamiki 1985, 145). That is, the Japanese government assured local Christians that bowing before the statue of Confucius was merely a display of nationalism and loyalty.

In 1939, Propaganda Fide, the same office of the Catholic Church that had condemned the Chinese rites as idol worship nearly three hundred years earlier, issued *Plane compertum est* with Pope Pius XII's approval. This pronouncement permitted Catholics to participate in public honors of Confucius. In regarding to ancestor veneration, it allowed bowing of the head and other gestures of respect before the deceased and their images on a family altar. It was announced explicitly that all previous decrees were thereby dissolved. With *Plane compertum est*, the Chinese Rites Controversy came to an end.

Pioneer Catholic missionaries in Vietnam viewed the practice of ancestor veneration quite differently. Had they been consulted, they would not have been in favor of *Plane compertum est*. In fact, they described Vietnamese ancestor veneration as the cult of ancestors and identified it as a Vietnamese indigenous religion. Alexander De Rhodes was probably the most influenced Catholic missionary in Vietnam in the early days. He was credited for coming up with the modern Vietnamese written language. He took great offense at the Vietnamese celebrations on death anniversaries (Phan 2005, 93). As an indigenous religion, ancestor veneration developed informally without an institutionalized structure of religious leaders or collection of sacred writings. It was and is both powerful and pervasive.

The Vietnamese Catholic Church quietly but closely followed the development of the Chinese Rites Controversy, because it would have direct implications on the tradition of ancestor veneration in Vietnam. On April 12, 1974, nearly thirty-five years after *Plane compertum est* was decreed, the Vietnamese bishops formally issued detailed instructions regarding ancestor veneration (Phan 2003, 124). The instructions allowed an ancestor altar to be erected under that of God, Mary, and

Jesus. They allowed the burning of incense and the lighting of candles. They permitted prostrating gestures with joined hands in front of the ancestor altar as filial piety. On death anniversaries they allowed the offering of things in a "commemorative" manner. During marriage ceremonies, the bride and groom are allowed to bow in front of the ancestor altar to express gratitude. Catholics are even allowed to participate in ceremonies according to local customs to venerate historical figures—benefactors of the village—as long as there is no superstition.

These ground-breaking guidelines were warmly received by the Vietnamese Catholic community as well as by the secular population. From then on, Vietnamese Catholics were free in their conscience to venerate ancestors. These guidelines also paved the way for them to interact with non-Christian family members, friends, and neighbors. On the surface, the hostility of others towards the Vietnamese Catholic Church was significantly reduced. However, the most important question remains whether her instructions are biblically faithful or whether they undermine God's truth and shove the church further into syncretism.

Commenting on the effect of *Plane compertum est*, Peter Phan, a leading Catholic theologian, who was also Vietnamese by birth, observed, "In spite of its short-term missionary gains, it [*Plane compertum est*] left unresolved many theological issues that are of great consequence for the project of liturgical inculturation" (ibid., 116).

Unlike other Catholic scholars who either denied or downplayed the religious significance of ancestor veneration, Phan fully recognized its religious nature. Nevertheless, he believed, "With its religious nature frankly recognized, it is possible to appeal to the doctrine of the communion of saints and enlarge it in such a way that the ancestors can find their appropriate place in this communion and receive due veneration" (ibid., 121). This perspective seemingly does not take into account the idolatry and superstitious nature of ancestor veneration. How can a non-Christian ancestor, living his life on earth worshiping idols, who died believing in works salvation and the mysterious outworking of reincarnation, possibly find his place in the communion of saints? To top it off, Phan appeals to the concept of popular religiosity and categorizes ancestor veneration as a popular religion that has its own liturgy and worship. Apparently he does not see popular religions as superstitious in nature.

Since 1974, altars have been allowed in the houses of Vietnamese Catholics. Approaching the altar, one would have to gaze very carefully at its upper part to determine if Christ or Buddha, Mary or Guanyin, is being worshiped. Close inspection is necessary because the rest of the altar is pretty much the same with ancestor pictures and various offerings. Christ is the functional substitute for Buddha; Mary is the functional substitute for Guanyin. The name of God is invoked in a time of need, rather than that of Buddha; barren women now pray to Mary instead of Guanyin. The convert is to be comforted to know that God is more powerful than Buddha; and that Mary is the mother of God, who can tell Jesus to fulfill the requests addressed to her.

In summary, while the Vietnamese Catholic Church might have been praised by the secular population for her cultural relevance, she would definitely receive a low score on biblical faithfulness from an evangelical position in the sense that she fails to present to the culture the heart of the gospel.

THE VIETNAMESE PROTESTANT APPROACH TO ANCESTOR VENERATION

Foreign Protestant missionaries and pioneer Vietnamese Christians were very aware of the peril of ancestor worship. They uncompromisingly established regulations for believers that they must not bow in front of their family altar, or eat food that has been offered to ancestors, or burn incense of any kind in veneration of their ancestors. The South Vietnamese Evangelical Church even officially discourages its members from participating in death anniversaries of their ancestors (South Vietnam Evangelical Church 2009, 82). She emphatically forbids any kind of altars. During marriage ceremonies, Christian brides and grooms are not allowed to participate in the traditional "ceremony of veneration toward the ancestors" in front of the ancestor altar. They are also forbidden to bow before living parents prior to leaving the house. In short, the Protestant churches take a strong position against any form of ancestor veneration. Practically speaking, they consider almost all forms of ancestor veneration to be idol worship and therefore to be avoided.

While not falling into external syncretism and truth compromises as her Catholic counterpart, the Protestant churches do not give enough room for healthy expression of respect toward ancestors. Believers are even criticized by the collective culture of Protestantism in Vietnam if they are caught crying at their parent's funeral. In a society that was established and preserved by relational networks, the Protestant approach alienates local Christians from their families and prevents them from reaching out to people in their sphere of influence. One of the most serious charges against Protestants is that they have forsaken and disrespected ancestors. Worse still, there have been instances of new Protestant converts who went home following their confession of faith and began to tear down the family altar. This is arguably one of the most desecrating acts that one could possibly do in Vietnamese culture.

In summary, the Protestant approach to ancestor veneration may receive a high score on biblical faithfulness from an evangelical perspective. However, it should get a low one on cultural relevance. There are a few ceremonies officially endorsed by the Protestant churches; most of them are Christian, such as baptism, Holy Communion, Christmas, etc. (ibid., 3). There is no approved ceremony that has an origin in the culture. The unwillingness to study Vietnamese culture with an appreciative attitude and with a sound theology of culture has unnecessarily isolated the Protestant churches from the mainstream of Vietnamese culture. They can be more culturally relevant without compromising the Scripture.

GUIDELINES FOR INTERACTION
WITH ANCESTOR WORSHIPERS

Regarding the impact of the gospel on culture, Craig Ott comments, "When the good news of Jesus enters a society, those who respond must decide what they will do with many of the old aspects of their culture" (Ott, Strauss, and Tennent 2010, 265). When Vietnamese people accept Jesus Christ as their Savior and Lord, they do not just accept him cognitively. The holistic nature of Vietnamese culture requires that all other aspects of life must also be transformed in response to the new faith. In particular, they need to decide what they must do with their cultural heritage, and old religious beliefs and ritual practices.

Without an appreciative understanding of local culture and a firm biblical knowledge, they may either discard the culture completely (and as a result alienate themselves from the environment they live in), or uncritically assimilate their indigenous beliefs and the Christian faith. Both are with severe consequences.

First and foremost, God is a relational God. In the Old Testament, whenever he introduces himself to the people of Israel, he always starts with this familiar statement: "I am the God of Abraham, Isaac and Jacob." He often causes them to remember what he has done for their ancestors and how their ancestors have followed him in the past. The nation of Israel was built on relational networks in which family has always been foundational. Respect due to parents and elderly people is not just a praiseworthy tradition but a solemn commandment with reward and punishment to follow. That commandment is reemphasized in the New Testament to become a universal truth for all times. God would agree with the Vietnamese saying, *"Uong Nuoc Nho Nguon"* ("Remember where you come from"). A thorough biblical study on the relationality of God is out of the scope of this paper. It, however, suffices to say that God would like his people to exemplify his character within their respective circle of influence. Within the family, God wants his children to respect parents and elderly people, not only verbally but also with tangible deeds.

The Bible encourages Christians not to follow the way of the world but to live according to the transformation of the mind (Rom 12:1,2). Living in a society in which relationships are the way of life, Christians ought to exemplify God's relationships without falling into the trap of ancestor veneration rituals that are superficial. Nghiem Van Doan, a well-known Vietnamese sociologist who researches and makes recommendations to the government on how to deal with religions, notes that Vietnamese indigenous religions are very ritual oriented. Being children of a relational God, Christians can go beyond specific moments of ritual activity to express real love and sincere care for parents and elderly people. This should bring praises to God and a fresh, new perspective on how one ought to respect ancestors. Hence the following guidelines are proposed in dealing with the tradition of ancestor veneration.

1. Indigenous culture must be studied carefully, respectfully, and appreciatively. There are many praiseworthy cultural traditions such as taking care of elderly parents, visiting and cleaning ancestor graves, and hosting family gatherings to commemorate ancestor contribution to the family heritage and the society at large. These can be used to strengthen family bonds and to build bridges for evangelism. There are also elements that are opposed to the teaching of Scripture and must be exposed in the context of grace. This study must be done in light of Scripture with an attitude of grace and love.

2. There are many healthy ways to express respect to parents and elderly people, whose hearts will be touched by authentic love and sincere care. Believers are encouraged to develop Christian rituals of the ancestors relevant to the culture without violating biblical faithfulness. For example, death anniversaries can be turned into an opportunity of thanksgiving both to God and to ancestors. Good deeds of ancestors can be recounted at such gatherings. It is also a good opportunity to strengthen family bonds, which can lead to genuine relationships among relatives, which in turn can give rise to many opportunities to present the gospel. As another example, taking good care and visiting ancestor graves can be a good Christian tradition.

3. While having an altar, offering food, and bowing in front of it is discouraged, having ancestor pictures and belongings as memorabilia or even keeping their ashes at home is a good thing and not against the Christian faith.

4. Christians should be proud of their heritage. A Buddhist ancestor worshiper after meeting Christ is still Vietnamese. Family should be the first to receive the good news. How can a Christian do that if family relationships are not preserved and promoted? In a ritual-rich culture as Vietnam, one of the best teaching moments is during rituals.

5. Believers are to model what the Bible means by respecting ancestors. Respect can take many forms without undermining the Bible. Having ancestors' pictures and personal belongings such as books around is not necessarily idolatrous and is therefore

acceptable. Believers with living parents and grandparents should demonstrate respect by regular visits and participation in care for them. This would be a powerful testimony to secular people who neglect their parents, especially in old age, while they are alive and then hold an extravagant funeral when they finally die. Believers have the responsibility to demonstrate to the world the family values taught in the Bible. Believers can contribute to the culture positively.

6. Believers have been bought with the blood of Christ and then delivered from the domain of darkness to the kingdom of light (Col 1:13). Their lives are completely under God's sovereign authority. With his cross, Christ triumphed over death and Satan. There is no condemnation for those who are in Christ (Rom 8:1). There is nothing to fear.

7. Believers are to please God and obey his commandments, including those pertaining to living parents and ancestors. The love and care they demonstrate within the family circle will bring praises from the society, which will ultimately give glory to God (Matt 5:16). On the other hand, if they were to neglect their duties to their families, God is the one who will hold them accountable. However, no one can execute curses on them. There will be no bad luck or illnesses or even death brought to them by the underworld power due their negligence. Moreover, the Bible teaches that the souls of the dead go to a certain place and do not hang around the world to either bless or harm the living (Eccl 12:7; Luke 16:20–31).

CONCLUSION

Ancestor veneration continues to be a stumbling block for Asians to come to salvific faith in Jesus Christ. Buddhism has negatively made it more superstitious and fearful. But it does not have to remain an obstacle. As suggested above, Christians can creatively and proactively develop Christian rituals of the ancestors. With compassion for the lost, Christians can go an extra mile in demonstrating real love and sincere care to living parents and elderly people in the extended family. When they pass away, remember them, honor them by keeping their belongings, and recount their good deeds at family gatherings. Furthermore, as family members get together, they can look forward to the day Christ returns, when we will see our beloved ancestors again. This is such an encouraging and hopeful vision to have on this side of heaven. In doing so, Christians venerate ancestors in a Christian way. In this paper, after reviewing the history of ancestor veneration in Vietnam and the historical approaches the Vietnamese Catholic Church and her Protestant counterpart have taken, guidelines for dealing with ancestor veneration were given. Implementation of these guidelines will require time, effort, and humility, but will allow believers to reach in to their families and reach out to the secular population.

REFERENCES

Dang, Nghiem Van. 2012. *Ly Luan ve Ton Giao va Tinh Hinh Ton Giao o Viet Nam* [Discussion on religions and the religious landscape of Vietnam]. Hanoi: National Political Publisher.

Minamiki, George. 1985. *The Chinese Rites Controversy: From its beginning to modern times*. Chicago: Loyola University Press.

Ott, Craig, Stephen J. Strauss, and Timothy C. Tennent. 2010. *Encountering theology of mission: Biblical foundations, historical developments, and contemporary issues*. Grand Rapids: Baker Academic.

Phan, Peter. 2003. *In our own tongues: Perspectives from Asia on mission and inculturation*. Maryknoll, NY: Orbis Books.

———. 2005. *Mission and catechesis: Alexandre de Rhodes and inculturation in seventeenth-century Vietnam*. Maryknoll, NY: Orbis Books.

South Vietnam Evangelical Church. 2009. *Giao Nghi cua Hoi Thanh Tin Lanh Viet Nam* [*Official book of prescribed ceremonies*]. Internal circulation.

Tran, Kim Trong. 1919. *Viet Nam Su Luoc* [The history of Vietnam]. Hanoi: Literature Press.

Truong, Lam Buu. 2010. *A story of Viet Nam*. Denver: Outskirts. Kindle edition.

CHAPTER 7

"I BELIEVE FOR 50%": NEGOTIATING SPIRITUAL AND SCIENTIFIC REALITIES IN CONTEMPORARY THAI COSMOLOGIES

DANIËLLE KONING

What do modern Thai cosmologies look like? Should Thai people be classified as "animist," "Buddhist," or "secular"? Before addressing these questions directly, let's look at a particular manifestation of contemporary Thai religion: the annual *phayanaak* ceremony in northeastern Thailand. The *phayanaak* is a legendary serpent-like creature that is widely featured in Thai religious art and architecture. Every year, at the end of the Buddhist Lent, there is a special ceremony around the mysterious phenomenon of fireballs that shoot up out of a stretch of the Mekong River that runs between Thailand and Laos, the supposed residence of the *phayanaak*. The traditional belief is that these fireballs are the breath of the *phayanaak*. Nowadays, this belief has become widely contested. Scholars have attempted to explain the phenomenon in naturalistic terms (e.g. as a result of gas reactions) but the most common theory now accepted by non-traditionalists, following an investigation that was TV-broadcasted, is that the balls are the result of Laotian soldiers firing tracer rounds into the air on the other side of the river. This TV-program greatly offended traditional believers and generated protests and lawsuits—likely not only religiously but also financially motivated as the *phayanaak* phenomenon boosts the local economy. After the TV-program, a movie was produced that portrays the various parties and their views—the elderly that live by tradition and bow down to the fireballs, the scholar that looks for natural explanations but gets questioned on his Buddhist identity, the masses that are undecided. The actual *phayanaak* annual ceremony itself is a mix of motifs:

it entails calling down the spirits and spirit possession, but the fireballs are framed by hip young presenters as a "natural" phenomenon.

The contestations around the *phayanaak* fireball phenomenon are an apt illustration of the paradox in contemporary Thai cosmologies. On the one hand, spiritual realities are more "real" to people than ever, considering that magical practices like fortune-telling, palm reading, horoscopes, amulet wearing, visits to spirit mediums and other forms are on the increase rather than on the decrease in modern Thailand (Kitiarsa 2012, McDaniel 2011, Mulder 2000). On the other hand, such "magical" aspects of Thai religiosity have been criticized and even discouraged by different segments of society as early as Prince Mongkut's religious reforms in the mid-nineteenth century, culminating in the present-day context where few Thai people seem to have a straightforward, naïve belief or trust in the reality of spiritual phenomena.

This volume centralizes the theme of "spiritual realities" in the Buddhist world. In this paper I argue that spiritual realities, as seen from a contemporary Thai perspective, cannot be understood apart from the specific ways in which science and modernity have shaped and are shaping Thai perceptions and experiences. Furthermore, a fruitful engagement with the missiological context of Thailand today requires an understanding of the ways in which the negotiation of spiritual and scientific cosmologies produces and is produced by conviction, action, and allegiance in people's day to day life.

To this purpose, I identify three different modes of navigating the divergent cosmologies, based on my research among Thai Buddhists in the booming city of Khon Kaen in northeastern Thailand: (1) reframing spiritual realities in scientific terms; (2) letting spiritual beliefs and experiences ambivalently coexist with scientific sensibilities; and (3) moralizing the spiritual domain. The paper will end with considerations for Christian missions in the modern Thai context.

REFRAMING SPIRITUAL REALITIES IN SCIENTIFIC TERMS

Supernatural notions and practices in Thailand are often legitimized by reframing them in scientific, secular terms. One expression of this mode is the reformist move to what could be called a "Protestant" type of Buddhism. In this expression of Buddhism, folk aspects of religion are stripped away and the emphasis shifts from supernatural explanations to reason and observation, and from ritual manipulation of the external world to internal understanding and awareness.

A long-standing example in Thailand is the Thammayut reform movement started by Prince Mongkut in the mid-nineteenth century, who aimed to purge Thai Buddhism from all "superstition" (a purifying response to modernity that has been called "pristinization"—a desire to go back to the origins of one's religion) (Yang and Ebaugh 2001). Recently I visited a Thammayut temple in the northeastern province of Roi Et. It was a temple completely unlike the scores of other temples I have visited in Thailand. The main hall was very sober. Absent were the usual colorful murals, scores of Buddha images and deities, and the sale of incense or flower garlands to make merit with. The "shrine" consisted of a life-size monk image and a few books and other objects, with a sign below saying in both Thai and English: "Please do not light candles or incense around the stupa. Bowing with a heart filled with devotion is the highest blessing." The other prominent "objects" in the large hall were engraved texts that centralized the practice of the Dharma as its central theme. The Thammayut philosophy focuses on personal practice and interior development towards overcoming *kileet* (desire or attachment). It explicitly distances itself from magical practices aimed at manipulating spiritual powers that are sought after for success and good luck.

"Protestant Buddhism:" Stripping Rituals, Magic and the Supernatural

Buddhadasa Bhikkhu, a highly influential twentieth century Buddhist reformer in Thailand, radically rethought Buddhist doctrine and similarly proposed a disenchanted and demythologized philosophy of Buddhism (Jackson 2003). To Buddhadasa, all references in Buddhist doctrine to supernatural entities, be they deities, *thevadas* (angelic beings), or evil spirits, should be understood as referring to psychological states rather than actual beings. The various levels of hells, for example, are simply deplorable states of the human mind. Brahmanic deities are not celestial beings but "A person free of suffering, who is beautiful, lives in ease and is glorious" (quoted in Jackson 2003, 77).

That such psychological reinterpretations of supernatural states and beings are not just reserved for intellectuals, but represent wider trends in Thai society is demonstrated by popular phrases such as *Sawan nai ok, narok nai jay*, meaning literally "Heaven is in one's breast, hell is in one's heart". In this view, heaven and hell are mental states in the here and now rather than physical places that one will go to in the future depending on one's level of merit making. One of the songs of the Thai rock band Ebola, entitled *Cotmaai Thung Phracaw* (letter to God), describes the Thai notions of heaven and hell as "tricks" that allure us but that we can do without.

One of the Khon Kaen University students that I befriended drew on this kind of thinking when I asked him what he thinks about Buddha foot prints, which are revered as places where the Buddha was present. Such foot prints usually are many times larger than human foot prints. His response was relatively emotional considering his generally phlegmatic spirit:

> Such things are just *wathu* [material]! People ask for blessings from *wathu*, like winning the lottery, but that is not right. The reason that such religious places exist is to remind us of the Buddha's teachings. *Khwaamsaksit* [holiness or sacred powerfulness] is not found in material things, but in the teachings of the Buddha about how to be a good person. The material things in themselves are useless!

Religious objects, in this kind of view, are not mediators of luck but mental aids to grow in understanding.

Spirits Made of Electrons: Thai Scientific Religion

Another expression of the mode of reframing spiritual practices in scientific terms is not to try to do away with spirits, supernatural objects and magical rituals entirely, but to legitimize such things by highlighting their congruence with scientific claims.

A point in case is a program called "spiritual jumping" developed by a Thai man who calls himself "the coach". The program entails people jumping in groups and being touched at the forehead and then falling backwards. The idea is that within ten seconds of falling, one's life will radically change. A TV program on spiritual jumping featured scenes of highly emotional people crying and hugging each other. Three ladies who participated in the program testified of the results it had in their lives: clearer goals, a *farang* (Caucasian) boyfriend, happiness, more optimism, and self-knowledge. The whole enterprise is highly reminiscent of certain forms of charismatic Christianity where devotees "fall in the Spirit" and receive instantaneous blessings in response to their actions. What is significant for our purposes here, however, is that this program is explicitly presented as scientific. On TV, "the coach" stressed that "this is science, it is about electrons, it is not *saiyasaat* [magic]." The videos on the program's website are full of images of sophisticated technology and the program is presented as the next step in human evolution that will fulfill humanity's dreams and ambitions. Though the scientific basis for the program's results seems obscure, it promotes itself as being on the cutting edge of science and technology.

The importance of underscoring one's being in harmony with science can emerge even in very intimate settings. A young lady with a background in pharmaceutical science and a strong bent towards a naturalistic worldview shared a special experience with me. When her grandfather died, she saw what she understood to be his disembodied spirit. This would seem to disrupt her scientific views, but since she believes in what her eyes can see, she thought through an alternative way of accounting for this experience. She now explains the appearance of her grandfather's spirit by referring to both science and Buddhist thought. She considers the spirit to be made of up electrons like everything else, but locates it in another dimension—in Einstein's dimension of time. She believes that science points to the possibility of the spiritual in many ways, such as in the discovery of antimatter, and that science has just not come to a full understanding of such things yet. To her, the idea of a "soul" could be a future scientific discovery. Buddhism, in her view, is in some ways more scientifically advanced than science—it teaches, for example, that the heart is faster than light and thereby enables people to see things that happened in the past or that will happen in the future.

It is common for Thai people to view Buddhism as a scientifical-ly sound religion, or even as the religion that is the best match with science. In a lecture by a Buddhist monk on the Thai TV-channel DMC (Dhamma Media Channel), Einstein was quoted as promoting Buddhism as a great fit with science (a widely-cited but false quotation). The monk described the Buddha as advanced in scientific knowledge through the practice of meditation. The Buddha, he explained, had insights that science took the "detour" to find out (i.e. through the ex-ternal rather than the inner world), such as the exact size of an atom or the fact that there are multiple galaxies. He described Buddhism as a religion not of *khwaamchuua* (belief, often used to refer to beliefs that cannot be proven), but of *prasobkaan phisut eeng* (proof through one's own experience).

AMBIVALENT COEXISTENCE OF SPIRITUAL AND SECULAR REALITIES

In many cases, spiritual intuitions and experiences simply coexist with scientific sensibilities, without making an effort to resolve their ambiv-alence. Hence people will say things like "I believe in amulets for 50%" or "I believe in reincarnation for 30%."

Deep Down I Wonder If the Spirits Are There: Believing Though Not Believing

One form of this ambivalent mode can be summed up in the phrase *mai chuua ko tong chuua*, which could be translated as "I have to be-lieve it even though I don't believe it". People who say this, report that they believe in things that they did not expect themselves to believe in. A middle-aged lady, who sells insurance, changed her name because a fortune teller told her that her own name was bringing her misfortune. This is not unusual in Thailand. The idea is that certain letters do not go well with certain days of birth, and that having such unfitting letters in your name could cause you problems. The proposed solution is then to adopt a new name without these letters. After this lady changed her name, her business success improved. She herself finds it hard to be-lieve in the connection, but her experience shows her it is to be believed anyway: *mai chuua ko tong chuua*. A similar dynamic was expressed by a grandmother I met who is a professional silk weaver. She narrated that in the past, she did not believe in spirits (*phii*), but this changed when she experienced that her deceased mother, who had also been a weaver, came to help her one night when she was weaving for hours and hours preparing for a big event. She had *khon luk* (goose bumps) as she recounted this experience. Stories such as these show the power of experiencing spiritual connections between actions and results or directly experiencing the presence of a spirit even when the person involved might not have a deeply enchanted view of the world. The experience cannot be denied, whether it makes sense or not it is there.

A case that reveals the depth of spiritual beliefs in Thai culture, even for those who try to rid themselves of those beliefs, is my friend Plooi. Plooi is a middle-aged man who promotes what he sees as "authentic" Buddhism—a Buddhism that is not defined by community traditions but directly based on the Buddha's teachings, which, in his view, are logical and rational. After half a year of listening to his frustration with Thai people's lack of understanding of "true" Buddhism, and his feeling that magical things such as a monk blessing a car or the belief in spirits are not properly Buddhist, he surprised me. I visited him at night and as we were talking over dinner, he shared that he had visited his monk teacher and asked him for *nammon* (holy water). Plooi rents out rooms and he observed that one of his rooms never has a stable renter, in contrast to his other rooms that have been rented by the same people for years. The monk, who adheres to the more orthodox Thai forest temple tradition, said he did not believe in holy water nor in the spirits that Plooi was trying to get rid of. Revealingly, however, Plooi said that he "forced" the monk to give him holy water, explaining that "even though there is no belief in spirits in Buddhism, deep down inside of me (*luk luk*) there is still something that wonders if they are there… it's like we cannot separate ourselves from this spirit stuff." Plooi, the lay advocate of demythologized Buddhism, confessed that you cannot do away with the spirits; you just cannot distinguish "proper," reasonable Buddhism from the engagement with the spiritual world.

Luck and Effort: Spiritual Power as Important but Insufficient

The mode of "ambivalent coexistence" is further expressed in practices and reasoning that show that spiritual power is important, but insufficient. Both "luck" and "effort" are needed to reach one's goal. Two teachers of traditional Isaan music instruments told me that a good performance is helped by *wai-ing* (to show respect by folding the hands) the god of arts, but still requires serious practice. One TV program featured two hip youngsters discussing the question: "On what hand and finger should I wear a ring considering the day of my birth and my gender so that I will be lucky in finding love?" After an elaborate discussion of who should wear what where (e.g. boys born on Saturday should wear a ring on their left hand pinky for good luck), the presenters said that next to the magic power of wearing the ring in the right place, you do need intelligence and money too in order to find the love of your life. They thus promoted a combination of supernatural and "earthly" tools, suggesting that spiritual tools are important, but insufficient—perhaps not more than just optional.

Whether it's Real or Not: Religion That Eases You

Finally, an important carrier of the mode of "ambivalent coexistence" is the fact that Thai people depict religious action primarily in terms of *sabaai jay* (being eased, relieved, unworried). From the time that my Thai language skills were still in their infancy, I picked up that the word *sabaai jay* was hugely important when people described merit-making activities like offering food to monks or releasing birds and fish. I have wondered whether the word in some ways sums up the nature of Thai popular religion—a religion that eases and unburdens you. Religious action does not in the first place depend on truth—e.g. whether your ancestors "really" receive a better place in heaven because of your donation to the temple, or whether the deities "really" exist and have the power to make you rich. Rather, the reward of religious behavior is embodied—people express how *sabaai jay* they feel when they follow what traditions and their modern adaptations delineate as a good and moral thing to do. It seems that this positive, deeply culturally embedded bodily experience tends to eclipse the sense of needing to negotiate or reconcile spiritual and scientific claims. It is therefore not surprising that it is perfectly possible for people to uphold a variety of apparently conflicting beliefs and practices, such as visiting a hospital and wearing an amulet, being a scholar and requesting ritual protection, being a cosmopolitan Buddhist and honoring local land spirits (McDaniel 2011, 226).

MORALIZING SPIRITUAL REALITIES: RESPECT, GOODNESS AND FAMILY

A third and important mode through which the relationship between spiritual and scientific realities is processed (in this case neglected) is moralizing the spiritual domain. This moralizing happens in two ways: through the value of "respecting" religion and through defining religion's core in terms of ethics and family responsibilities.

One day I watched a movie about the popular Thai legend of the *Mee Naak* ghost with my college age friend Pin. When we were done, my analytical mind was still wondering about some of the logic in the movie and so I straightforwardly asked Pin: "So the monk captured the spirit of the ghost in his amulet and that amulet was then used as a source of power for many centuries. But how is that possible considering that the ghost would probably reincarnate at some point?" Pin looked at me a little fearfully. With a quiet voice, she responded: "I don't know... we don't really talk about such things in Thailand... because this kind of question is like *lopluu* (looking down on something). I would actually like to know the answer too, but I do not dare to ask and would not know who to ask."

This experience taught me the deep significance of the Thai idiom *mai chuua yaa lopluu*, which means: "if you don't believe it, don't look down on it". If *sabaai jay* is a big marker of Thai religion, then respect is another. The value of respect is expressed in the idea that it is very impolite to even subtly question or critique religious beliefs and practices (which is what I had done in regard to the *Mee Naak* movie). For instance, comments that might *seem* critical about religious practices are often prefaced with "I am not critiquing this, but..." Even the presenter of a TV program with the challenging title *chuua ru mai* (do you believe it or not?), which explores all kinds of religious phenomena in Thailand, ends his shows with: "Like I always say: *mai chuua yaa lopluu.*" Though as we have seen, the deep-seated value of respect has not prevented "anti-superstition" movements from emerging in Thailand, it seems that Thai people's deep internalization of this value in some ways protects spiritual realities from being widely probed and "dismantled" by scientific or other critiques.

In addition to respect, belief in spiritual realities is further moralized by the idea that religion's core business is to teach people how to be good people (*pen khon dii*). A middle-aged lady allowed me to probe her belief in the "reality" of the existence of *Mee Thorani*, the earth goddess. She responded: "We have never seen her. We cannot prove her existence. But the belief is in our heart. It helps us to do good things. We have to respect the water and the earth because we depend on it." Many Thai people seem to think like social constructivists - they recognize the constructed nature and social functions of religion. However, rather than translating this observation into skepticism about the truthfulness of religious claims, they translate it into respect because of religion's embraced moral purpose: believing is good because it helps one to be a good person.

Being a good person by being religious includes the important responsibilities one has towards one's parents and ancestors, to whom Thai people feel a great sense of indebtedness. This explains the importance of practices like *buat* (becoming a monk) or *taakbaat* (offering food to monks), the merit of which is devoted to deceased loved ones, though participants in such events may lead otherwise largely secular lives. Here, again, the moral center of religious practices renders reflections about their compatibility with science or modernity peripheral.

IMPLICATIONS FOR MISSION

In this chapter I have sought to trace the various ways in which spiritual realities, the theme of this volume, are "real" for modern Thai people who are well aware of scientific perspectives. We have seen spiritual realities stripped from their supernatural features, reframed as congruent with scientific claims, believed in in spite of unbelief, treated as important but insufficient, embodied (and left uncriticized) in the experience of *sabaai jay*, protected by the value of respect, and moralized as a metaphor of goodness and the site of family responsibilities.

The complexity of ways in which spiritual realities are contested and appropriated by modern Thai people should inform ministry practices in Thailand. First, it must be recognized that the Thai missiological context is complex—it does not suffice to depict and respond to it as simply "animist," "Buddhist," or "secular." Instead, what I have attempted to show in this paper is that Thai cosmologies are produced by and produce intricate negotiations between the spiritual and the scientific, the cognitive and the bodily, the religious and the social. Second, a good missiological response is mindful of and should step right into these tensions:

1. Missionaries in contemporary Thailand, and perhaps larger modern (urban) Asia, must be as ready to address actual spiritual realities as skepticism about such realities. In the context of the widespread influence of scientific ways of seeing the world, Thai people are apt to wonder how credible a religion is that centralizes "God" as a supernatural being and has lots of miraculous stories and doctrines. Christianity is commonly depicted as centered in *khwaamchuua* (again: belief, often used to refer to beliefs that cannot be proven) while Buddhism, as we have seen, is viewed as a religion that *mi heet mi phon* (is logical and rational). In fact, in the history of Buddhist-Christian dialogue in Thailand, the argument that Buddhism is more rational than Christianity has been a consistent one. Zehner (2003) observes that the worldview of early missionaries to Thailand was more "rational" than the worldview of those they wished to evangelize, e.g. some tried to teach people that local spirits were not real. However, today it seems that the tables have turned: contemporary missionaries in Thailand are now less "rational" than the society in which they work, considering that they believe in God and angels and miracles, whilst many Thai highly esteem naturalistic views of the world.

2. Missionaries in Thailand must grapple with the challenge of facilitating a historical understanding of the Bible. Considering the trend to reframe spiritual realities in scientific terms, plus the widespread Thai understanding that religion equals ethics, Thai people who engage in Bible studies tend to interpret Bible

stories allegorically. The allegorical approach glances over scientifically problematic passages and focuses on the moral lesson rather than the historical description. For example, the Fall in Genesis 3 is seen as a poetic depiction of human "attachment" and desire (a Thai Buddhist reading) or simply a moral tale about the importance of obeying God (a Thai Christian reading), rather than an actual, world-changing event that took place in the beginning of human history.

3. Even though mission responses must be mindful of the scientific sensibilities in Thailand as outlined in point 1 and 2, "power encounters," which highlight the importance of the spiritual world, are still an important part of missions in Thailand. The research material shows that in spite of the scientific alternative, which always seems to be readily present mentally when my Thai friends analyze "how things are", there is still a strong sensitivity to spiritual realities, as well as a quick tendency to search for help from spiritual realms in times of need or just to feel *sabaai jay*. Prayer, then, should be promoted as a key aspect of ministry. Thai people generally enjoy being prayed for, being open to the option that true blessings may come from the spiritual world through the lips of a Christian mediator. The importance of power encounters is evidenced by the relative success of charismatic Christianity in Thailand and the prominence of spiritual power as a motif in conversion stories. However, the influence of power encounters must not be overrated—an encounter with the God of the Bible is only one of many other encounters in the Thai spiritual landscape and it does not necessarily forge an exclusive or ongoing bond beyond the temporary need to clear one's indebtedness to him (ibid.).

4. We have seen that tensions between spiritual and scientific perspectives can get eclipsed by the fact that Thai people chiefly experience religion as bodily (it eases you) and moral (it makes you a good person). There are many missiological implications here that are beyond the scope of this paper, but it seems clear that to offer Christianity as both a sensory experience and a deeply moral lifestyle are important bridges that must be explored.

As both spiritual and scientific perspectives are "real" to Thai people in diverse ways, mission workers have the opportunity to discover the many meanings of salvation—from being set free from the attacks of a demon, to the rediscovery of the awe-inspiring in a world of logic.

REFERENCES

Jackson, Peter A. 2003. *Buddhadasa. Theravada Buddhism and modernist reform in Thailand.* Chiang Mai: Silkworm Books.

Kitiarsa, Pattana. 2012. *Mediums, monks and amulets. Thai popular Buddhism today.* Chiang Mai: Silkworm Books.

McDaniel, Justin T. 2011. *The lovelorn ghost and the magical monk: Practicing Buddhism in modern Thailand.* New York: Columbia University Press.

Mulder, Niels. 2000. *Inside Thai society. Religion, everyday life, change.* Chiang Mai: Silkworm Books.

Yang, Fenggang, and Helen R. Ebaugh. 2001. Transformations in new immigrant religions and their global implications. *American Sociological Review* 66 (2): 269-288.

Zehner, Edwin R. 2003. *Unavoidably Hybrid: Thai Buddhist conversions to Evangelical Christianity.* PhD diss., Cornell University.

CHAPTER 8

RITUALS FOR BLESSING AND DESTRUCTION AMONG THE RGYALRONGWA OF SICHUAN, CHINA

DAVID BURNETT

During the turmoil of the Cultural Revolution, many of the monasteries and traditional festivals in China were suppressed as being expressions of the old way of life. Since reform and opening up in the late 1970s, there has been a growing interest in traditional customs, especially with regards to the minority peoples of China. This paper will discuss the contemporary rituals of the Rgyalrong (Chinese: Jiarong) people of western Sichuan province (Burnett 2014).

THE RGYALRONG VALLEY

The Rgyalrong people live in the so-called "Ethnic Corridor" that runs along the eastern margins of the Qinghai-Tibetan plateau from the province of Gansu in the north, through Sichuan to Yunnan in the south. This is a mountainous region with the Tibetan grasslands to the west and the plains of Sichuan to the east. After the "Liberation of Tibet" by the People's Liberation Army (PLA) in 1950, the region was formed into four Chinese provinces: Gansu, Qinghai, Sichuan, and Yunnan.

Rgyalrong is a shortened form of a Tibetan alliteration of *Jia Mo Ca Wa Rong*. *Jia Mo* refers to a queen, who according to legend ruled this area during the Tang dynasty (AD 608–917), and *Ca Wa Rong* refers to a river valley. The name can therefore be understood as "The Queen's River Valley." An alternative Tibetan transliteration is *gyalrong*, and the people would be called *gyalrongwa*. Defining the term "Rgyalrong" has many difficulties. Rgyalrong is not a self-appellation but a loanword from Tibetan, which can carry different meanings, depending on whether it is defined by historical, political, or geographical arguments.

I will use the term "Rgyalrong" to indicate both the historical and political entity of eighteen principalities and the area of distribution of the Rgyalrong language. This last usage of the term has only recently become more commonly used as a result of linguistic work published both inside and outside of China suggesting that Rgyalrong is a distinct language belonging to the Qiangic branch of the Tibeto-Burman family. There are currently an estimated 150,000–200,000 Rgyalrong speakers (Prins 2006).

The region consists of five deep valleys over two thousand metres above sea level and stretching for more than two hundred kilometres, forming the pattern of a star with the county town of Danba at the centre. The main basin of the valley is formed by the river Dajinchuan (literally "Big Gold River") that flows from the north in a southerly direction. At the point that it reaches Danba, it merges with the Geshizhaha River and makes a sharp bend through gorges until it meets another large tributary, the Xiaojinchuan ("Little Gold River"), which comes from the northeast. The river then becomes known as the Dadu River and runs southwards along a gorge so narrow that the river occupies the whole width of the river basin. There is a road on the west side of the river, but this is often washed away in the rainy season as the river floods or the rains cause rockslides. In recent times the region has been divided into two administrative areas: in the north is the Aba Prefecture, and in the south the Ganzi Prefecture. In total the population may number as many as 100,000 persons, and the present administration defines them all as part of the Tibetan nationality (*minzu*).

The majority of the Rgyalrongwa continue to live in the rural areas, often situated high in the mountains overlooking the main valley. The main religious traditions of the region are generally classed as Bön and Tibetan Buddhism. Chinese settlers live in the towns like Danba and Ma'erkang (Barkham) where modern-style concrete buildings line the valley basins. Until recently the main economic activity of the region was timber, but the central government banned logging in the area in order to conserve the environment. To provide jobs the local authorities have encouraged tourism, but the majority of young people have chosen to find work in the cities.

Three types of rituals will be discussed that are part of a quest for blessing and protection. The first relates to those performed by members of the *sangha* either in the monastery or in the local community. The second are calendar festivals organized by the local community to ensure blessing for the coming year. Finally, there are the many local rituals often placed under the general title of "folk religion."

MONASTERY AS A PLACE OF RITUAL

In the Kham and Amdo areas of Tibet there are several monasteries with upwards of fifty to several hundred monks. In the Rgyalrong region about 5–10 percent of the male population are monks, and a much smaller percentage of women are nuns. Although the overall number of monks is relatively small, their influence is still very significant. This study draws mainly on research undertaken at the dGelugpa monastery at Caodeng, which is one of the largest in the Rgyalrong region, located in the extreme north in Ma'erkang County close to the region of Amdo.

The dGelugpa tradition has made the ethical and monastic discipline of the *vinaya* a central part of its spiritual practice. A person may only start to perform Tantric practice once they have received the appropriate empowerment (Tibetan: *wang*), which involves a series of consecrations in which a lama's spiritual energy (Tibetan: *chinlab*) is transferred to the student. Although the monk is ideally on a quest for his own enlightenment, through his training and contemplative preparation he is able to perform a pragmatic role in the community. In the *ch'am* rituals the malevolent spirits are suppressed through the power of the Buddha and the Tantric deities.

As Beyer writes, "Thus the monastery acts as a service group—a pool of ritual talent—for the lay community, and suitable recompense in the form of food, tea, and money is given to the monks for any special call upon their professional services" (1978, 68). This must not be confused with another monastic task, which is that of allowing laypeople to gain merit. Although, the *vinaya* forbids monks and nuns from engaging in practices such as astrology, medicine, or ritual performance, over the centuries these practices have flourished. In Tibetan Buddhism the great majority of monks adopt such a priestly function

(Dreyfus 2003). As Beyer discovered in his research, "Buddhism is basically a performing art" (1978, xii). This may surprise many who think of monasteries as places of rational philosophy and meditation. Most monasteries are devoted to meeting the ritual needs of the laity of the area, and hence their schedule revolves around ritual. Even in the large monasteries, rituals take precedence over everything else. It is because the monasteries so emphasize ritual that those monks who want to focus on meditation leave the monastery to go to some isolated hermitage. Most rituals are performed in the assembly hall at the centre of the monastery, where all the monks can gather.

There are various classes of ritual activities. For the dGelugpa the first category of rituals are those prescribed by the *vinaya* and focus upon the monks' own contemplation. The most important of these is the confession held every fortnight. Here monks confess any failure in fulfilling the 227 rules set out in the *vinaya*.

A second group of rituals relate to annual events such as the celebration of the Buddha's birth, enlightenment, and *parinirvana* (passing away), which usually occurs in May. Monasteries also celebrate the passing away of their founder. For example, dGelugpa commemorate Dzong-ka-ba's passing away and Nyingma Padmadambhava's passing. An important festival that occurs in Caodeng in May is the "Grand Auspicious Prayer," which aims to bring blessing upon every region of the local biosphere. At the beginning of the period the surrounding land is brown and barren, but by the end, colour is coming to the landscape as new shoots emerge. In 2013 some three hundred monks and seven hundred laypeople attended, and the rituals continued day and night for seven days. During that time the participants repeated the great mantra *Oṃ mani padme hum* 200 million times. Chanting or listening to chanting is considered an important act that brings blessing in all traditions of Buddhism. In actual fact the festival has more associations with Bönpo than dGelugpa. The lay people see the ritual as the spiritual force that brings about the spring growth. This can also be a time when epidemics are common, and so it is considered to be an auspicious activity to prevent disease.

A third set of rituals are those specific to a particular monastery. Each monastery has its own daily ritual cycle, which include rituals performed by the majority of the resident monks. Some of these rituals are those for the lamas or monks of the lineage of the monastery, and the monastery usually begins with a prayer to the entire lineage. Other rituals relate to the high patron deities who preside over the great Tantras of the Highest Yoga, and the "protectors of the dharma."

A fourth category of rituals, which are of the greatest number, are those called "foot firming" (Tibetan: *zhabs brtan*), which have various pragmatic functions. These may be to cure disease, repel evil spirits or bring luck in various activities, etc. These could be requested by the laity, or monks, or by corporate entities such as the Tibetan government. Their timing is determined either by consultation of an astrological calendar or divination performed by a monk. If they are to be performed by the entire monastery, all the monks gather in the assembly hall. In return, they at least receive tea from the sponsors, and sometimes food and money. These rituals may alternatively be performed by a few monks in the sponsor's home. These rituals build a network of supporters who come to rely on the monastery in times of crisis and are therefore willing to be quite generous. They are an important source of income to the monastery as a whole. Some monks may spend much time on these rituals and gain a reputation for their skills.

For the practitioner, there are two approaches to spiritual power: evocation and offering. In evocation the practitioner generates the power within himself as he visualizes himself as the deity and so, in effect, transforms the power into the world of events. He is then able to evoke the same deity to place this power in some material object or person. With the offerings there is no self-generation or manipulation of power, but the deity is approached and through the effectiveness of mantras, offerings, and prayers the spiritual power is requested. As with the performance of all rituals, these need to be performed by monks whose vows are unbroken, who have been duly initiated, and who have gone through the prior ritual service to the deity.

Access to the powers of the ritual are available only to those able to invest the time required for the contemplative training that alone makes one fit to use them. The motive power of the ritual is always the contemplation of the deity, which requires the ability to form a vivid, stable mental image of the deity being contemplated in the ritual.

The ability to achieve a single-minded visualization requires long practice, especially as this is performed whilst the practitioner is reciting a text. The practitioner is in effect creating a nonempirical state of reality in a way like some psychologists would say a schizophrenic creates a reality that is unshared. This contemplative reality enables the spiritual power to be manifest.

DANCE OF THE THIRTEEN FIGHTING GODS

Turning to the place of spiritual powers in the lives of the community, the illustration taken here is a festival that takes place in a small village in the hills high above the Dadu River valley. This basically consists in the creation of a *mandala* of deities in which the evil spirits are offered as a sacrifice. The principal dancers represent the central figures of the *mandala* (Samuel 1993, 266). This type of ritual shows how the power is directed to destroy the spirits that cause harm to a village. The large *ch'am* ritual dances performed by monks in the monasteries have been studied by Cantwell (1992) and Schrempf (1999). Outside the monastery these dances are performed by lay practitioners with the dance of the thirteen fighting gods.

Before the dance takes place, monks from the small local monastery chant continuously for twenty-four hours. I was informed that in earlier times it was a shaman and not the monks who chanted, which shows how the monks have adopted non-Buddhist shamanistic practices found in many Central Asian societies. The chanting is believed to draw the evil forces of the region to gather in the dance area where they can be dealt with at the dance. There are many words in Tibetan for malevolent powers, but two words are particularly used in this case: *doerma* and *dongi*. *Doerma* are spirits or local deities that can cause problems for the community. These spirits are believed to be active in the world and, although they cannot be destroyed, they can be brought under control and expelled from the village so that they no longer cause harm. *Dongi* are best understood as being ghosts—the spiritual essence of deceased people who afflict misfortune upon the living. Unlike the *doerma*, the *dongi* can be destroyed, and the ritual seeks to do this. In this way blessing is brought to the people for the coming year.

The dance commences in the afternoon of the tenth day of the first month of the Chinese lunar calendar. In the centre is erected a twenty-metre-high pole that is adorned with prayer flags and topped with the national flag of the People's Republic of China. Around this flagpole are arranged tables on which alcohol, fruit, and other items are placed. The dancers are led into the ground by a prancing snow lion animated by two dancers. Following them are the two monks currently resident in the area and then the elders of the village. The thirteen dancers follow in the procession, which circles the dance area. White silk scarves are then given by the monks as tokens of respect to the people who had arranged the particular dance. The people then seat themselves as the thirteen dancers take their positions in a wide circle around the central pole. In Tibetan culture the number thirteen has positive religious and cosmic significance, and not the negative value found in the Judeo-Christian tradition (Ekvall 1959).

The dancers wear ancient military-style dress and coloured helmets with long bird feathers but, unlike the *ch'am* dances performed in the temple, these dancers do not wear masks. On their backs they carry a decorated shield, and in their hands they hold a bow but no arrows. Strapped to the waist of each dancer is a sword. Two musicians with drum and cymbals start to play. The dance is vigorous and demands strength and stamina, as one would expect from soldiers. The sweeping movements often end in a kneeling position in which the dancers draw their bows as if shooting an arrow. As the dancers do not have any arrows, their swords are used in their place.

The final stage of the dance is perhaps the most symbolic. The dancers gradually move in a spiral pattern closer to the centre of the circle and, when within a couple of metres of the post, they thrust their swords into the ground. The dancers then back away to the outer part of the dance area, leaving thirteen swords stuck into the ground around the central post. The dancers then move back to their swords. They do not simply pick up their swords but jump back with a shout as if they are hesitant to again take up their swords. They then move forward a second time, and this time they withdraw their swords, and then the dance ends.

Thanks are then given by the master of ceremonies to the team for filming the dance, and white scarves are once again given before the second and shorter section of the dance begins. In this dance the old man seated at the edge of the circle sings with a clear voice. The dancers respond while moving around in a less vigorous circular dance. After some ten minutes the dance comes to an end, and the warriors walk from the dance area. The performance ends with photographs being taken of those who had arranged the event and the monks seated in the place of honour.

The dance can be regarded as being like that of *ch'am* with the formation of a *mandala* in which the thirteen dancers take their place. The vigour of the dance demonstrates the power of the gods and their final destruction of the malevolent spirits. However, the villagers did not explain the dance in this way but merely reported that the symbolism had been lost during the Cultural Revolution. In fact the dance seemed to have lost much of its religious meaning as illustrated by the fact that in 2007 there was a controversy in the community as to the relevance of the dance. Critics saw it as costly and time consuming, but they did acknowledge its potential as a tourist attraction. People were, however, uncertain about the financial rewards of the dance, even though all had heard of the gains made by other minority communities in the south of China. This village is only accessible by a very narrow road that zigzags up the steep hillside. The dance would seem to be the only item of interest for tourists apart from the beautiful scenery, but since 2007 few tourists have come. Nevertheless, the dance has continued despite the lack of tourists, which shows that there are other reasons why the people want to conserve the performance.

It was not until about the year 2000 that this village was caught up in the changes that have been sweeping China. It was then that many of the children went out of the village for their schooling and young people went to the cities to find work. The younger generation has been impacted by the secular teaching in schools and have adapted to a lifestyle associated with the Han Chinese. In the light of this, the older generation wants to hold on to their traditions, and this has become a matter of general discussion and concern. Many of the older people are also beginning to learn Tibetan writing and are studying during summer and winter periods when farm work is less busy. This is encouraged by the dGelugpa monks, for whom the Tibetan script is an important part of their literal tradition. Although the people consider Tibetan to be an important part of their heritage, other evidence shows that this is not the case, and that the people have traditionally been part of the Rgyalrong language cluster. The old people therefore seem to be adopting more of Tibetan culture in order to retain something of what they imagine to be their traditional culture. One can therefore see that, during the period from about 2000, the religious aspect of their culture has become more Tibetan while the economic aspect has become more Han.

Returning to the dance itself, as with many aspects of Tibetan religion, it can be understood on a variety of levels. Pott (1965), for example, sees *ch'am* representing the bringing under control of the different aspects of the personality of the individual on the path to enlightenment. This sophisticated interpretation is very different from that of the majority of the people of the village. The older people see the dance as a way of dealing with malevolent spirits and the bringing of good fortune in the coming year. For the young people, however, the dance has become secularized and lacks any real spiritual reality. It is only at the request of their parents that the young people come home for the dance. The first few days of the Chinese Spring Festival are a busy and lucrative time for the young people who are dancers and singers, but they come home for the final part of the two-week holiday.

FOLK RITUALS

To the Rgyalrongwa the world is inhabited not only by humans and animals but also by countless other beings that might be described as gods, spirits, and ghosts. There is a constant threat to life and property, and much family ritual activity is directed towards protection from malevolent spirits. Rituals are held to bless a new house, protect a family after a death, and to bless the new bride as she enters the home of her husband. Folk religion has many facets reflecting the various interactions with the indigenous shamanism. As Swearer writes, "The dialectic relationship between Buddhism and indigenous animism such as Bon of Tibet led to the parochialization of Buddhism, but also changed the face of those native traditions encountered" (1989, 352).

Divination (Tibetan: *mo*) and the reading of omens (Tibetan: *tendrel*) are common in the Tibetan region (Ekvall 1963). Divination offers a means of finding answers to questions of misfortune, and this is especially significant with the Buddhist connection of cause and effect through the karmic link. As all things are connected, it is possible for a skillful observer to read the signs and discern if a particular date or time is auspicious. For example, a Rgyalrong farmer may come out of his house in the morning and hear the sound of monks chanting in the monastery nearby, and this would bring him a sense of well-being. If, however, he comes out and sees a black cat in the corn, or a crow cries above his head, he may consider that the day is inauspicious and decide to change the task he had planned for the day.

In addition to reading the signs (*tendrel*) there are specific techniques of divination to discern whether or not a situation is auspicious. Some of these are very general and can be performed by anyone, lay or monk. They could be as simple as counting the beads on a rosary, or maybe could only be performed by a monk or lama on behalf of the laity. Methods used by the lama include mechanical techniques such as the casting of divining arrows or divining dice, and some lamas are believed to have spiritual powers that enable them to divine without the use of any specific apparatus.

Astrology is another common phenomenon in the Tibetan region where it combines techniques from both India and China. Expert knowledge is only associated with the monastery and lamas. The most spectacular form of divination is that of the spirit medium when a lama is possessed by one of the major protective deities of the monastery. Spirit mediums (*powa*) are found in villages throughout the Tibetan region. These are usually men and function like the local shaman. The shamans claim to be possessed by mountain deities and are often involved with healings relating to the calling back of the *la* [the "pulling in"] that may have been lost from a person. One of their most important tools in this practice is the one-sided drum, which is common among many of the Siberian shamans.

Another common figure in the Rgyalrong area is the fortune-teller (Chinese: *suan ming xian sheng*). Every New Year the family would invite the fortune-teller to come to their home and tell them their fortune for the coming year. Knowing their birth date and consulting two books, he would draw up a square matrix into which he would place the various members of the family. From this he would be able to give each advice on various aspects of their life and behaviour.

First, what foods they should eat or avoid during the coming year. For example, during one year the older sister in the family I knew was told to avoid eating fish, while the younger sister was told to avoid eating chicken. Second, particular places they should avoid. A person may be told to avoid water or any houses that are being constructed. This seems to result from a danger of harm resulting from being in one or other of these locations. Third, the fortune-teller will give advice on particular auspicious colours that the person should wear during the year. One informant was told that she should wear red or yellow during the current year, and so she ensured that she always wore at least one article of clothing with these colours. Fourth, advice could be given on appropriate speech and behaviour. Usually this is that a younger person should always speak respectfully and humbly to an older person. Finally, there is an element of specific predictions and warnings. For example, a person may be told that during the coming year they may lose some money or have problems with their education. As with horoscopes in all societies there is an element of ambiguity, which allows the client to apply the words to their own particular situation.

DISCUSSION

Contemporary religion in the Rgyalrong region can be seen as complex and diverse. The atheistic teaching taught in schools has not deterred students from going to the monastery or temple to request a blessing. Neither does it deter officials of the Chinese Communist Party from taking part in celebrations or even going on pilgrimage. These practices are conveniently placed in the official category of culture or superstitions rather than religion. Many people therefore operate within dual worldviews: one relates to the government, science, and education; one relates to the village, family beliefs, and requests to the local gods for help and blessings. Terwiel in his study of village Buddhism in Thailand made the useful distinction between what he calls "syncretistic religion," which is similar to what we have here been calling "folk religion," and "compartmentalised religion" (Terwiel 1994). This distinction usefully describes what is found in the Rgyalrong region.

The issue of the reality of spiritual powers continues to perplex Western scholars and generates heated debate. In seeking to contribute to this discussion, I want to discuss three theories that seek to give insight into this subject: functionalist, archetypical, and symbolic.

Bronisław Malinowski was a major exponent of the functionalist view who contended that every person uses both magic and science. He made a clear distinction between the "sacred" and the "profane" or "magic/religion" and science, and argues that feelings of reverence and awe rely on observation of nature and is a type of science. Both magic and science are based on knowledge; magic is knowledge of the self and of emotion, while science is knowledge of nature. According to Malinowski, magic and religion are also similar in that they often serve the same function in a society. The difference is that magic is more about the personal power of the individual and religion is about faith in the power of God. Malinowski further argued that the potency of magic is felt to lie in words (spells), which he demonstrated from linguistic data (1965). To the question "why magic?" Malinowski answers, "Magic supplies primitive man with a number of ready-made rituals, acts and beliefs, with a definite mental and practical technique which serves to bridge over the dangerous gaps in every important pursuit or critical situation" (ibid. 1948, 90).

In Christian circles the ideas of Charles Kraft have been influential with the concepts of "form" and "meaning (1979, 64–80). He states that "form" refers to any cultural element—a material object, a word, an idea, or a ritual—and "meaning" refers to that which the form conveys. This model has been particularly used in linguistics. For example, in English the sound "dog" gives to the hearer the meaning of a four-legged canine animal. The problem with this model comes when it is applied to a religious or magical practice. Does a statue, for example, have any inherent spiritual reality, or does this only depend on the meaning understood by the observer? In many cases sacred words are different from the language of ordinary use and have been imported from a foreign or archaic language. Malinowski asserted that magical language was an emotive use of language. This is as a result of the emotional tension of particular situations out of which spells and rituals express a spontaneous flow of emotion (1948, 53). The functionalist model, however, struggles to provide an explanation as to how there can be any spiritual power in this form/meaning relationship. "Spiritual reality" is merely portrayed as a distinct, unseen alternative reality to that discussed as form and meaning, which is affected by the spontaneous flow of emotions.

A second approach comes from the archetypical view of Carl Jung, who holds to the understanding that the human unconscious consists of two layers: the personal and the collective. The personal layer ends at the earliest memories of infancy, but the collective layer comprises the pre-infantile period, which he proposes is the residue of ancestral life. He writes,

> When, on the other hand, psychic energy regresses, going beyond even the period of early infancy, and breaks into the legacy of ancestral life, the mythological images are awakened: these are the archetypes. An interior spiritual world whose existence we never suspected opens out and displays contents which seem to stand in sharpest contrast to all our former ideas. (Jung 1967, 1991)

Basic to Jung's psychology is the belief that the psyche is equipped with a "religious function" as universal and invariable as our biological functions.

Mircea Eliade developed Jungian ideas into the realm of religion, and in *Myth of the Eternal Return* he lays out his argument that humanity is divided into two polar types—modern and archaic (1971). Modern man has become conditioned by the secular approach such that the symbolism of the archetypes has lost its significance. Archaic man, in contrast, reaches out to the archetypes, which are the basis of symbols, myths, and rituals that are beyond change. The manipulation of these archetypes has a psychic power that provides a way of understanding the working of magic and religion. This approach has been widely used by western Buddhists ever since Jung wrote the introduction to the first publication of Evans-Wentz's *The Tibetan Book of the Dead* in 1927.

This approach provides a way of relating what we have called "spiritual realities" into the human psyche through the use of archetypes. Both Jungian psychology and Tibetan Buddhism emphasize the psyche (or mind) as the primary means through which liberation (in the Tantric tradition) and psychic wholeness (as in Jungian psychology) is pursued. Each emphasizes the realm of dreams, and meditative visualizations are designed to effect a reconciliation of opposites. The material world ("seen") is thus united with the spiritual realm ("unseen").

The third approach is the symbolic view proposed by Victor Turner, who built upon the ideas of van Gennep but moved from considering the mere function of ritual to study its symbolic nature. Turner's major study was on the rituals of the East African Ndembu people in which he mapped the rich structure of their symbolism (1981). He especially studied the transition stage in the rites of passage, which he called the *liminal* period. During this period people are thrown together as a result of the stress and change of identity, and undergo a mutual experience he calls *communitas*. This realm is without clearly defined laws and may be understood as a sort of "other reality"—the realm of anti-structure. Symbols are more than ritual markers or statements about the world, but rather triggers of the liminal condition. In ritual, individuals are taken outside normal space and time to a liminal state. There they undergo an embodied experience built up of a complex set of symbols, in order that the ritual leaders may impart a particular worldview (or, more likely, a portion of such a worldview) and life lessons (1969). The result, and the reason, of the ritual is to build *communitas*—to make the candidates members of a particular cohesive social group, which continues to hold meaning for them after their return to everyday space and time.

Victor Turner's most well-known study was the Ihamba affliction that was carefully documented in *The Drums of Affliction* (1981). Among the Ndembu of Zambia a tooth of a dead hunter is sometimes kept as an amulet helpful for hunting. However, if the tooth is neglected, so the Ndembu say, it enters someone's body and travels along the veins biting and inflicting a unique disease. This thing is both a spirit and a tooth. It is removed only after a lengthy ritual in which cupping horns are placed on the afflicted area to draw out the tooth. Victor Turner sought to understand rituals in terms of its social and psychological functions, but dismissed the Ndembu view that the real context of Ihamba is spiritual. His wife, Edith, who was also a trained anthropologist, returned to Zambia in 1985 some thirty years after their previous period of research. This time she actively participated in the ritual, and she records how she finally saw the Ihamba come out of a person. This was something that neither she nor her husband had observed before. The difference this time was that she was not merely observing the ritual but was actively taking part in the clapping with the other women. The discussion raises some important issues concerning subjectivity as Edith Turner notes in her book *Experiencing Ritual* (1992). Anthropologists are generally divided about subjectivity. Even those who have an experience will be uncertain about where such a sense impression comes from. The back cover of Edith Turner's book makes a fascinating statement: "Through her richly detailed analysis, she presents a view not common in anthropological writings—the view of millions of Africans—that ritual is the harnessing of spiritual power" (ibid.). For those who actually participate in rituals, they may have more significance than that of the social function and symbolic meaning.

Africa is a long way from the Buddhist contexts we have been discussing, but there are relevant associations. Buddhism is a path of transformation, which means that it is not enough to understand the dharma intellectually, but that individuals must actively engage the emotions and the imagination. This means having devotion or faith, and implementing ritual is a way that directly engages the emotions. In the past, spiritual power was only accessed by the shaman, but with the coming of Vijrayana Buddhism into Tibet a new rational perspective was introduced with regards to spiritual powers. Could it be that the active participation of individuals in the manipulation of symbols produces a psychic state which makes spiritual powers a reality?

REFERENCES

Beyer, Stephan. 1978. *The cult of Tara: Magic and ritual.* Berkeley: University of California Press.

Burnett, David. 2014. *Rgyalrong: Conservation and change; Social change on the margins of Tibet.* n.p.: Lulu.

Cantwell, Cathy. 1992. A black hat ritual dance. *Bulletin of Tibetology* 1: 12–23.

Dreyfus, Georges B. J. 2003. *The sound of two hands clapping: The education of a Tibetan Buddhist monk.* Berkeley: University of California Press.

Ekvall, Robert B. 1959. Significance of thirteen as a symbolic number in Tibetan and Mongolian cultures. *Journal of the American Oriental Society* 79, no. 3: 188–92.

———. 1963. Some aspects of divination in Tibetan society. *Ethnology* 2, no. 1: 31–39.

Eliade, Mircea. 1971. *The myth of the eternal return.* London: Taylor & Francis.

Evans-Wentz, Walter Y. 1960. *The Tibetan book of the dead.* Oxford: Oxford University Press. First published 1927.

Jung, C. G. 1967. *Collected works of C. G. Jung.* Vol. 7, *Two essays on analytical psychology.* Princeton, NJ: Princeton University Press.

Kraft, Charles H. 1979. *Christianity and culture.* Maryknoll, NY: Orbis Books.

Malinowski, Bronislaw. 1948. *Magic, science and religion and other essays.* Boston: Beacon.

———. 1965. *Coral gardens and their magic.* Bloomington: Indiana University Press.

Pott, P. H. 1965. Some remarks on the "terrific deities" in Tibetan "devil dances." In *Studies in esoteric Buddhism and Tantrism,* ed. Y. Matsungnaga, 269–78. Koyasan, Japan: Koyasan University Press.

Prins, M. 2006. The Rgyalrong New Year: A case history of changing identity. In *Tibetan borderlands,* 1–27. Leiden: Brill.

Samuel, Geoffrey. 1993. *Civilized shamans.* Washington, DC: Smithsonian Institution Press.

Schrempf, M. 1999. Taming the earth, controlling the cosmos: Transformation of space in Tibetan Buddhist and Bon-po ritual dance. In *Sacred spaces and powerful places in Tibetan culture,* ed. T. Huber, 198–224. Dharamsala, India: Library of Tibetan Works and Archives.

Swearer, Donald K. 1989. Folk Buddhism. In *Buddhism and Asian history*, ed. M. Eliade, 351–57. New York: Macmillan.

Terwiel, Barend Jan. 1994. *Monks and magic: An analysis of religious ceremonies in Central Thailand*. Bangkok: White Lotus.

Turner, Edith. 1992. *Experiencing ritual*. Philadelphia: University of Philadelphia Press.

Turner, Victor. 1969. *The ritual process: Structure and anti-structure*. New York: Aldine De Gruyter.

———. 1981. *The drums of affliction*. London: Hutchinson.

CHAPTER 9

AN EVANGELICAL CHRISTIAN ANALYSIS OF THERAVADA BUDDHIST SPIRITUALITY EXPRESSED IN THE ALMSGIVING CEREMONY

G. P. V. SOMARATNA

This chapter deals with one aspect of spirituality of Theravada Buddhism practised in Sri Lanka today. Its main focus is on the *dana* (almsgiving) ceremony in a traditional Sinhalese Buddhist village. The facts are selected to inquire avenues to detect spiritual activities of Buddhists in order to develop a friendship with them. The main purpose of the paper is to seek ways and means to communicate the Christian ethos without disturbing the traditional Buddhist worldview in the village.

SPIRITUALITY

Conventionally spirituality has been described as a procedure of the adjustment of personality in accordance with religious teachings. "It is a human activity subject to a rationale which one believes to be real" (Houston 1993, 4). True spirituality is found deep within a person. It is a subjective and blissful experience. It is about the development of a sense of identity, self-worth, personal insight, meaning, and purpose. Whether it is personal or collective, spirituality concerns a fully integrated approach to life. While inherently being a social matter, it is also an individualistic aspect of life. The spiritual goals are driven by the human desire, which is more than what one can achieve physically and intellectually.

Christian spirituality may be explained as a personal relationship with God and Jesus Christ, and it is a lived reality within that relationship. In Christianity itself there are different ways in which spirituality is expressed. Roman Catholic, Eastern Orthodox, Protestant, and Pentecostal are four broad categories. Within these categories also there are differences. They represent the ways of living the Christian life based on what they perceive to be the significant concerns in their understanding of religious faith. In these practices the common denominator is the Christian's experience of God through a relationship with Jesus Christ.

Since spirituality is a lived experience, it is the domain of any religious person, either Buddhist or Christian. A discussion of spirituality would speak to the adherents of these two faiths regarding their deep feelings about their religious life. The spiritual formation would indicate the change of behaviour of individual believers in a positive way. Spirituality being a subjective experience, it is not easy to take note of and to assess the internal state of a person's heart in the individual's spirituality. Yet it affects an individual's personal and social behaviour.

Spirituality is a significant theme in dealing with issues between religions. Spiritual activities make it feasible for religions to launch connections where doctrines differ considerably. This has been considered to be the most cherished point of contact between the supporters of different religions (Dumoulin 1990, 111). Familiarity with each other's spirituality would enable the adherents of the two religions to appreciate and learn from one another. Historical evidence shows that the Buddhists are willing to appreciate and sanction Christian spirituality when outward signs of spirituality are not offensive to them.

This chapter is concerned with some aspects of the spirituality of Theravada Buddhism. The Theravada school of Buddhism is centred on the personality and the teaching of Gautama Buddha. The devotees focus their spirituality to fulfil the tasks stipulated by his teaching. Therefore the spirituality of Theravada Buddhism is based on the Buddha and his teaching, which is dharma, and the sangha, the depository of that teaching. This is nibbanic Buddhism which, in practice, is regarded as the highest. Most Buddhists are expected to aspire for it. It is in this tradition that Buddhist spirituality rests. The main purpose of Buddhist spirituality is to gain merit (*punna*) and to combat dukkha (human misery). The concepts of samsara (the eternally repeating cycle of birth, life, and death) and reincarnation are pivotal in Buddhism. Samsara arises out of *avidya* (ignorance) and is characterized by dukkha. The Buddha's Four Noble Truths explain the path to salvation.

The popular form of Buddhist spirituality is not taken into account in this paper. Popular Buddhist ceremonies do not deal with merit making by the participants. Its agents are gods, planetary deities, and demons and spirits, who in fact need the merit earned by the living humans. Thus they depend on the good works of the devotees on occasions of merit-making ceremonies. The theme taken in this study, *dana*, falls within the tradition of philosophical Buddhism with popular sentiments embedded in it. It is a spiritual activity which aims at earning merit.

BUDDHISM AND CHRISTIANITY

The form of Buddhism that is found in Myanmar, Sri Lanka, Laos, Cambodia, and Thailand is the Theravada school. Theravada Buddhism is a religion of practice. The spirituality of Theravada Buddhism has to be observed in the light of its self-salvific philosophy. It is a nontheistic religion where there is no belief in an eternal God. This means that in order to derive benefit from the religion one needs to exert oneself without external aid. To call oneself a Buddhist without trying seriously to follow Buddhism will not mean much in terms of practical results.

Through its long history Buddhism in Sri Lanka has been exposed to various cultural forces and traditions of colonial powers. Buddhism has demonstrated its excellent resilience throughout and has survived the most trying developments under three colonial regimes lasting nearly five centuries.

Historical evidence would show that Christian spirituality has not attracted any significant number to the Christian faith in all the Theravada Buddhist countries. Despite the evangelical work among them for the last two centuries, Christianity has not penetrated into the centre of Theravada Buddhist society. The success of Christianity has taken place mostly in the periphery of the Buddhist societies since the majority of the converts have come from the tribal areas in the South and Southeast Asian nations. In the case of Sri Lanka also, it can said that the success is in the peripheral sectors of the Buddhist society. Formerly when the missionaries were active in Sri Lanka they tried to reach the grassroots levels of Buddhist society through their paid workers. This discouraged the Buddhists in villages from getting too close to

Christianity. Today it is not the paid worker who is in the forefront of evangelism but local people with Christian convictions. Nevertheless they are blamed for the errors committed in the colonial period.

Lankan Buddhism

Sri Lanka is generally regarded as the home of the pure Theravada form of Buddhism, which is based on the Pali Canon. This school of Buddhism emphasizes the Four Noble Truths as the framework of Buddhist doctrine, and the Noble Eightfold Path as the direct route to nirvana, the salvation taught by Buddha. The corollary to that is the belief in the cycle of rebirth caused by one's karma. However, side by side with this austere, intellectually sophisticated Buddhism of the texts, in practical life the gap between the "great tradition" of canonical Buddhism and the average person's world of everyday experience is bridged by a complex round of ceremonies, rituals, and devotional practices. The doctrinal Buddhism of the Buddhist texts, though not understood fully by the average Buddhist, continues to guide the thinking of the people.

One may notice that there are gods in Buddhism, but they are mere mortals who exist in one of the heavens for a limited period. These gods would become other beings when their merits are depleted. They enter the cycle of births and deaths until they are able to attain nirvana (Hoffman and Mahinda 1996, 24). According to Buddhism, everything in the universe is impermanent. The doctrine of impermanence shows that these gods are transient. None of these gods are redeemers (Gowans 2014, 20). They cannot offer any form of merit to devotees to achieve salvation. Buddha, who is far superior to all these beings, no longer exists, as he has attained Nirvana. Thus he has moved out of the cycle of samsara. Since Buddhism does not believe in a God, the universe has no Creator who brought it into being and directs its action. In contrast, the Christian God directs the destiny of humankind. For the Buddhist there is no God to whom humans can turn for salvation. There is no vertical relationship in Buddhism to a Supreme Being. In addition it has no especial place for human beings in the cycle of samsara. As a result the personal dignity of humans is reduced by including animals as sentient beings equally significant.

Each person must save himself or herself without the help of an outside force. Since there is no supreme reality, everything in the universe is in a flux. There is no Supreme Being worthy of one's reliance to eradicate endless rebirth.

Buddha denied the existence of any soul or self as well as a Creator God. No soul means that man is an aggregate of five material factors, which at death disintegrate without any residue. Buddhism therefore has been interpreted as an ethical religion similar to humanism and modern ethical culture (Ichimura 2001, 54). The ideal of Buddhism is to aspire to the extinction of existence and to end the endless cycle of rebirth. For one to attain it would take an innumerable number of births and deaths in various life-forms. For some it is not a task that can be achieved in their entire samsara.

Bridges

One may at first glance find that Buddhism and Christianity are diametrically opposed to each other in their expression of spirituality. A superficial look at the pessimistically inclined Theravada form of Buddhism would seem to indicate that a gap separates Buddhism and Christianity. These phenomena differ not only in meaning and content but also in value. The relational aspect of Christian spirituality would be difficult for a nontheistic Buddhist to comprehend. A pious Buddhist would find it hard to understand the Christian spiritual practices of singing, weekly congregating like school children in a classroom, the seeming lack of respect for the things of religion, and so on. This is because they cannot grasp the theistic worldview of Christians.

More than anything, what keeps the Buddhist away from Christianity is its links with foreign powers in the past and the association with foreign forms at present. The Christian vocabulary and social behaviour are understood by them as non–Sri Lankan. These differences should not forestall the great advantages that Buddhists and Christians could gain from understanding one another's approaches to spirituality. They have many overlapping features, and spirituality is a fruitful area of common ground that can lead to satisfying conversations and mutual learning.

While Theravada Buddhism denies the existence of any Creator God, Christianity teaches the existence of a God who is willing to help the believer holistically. Although Theravada Buddhism considers this life as a part of an unending cycle of births and deaths, Christianity teaches that this life is the only life in which one can accept or reject the salvation which is linked to faith in Christ. While Christianity promises happiness and eternal bliss, the Theravada insists that all experience is implicated in never-ending suffering. Even an uneducated Buddhist would utter the expression *"aniccan dukkhan samasaram"* (samsara is impermanent and sorrowful) in times of crisis. Christianity teaches that the satisfaction of certain desires is the mark of salvation, while Theravada Buddhism teaches that the extinction of desire is the prerequisite to gain salvation. For the Christian, eternal life is the consequence of redemption, while Buddhism wishes to annihilate any possibility of continuation of life in any form in its final aim of nirvana.

Theravada Buddhism teaches that in this quest one can rely on no one and on nothing but oneself. Priests, gods, church sacraments, faith, works are of no avail. It is true that Paul says that you must "work out your own salvation with fear and trembling" (Phil 2:12 RSV). At the same time, the next verse continues to state, "For God is working in you, giving you the desire and the power to do what pleases him."

Practical

Buddha rejected any involvement with metaphysical disputations. His concern was a practical one since his desire was to escape from the existential situation of suffering of all beings. Therefore the individual's own effort was necessary to reach the desired object. He introduced a practical spirituality to escape from the existential state of suffering. The emphasis of Buddhist spiritual exertion is directed toward the eradication of suffering and its causes. Unlike theistic religions, which rest upon faith in a supreme benevolent being, the Buddha formulated his teaching in a way that directly addresses the critical problem of suffering, which he believed is at the heart of human existence. He taught that those who follow his teaching to its end would realize here and now the highest happiness and peace. All other concerns apart from this, such as theological dogmas, metaphysical subtleties, rituals, and rules of worship, were waved aside as irrelevant to the task at hand, the unravelling of the predicament of suffering. The Buddha told Malunkyaputta (Bhikkhu Nanamoli and Bhikkhu Bodhi 2009, 648) that the spiritual life did not depend on any answers to these questions, which were mere distractions from the real challenge of following the path.

As we noticed earlier, Buddhist spirituality is based on two foundations. Firstly, that all beings belong to an endless samsara of life and death. Buddha's Four Noble Truths say that this samsara is full of *dukkha* (human misery). One has to make his or her own effort to terminate this cycle. Secondly, the quality of one's status in the samsara would depend on one's karma; therefore, meritorious acts play an important role in Buddhist spirituality.

The goal of self-focused spirituality of monastic Buddhism is for gaining one's own merit. In the case of monasteries it is the training of the mind that would lead to the goal of Nirvana. A monk can reach a state of perfection worthy of veneration and free from all desire and from the cycle of rebirth. On the other hand, the common man's spirituality is focused on the merit-making process not leading to Nirvana. However, it is believed that the merit generated would have a cumulative effect.

The majority of Buddhist laypeople practise a popular form of Buddhism. They find fulfilment of their spiritual needs in the popular religious practices in all Theravada countries. They are practical and useful for the individual and community. They serve to alleviate the suffering in daily existence. The devotional approach (*shraddha*) to the dharma has its roots in lay Buddhist practice during the time of the Buddha himself. Devotion being the intimate inner side of religious worship, it had a place from early Buddhism. For Theravada Buddhism, devotion is an ardent feeling of love and affection (*pema*) directed towards the Teacher who showed the way to freedom from suffering. Such an attitude inspires the devotee to follow the Master's teaching faithfully.

Dana

The highest form of Theravada Buddhist activity is meditation, but it is beyond the capability of the ordinary Buddhist. Therefore they take the other alternatives which are less important but which nevertheless help them in bettering the status of their next birth. Thus for Sinhalese traditionalists, Buddhist spirituality often means merit-making activities such as offering food to monks, contributing to the construction projects of a monastery, or a similar merit-making project. Taking part in Buddhist festivals and ceremonies is also considered a meritorious act. The devout chant five precepts every day, which every lay Buddhist is expected to follow. However, they usually lack intellectual understanding of the Buddha's teachings. Temple fairs and celebrations provide them with cultural entertainment and more opportunities to make merit. These people are more or less content with the status quo and expect little from their involvement with the religion other than the accumulation of merit. However, they do contribute in no small measure to the preservation and maintenance of the Buddhist institutions in the Sinhalese culture.

Dana is considered important to the ethical life of a Buddhist individual. It is the first of the three ways of acquiring merit, others being *sila* (morality) and *bhavana* (meditation). It is the first of the ten *paramita* (perfections) of a person who aspires to be a Buddha (Sivaraksa 1998, 63). There is another meritorious act called *pattidana* (donating merit), where others are invited to take shares of the merit by associating with it. One's own merit is not decreased even though shared with others, just as a light out of a lamp does not diminish although another lamp is lit from it. Merit accrued at a *dana* ritual is for the profit of the donor and the deceased as well as for others who take part in it. Usually such a ceremony would last two days. The first day is set aside for the chanting of *pirit*. On the second day breakfast and lunch are offered to monks (Kariyawasam 1995, 23).

Merit-making value

"The offerings made by the laity to the sangha are defined in all Theravada traditions as having the supreme moral acts through which laity acquires merit" (Keyes and Daniel 1982, 274). Tambiah noticed that Thai Buddhists give a very high place to the *dana* as a merit-making process. His informants stated, "On the whole then we must conclude that merit through gift giving is more valued than the pursuit of

Buddhist ethical aims" (Tambiah 1970, 148). Burmese Buddhists also considered giving *dana* to be the primary means of acquiring merit. "When asked to list the ways in which merit can be achieved, the Burmese, almost without exception, mention *dana* to the exclusion of anything else" (Spiro 1982, 103). Sri Lankan Buddhists also have the same attitude (Langer 2007, 87). Buddhist monks are unpaid as volunteer spiritual teachers residing at centres. They are supposed to be supported by their local communities. Lay followers acquire merit by providing food in addition to clothes, lodging, and medicine to them (Bechert and Gombrich 2008, 17).

Occasions for *Dana*

Dana is offered by Buddhists on occasions of family events. Such a ceremony may be performed on important occasions, a wedding in the family, a ceremony to occupy a new home, and to offer merit to a dead relative. The commemoration of a dead relative is done seven days, three months, or annually after the death. Some people offer *dana* to monks after a good rice harvest. There are people who think that they should offer a *dana* at regular intervals just to gain merit. The ceremony of almsgiving is very often preceded by a ceremony of *pirit* chanting. It is generally known as *sanghika-dana*, meaning "the alms given to the community of monks." In the case of memorial *dana*, the ceremony is supposed to ensure the well-being of the dead person in the spirit world.

Ceremony

A considerable effort is made by the family before the *dana*. The floor of the house will be washed and sprinkled with water mixed with saffron powder. A day or two before the ceremony additional chairs, plates, cups, glasses, and other items would be collected. The usual practice is to borrow from the neighbouring houses for the occasion. Neighbours happily offer them as they are going to be partakers of a merit-making event. Nowadays there are places where these items can be hired for a fee. A large brass lamp with the sign of a rooster would be brought from the temple.

The monks are brought from the temple in a procession. A minimum of four ordained monks (*upasampada*) must participate in the *dana* ceremony in order for it to be valid as a traditionally accepted *sanghika-dana*.

A layman, usually a member of the host family, leads the procession, with the relic casket, representing the Buddha, borne on his head under an umbrella or canopy. This is accompanied by a short procession with drummers and flute players. In the same manner the procession would leave the house after the monks have received the *dana*.

The monks are respectfully conducted to the *dana* house. As they approach the particular household they are received by the host. Before the monks step into the house, a male person washes their feet, while another wipes them. The monks are then escorted to the cushioned seats arranged on the floor of the hall. Alms are first offered to the Buddha in a separate bowl, and are placed on a separate table on which the relic casket, containing a relic of the Buddha, has been set. All the items of food are served on plates and placed on mats in front of the seated monks.

A senior monk administers the Three Refuges and the Five Precepts to the assembled gathering. This has become the established custom with which any Buddhist function commences. After he has given a short address on the significance of the occasion, the food is formally presented by getting the chief householder to repeat a Pali statement that they offer to the whole community of monks. The monks would be served food by the householders. According to *vinaya* rules the eating part of the *dana* by monks should be completed before noon.

When they have finished eating, the other requisites (*parikara*) would be offered. The most important item among these offerings is what is traditionally known as "the eight monastic requisites" (*ata-piri-kara*): the alms bowl, three robes, belt, razor, water strainer, and sewing needle. This offering is regarded as especially meritorious. As it is expensive and therefore difficult to offer to all the monks, generally one *ata-pirikara* is offered to the chief monk; and other items such as books, towels, pillowcases, umbrellas, sandals, etc., are presented to the other monks.

Benediction

Once this is over, another monk administers what is known as *anu-modan* (transferring of merit). In this ritual all those who are connected with the ceremony are requested to partake in the merits generated in the *dana* for their own benefit. The participants are also called upon to transfer the merits they have thus acquired for the well-being of their dead relatives and friends. The transfer of merit to gods and spirits for their benefit is an important part of this ceremony. It is believed that the deities protect the donors out of gratitude for receiving merit.

The relic casket and the monks are conducted back to the temple in the same manner in which they were brought, and the proceedings are concluded. All those who are present in the house are offered food prepared for the day. The neighbours also would be sent adequate food for their families. Even Christians are invited to partake in the meal.

Preparation and the Christian

The neighbours come with plates of rice prepared in their homes and serve it on the *dana* food table. A small part of this food is also taken when the bowl of food is prepared for offering to the Buddha, in front of the relic casket at the time of the *dana* proper. The purpose here is to get the neighbours and outsiders also to participate in this merit-making ceremony. Christians can avoid taking part in it without offending the host family. The offering to the monks involves worshiping them. The Christians, however, can make provisions to the process without taking part in the merit-transferring process.

PASTOR AS A SPIRITUAL LEADER

There is a tremendous respect for spirituality among Buddhists in Sri Lanka irrespective of religious differences. The Kandyan king Vimaladharmasuriya II (1687–1707) built a church for Joseph Vaz (1651–1711) when he realized that the Catholic priest was a saintly person. There are recent reports in the country that the Buddhists went to the extent of protecting Christian ministers in villages when Buddhist extremists who came from outside attempted to harass them. However, the pastor must have the reputation of being a person of spiritual standing in the community. The Buddhist believes that respecting and honouring any religious leader is meritorious.

In our interviews with pastors in rural Buddhist areas it became clear that they were able to win the hearts of their Buddhist neighbours by taking part in the Buddhist ceremonies of villagers including *dana*, except in areas where Buddhist worship was involved. Their view is that the neighbours admire the help of the Christians, not only because of the assistance they receive but also the principles followed by Christians in not taking part in Buddhist worship sections. In these interactions with Buddhists in their ceremonies it has been found that any religious discussions, debates, and arguments have been destructive. It is advisable to refrain from any word condemning Buddhist rituals.

The food for the *dana* is prepared in the house. Several days before that, sweet meats are prepared for the monks as well as for guests. Fish is prepared a week before the ceremony and preserved in special clay pots. On the day of the *dana* itself, the relatives and neighbours bring items of food. In all this preparatory work a Christian neighbour can offer help and would be appreciated. In this period the pastor and some members of the congregation could visit the home and inquire about the ceremony and see if there are ways that the church can help as neighbours. In fact the pre-ceremony period is pivotal to the householders as they are grappling with the arrangements without the help of the relatives who would come in time for the ceremony and leave soon after.

Christian ladies can help in the work of the females in the household such as cooking, preparation of tables, and helping the householders. The dress of the ladies should agree with the Buddhist religious atmosphere. Immodest clothes that they might wear to outside events would be unwelcome and may cause a bad reputation in the village. While making friends with them, it could be used as an opportunity to show the personal strength the Christians have in their faith. Even after the *dana* ceremony Christians can be of help to the family, as most of the relatives and friends would depart after the *dana* ceremony, leaving the family to put the house in order.

If there is an opportunity to talk of the gospel, Christians must have a good grasp of the reasons behind Buddhist practices in order to prevent any misunderstanding and rejection. If one is going to point to the strengths of Christianity without showing sympathetic concern for the Buddhist way of life, Buddhists would refuse to talk to the Christian.

The overriding perception of an average Buddhist is that the local Christians are agents of foreigners. Thus their feelings are even filled with suspicion. Under such circumstances dealing with the Buddhist neighbour in real life may not be easy. Some pastors who work among them have stated that the village people smell, they are dirty and unpredictable; they may even take your help and use it as a weapon against you, stating that you came with a view to convert people with material help. The typical bad habit of Christians has been charity from aloofness, loving those who are far away with no direct participation. The involvement in a *dana* ceremony may be difficult where one has to rub shoulders with the householders. The Buddhist householders may hold numerous prejudices regarding Christianity. They are embedded in Buddhist culture and are ethnocentric and may entertain caste prejudices. Their vocabulary is full of popular Buddhist concepts and intolerance. Even the *dana* ceremony is arranged according to astrological charts. In their words of thanking they would use "May you gain merit" or "May the Triple Gem bless you" and so on. When the Buddhist monks arrive in the house, the crowd will kneel or get into a squatting position to receive a Buddhist blessing. Everyone worships the monks. Customs and words are pregnant with Buddhist concepts.

Even within such a difficult environment the *dana* ceremony is one occasion where a Christian can show solidarity with his or her neighbour without going into theological issues or superstitious practices. Participation in a *dana* ceremony of a Buddhist neighbour would provide a chance to talk about Christianity on a personal basis. Very often the participants in a *dana* ceremony would fall into three levels—beginning, intermediate, and advanced. Understanding the Buddhist neighbour would open the line of communication between the two groups. This allows both parties to establish a good interpersonal relationship.

For most of the Christians in Sri Lanka, choosing Christ could mean shaming parents and losing family. In cultures in which family is central, this is a demoralizing loss. In Christianity we have the words spoken by Jesus, who said, "If anyone forces you to go one mile, go with them two miles" (Matt 5:41). Thus one must assume responsibility for the "other" without expecting a thank-you or anything in exchange. Real Christian compassion does not consist in reciprocity.

We are to see people as created in the image of God (Gen 1:26). They are objects of God's love (John 3:16) and deserving of ours as well. It is said that the message and messenger must be incarnate in the receptor culture (IJFS 1993, 136). This includes personal lifestyle; an attitude of empathy and sensitivity to people whose faith is as devout and sincere as our own; and an outgoing, friendly spirit that accepts people as they are.

As we mentioned earlier, *dana* ceremonies are performed on an issue significant to the family. It can be a time of remembering a dead relative, an occasion of some successful achievement, maintaining a family tradition, or to ward off some disaster predicted by an astrologer. The Christian should be concerned about these even to the extent of showing his sympathy with the family. The best witness will be personal people contact. The witness can be more visual and less verbal in a situation like a *dana* ceremony. In limited-access areas like Sinhalese Buddhist villages, an individual witness would carry the message of the gospel, which would later develop into praying for the sick and even power encounters.

In Buddhism the idea of *dana* is directly linked to the concept of friendship and compassion. It also helps the donor by accruing the benefits that follow both in this life. Twofold benefits that the recipient gets are also emphasized in the *Anguttara Nikaya*, which states that there are five benefits that a donor would accumulate. They are:

> The donor becomes acceptable to many people, peace loving good people like to associate with him, a good reputation would spread about them, he could be happy that he would be reborn in a good state, in heaven. A person who gives another a gift of food thereby gives the recipient long life, complexion, happiness, strength, and promptitude and having given these five things, the donor, too becomes endowed with the same things in a future life. (AN 3:3)

This is an excellent opportunity for the Christian to make full benefit of this Buddhist teaching.

Confrontation with ideas and attitudes is not suitable when dealing with Sri Lankan villages. Christians are being watched by non-Christians around them, no matter what, who, or where they are. Both spiritual and cultural obstacles can prevent Buddhists from accepting the gospel. As much as you try to bridge the cultural gap through relationship and understanding, barriers will likely remain. Christian workers have to spend years learning culture and language in order to communicate the gospel in a way that least-reached Buddhists can understand, yet they still fight the perception that Christianity is a Western religion.

CONVERSION

Buddhism is intertwined with the local culture. If believers of Buddhist background do not lose their families, they often repeatedly face situations in which they feel that leaving Buddhist practices behind will offend family members or bring dishonour or embarrassment. For instance, churches and fellowships in Sri Lanka are full of believers who are the only Christians in their families; their families expect them to participate in Buddhist rituals which are contrary to faith in Christ. In addition to cultural barriers, Ephesians 6:12 tells us that "our struggle is not against flesh and blood, but against the rulers, against the authorities, against the powers of this dark world and against the spiritual forces of evil in the heavenly realms." We cannot begin to understand the spiritual conflict that is taking place over the hearts of our Buddhist friends. Whether spiritual or cultural, these obstacles are monumental and can only be overcome through magnanimity and love.

Behaviour

Christians who wish to make an impression on Buddhists about their Christian neighbourliness should be careful with regard to the respect shown to any religion. Buddhists usually respect any sacred object or action. When it comes to Buddhism itself, they are extremely careful to offer the utmost respect. They use a special language to offer respect to Buddha and Buddhist monks. They do not refer to Buddha without the suffix -*vahanse* (venerable sir). The traditional mode of address used for *bhikkhus* in the time of Lord Buddha, and still used in Sri Lanka, is *Bhante* in Pali and -*vahanse* in Sinhala. In addition they have special words to refer to sacred objects differing from the use of ordinary and mundane matters and people. For example, with a Buddhist monk they would say *valandanava* to refer to the monk's eating, whereas it is *kanava* for an ordinary person. Sacred language is never used of ordinary people. The Christian who wishes to participate in *dana* or any other

Buddhist ceremony should guard against the use of the wrong word, as any error in this regard would be interpreted as an insult.

Address

They also should be careful with the use of Christian vocabulary in Buddhist places, especially on religious occasions. Christians have a habit of referring to their Christian friends as brother, sister, and so on. The Sinhalese Buddhist society would not like such usages as they would be treated as Christian and alien expressions on a Buddhist sacred occasion. The Buddhist usually uses family relational titles to refer to people of different age structures as well as to distinguish sexual differences. Therefore if the Christian uses the term *aiyaya* (elder brother) or *akka* (elder sister) to refer to people older than them but in the same generational range, it would be taken as acceptable. If the people referred to are of an older generation, they need to use relevant relational terms. In that manner the Christian would be able to receive acceptance in the Buddhist gathering.

Dress

Buddhist shrines and festivals have their own dress codes. Usually the devotees and participants of the ceremonies wear white. The dress is normally sober. Females are expected to cover their bodies modestly. They cannot wear the kind of clothes that they wear to church. When they enter a shrine they are expected to remove their footwear.

On the occasions of *dana* the monks are normally seated on a higher level than the laity. Those who partake in the ceremony are expected to be quiet in the period they have the function. This may be a difficult thing for Christians who whisper in the congregation of the church.

CONCLUSION

Dana is an occasion where even the poor can become participants in the spiritual event of the host family. It can be the provision of material or labour which is meritorious and a spiritual act in the Buddhist sense. The host family would gladly accept the participation of others in their meritorious act. Thus there is cordiality and friendship irrespective of caste, creed, and racial barriers. This joyous situation is a part of Buddhist spirituality of sublime joy, which is completely devoid of carousing or partying. This aspect of *dana* which brings sublime joy to the Buddhists has been largely misunderstood by the Christians, as they are unable to comprehend the spirituality in this tradition. It is an integral part of the Buddhist ethos. The *dana* activity among Buddhists is also a familiar event, as it is often linked with life-cycle events. Christians can easily mingle with the Buddhists and share their joy with them on these occasions. Christians in the village should make better use of this opportunity, without staying aloof and alienating themselves from the rest of the community as they have been prone to do.

Spirituality is about experience. Buddhist spirituality is concerned with the end of suffering through the enlightened understanding of reality. The spiritual practices of the Buddhist tradition are oriented toward ultimate freedom from suffering. It is not necessary to believe in God or to deny God's existence to practise Buddhist spirituality. There is no demand to take the Buddhist path, to reject prior faith commitments, or to adopt new ones. Holding a particular belief is not paramount for living the holy life. Buddhists accept that spiritual persons can hold all sorts of beliefs. They respectfully recognize saints in Christian, Jewish, Muslim, and Hindu religions. Buddhists acknowledge that other perspectives and practices can genuinely mediate salvation. Participation in a practical spiritual event like *dana* would help to alleviate many of the prejudices that Buddhists have against Christianity while at the same time make it an opportunity to show the Christian side of spirituality even amidst Buddhist rituals.

REFERENCES

Bechert and Gombrich 2008. *The World of Buddhism.* Thames and Hudson, London and New York.

Bhikkhu Nanamoli, and Bhikkhu Bodhi, trans. 2009. *The middle length discourses of the Buddha: A translation of the Majjhima Nikaya.* Somerville, MA: Wisdom Publications.

Chan, Simon. 2009. *Spiritual theology.* Grand Rapids: IVP Academic.

Dumoulin, Heinrich. 1990. *Christianity meets Buddhism.* La Salle, IL: Open Court. First published 1974.

Egg, James R. 2013. *Religious giving and the invention of karma in Theravada Buddhism.* New York: Routledge.

Gowans, Christopher W. 2014. *Buddhist moral philosophy: An introduction*. New York: Routledge.

Hoffman, Frank, and Deegalle Mahinda. *Pali Buddhism*. 1996. London: Routledge.

Houston, James M. 1993. *Holy Spirit in contemporary spirituality*. Bramcote, England: Grove.

Ichimura, Shōhei. 2001. *Buddhist critical spirituality: Prajñā and Śūnyatā*. New Delhi: Motilal Banarsidass.

Kariyawasam, A. G. S. 1995. *Buddhist ceremonies and rituals of Sri Lanka*. Kandy, Sri Lanka: Buddhist Publication Society.

Keyes, Charles F., and E. Valentine Daniel, eds. 1982. *Karma: An anthropological inquiry*. Berkeley: University of California Press.

Langer, Rita. 2007. *Buddhist rituals of death and rebirth: Contemporary Sri Lankan practice and its origins*. New York: Routledge.

Lefebure, Leo D. 1993. *The Buddha and the Christ: Explorations in Buddhist and Christian dialogue*. New York: Orbis Books.

Nyanaponika Thera. 1962. *The heart of Buddhist meditation*. Kandy, Sri Lanka: Buddhist Publication Society.

Sivaraksa, Sulak. 1998. Buddhism and human freedom. *Buddhist-Christian Studies* 18: 63–68.

Spiro, Melford E. 1982. *Buddhism and society: A great tradition and its Burmese vicissitudes*. Berkeley: University of California Press.

Tambiah, Stanley J. 1970. *Buddhism in the spirit cults in North-east Thailand*. London: Cambridge University Press.

Thomas, Merton. 1971. *Contemplation in a world of action*. London: George Allen & Unwin.

PART III

MISSION
STRATEGY

*I revealed myself to those
who did not ask for me;
I was found by those
who did not seek me.
To a nation that did not
call on my name,
I said, 'Here am I, here am I.'*
Isaiah 65:1

*From one man God made all the nations,
that they should inhabit the whole earth;
and he marked out their appointed times in
history and the boundaries of their lands.
God did this so that they would seek him
and perhaps reach out for him and find him,
though he is not far from any one of us.*
Acts 17:26,27

*Now faith is confidence
in what we hope for
and assurance about
what we do not see.
This is what the ancients
were commended for.*
Hebrews 11:1,2

CHAPTER 10

A POST-3/11 PARADIGM FOR MISSION IN JAPAN

HIROKO YOSHIMOTO,
SIMON COZENS, MITSUO FUKUDA,
YUJI HARA, ATSUKO TATEISHI,
KEN KANAKOGI, TORU WATANABE

March 11, 2014. We are sitting in a meeting room in northern Japan. The room is part of a temporary housing complex for those who lost everything in the 2011 Tohoku earthquake and tsunami. Some friends of mine are holding a Bible study, and I think most of the people who have come are there out of gratitude for the aid they received.

After a very dull Bible study where the "teacher" kept on talking, people are randomly chatting over cups of tea. Suddenly one lady says
> "Oh, by the way, the other day, something very interesting happened to me. I was feeling down, thinking about all the things that I lost in the tsunami. Then this Jesus that you talk about came to me and said, 'Those things are gone, so do not worry about them. But in the future, there will be a clear river flowing for you.'"

A man shows up at the house of some Christians who moved there right after the disaster and says, "Jesus appeared in my dream and told me to come to you."

Another man, when he talks about his experience, says that God pulled him out of the water when he got swallowed by the tsunami. As he says the word "God," he pulls out a necklace that he has on. It has a cross hanging on it. The combination of "God" and the cross is extremely unusual in Japan. Obviously, he recognizes that the God who pulled him out of the water has something to do with the cross.

The disasters which hit the Tohoku region on March 11, 2011, changed the physical landscape of Japan. But it is becoming clear that they also marked a change in the spiritual landscape of the country. In the past, missionaries had seen very little fruit for their efforts over many centuries. Now we are beginning to see a new understanding of mission emerging in Japan—one which God himself is initiating and leading.

One pastor who has been planting churches in the area described the change as "a kind of powerful force moving them on." He refers to the current mission practice in Japan as being in a state of "paralysis"— shocked, standing still, and unable to move effectively. He realizes that God is calling us to have a paradigm shift. We need a paradigm shift to understand what God is doing right now and also to reach Japan at such a time as this.

THE NEW PARADIGM

Much of the current practice of mission in Japan has not changed for the past two centuries of Protestant mission. Missionaries and pastors have first established churches as beachheads of the kingdom, and set them apart from the society that they have seen around them. They then— deliberately or inadvertently—positioned their churches as places of culture, learning, and spiritual purity. They sought to attract people into churches on the basis of these advantages. Those who came to the churches and wanted to understand the faith of their "hosts" would then be trained through Bible study until they professed faith them-selves. After that, they would take a generally passive role as church members, mostly restricted to the attendance of Sunday services.

We could summarize the mission strategy to date under the fol-lowing six areas:

1. Calling people to gather with us
2. Not being involved in the local society
3. Building a church separate from the local society
4. Creating encounters with the Bible
5. Missionaries talking about Jesus
6. Prioritizing an intellectual understanding of the gospel

FELLOWSHIP

An effective missional movement needs to continue to reach outwards. When it turns in upon itself, it dies. In the past, the typical response of Christians toward a person who has shown interest in Christ was to first invite him to church or events sponsored by the church. The idea was that the person would meet other Christians and become touched by the love and the kindness of Christians. They would have a nice meal at the church. Slowly they would get pulled into the Bible study group and the other programs at the church. Unfortunately the initial experiences of fellowshiping with Jesus would gradually be replaced by Christian activities. God becomes replaced by Christianity, meeting Jesus with church meetings.

At the same time, we cannot deny the importance of fellowship with fellow believers. How do we make sure that the movement continues to reach outwards, and yet also allow for believers to encourage and strengthen one another? As this paradigm is still developing and we are still discovering how to work effectively within it, we can only offer some tentative suggestions.

One approach is to introduce someone who has heard from God to one person who understands this new paradigm. One person will continue to ask him what he has been hearing from Jesus and how he has been responding. They will pray together. Meet and pray with only one person? Is that enough? We would dare to say yes, if this one person has the new paradigm. Because one of the characteristics of those who experience Jesus supernaturally is that they cannot keep their mouths shut.

Mr. M is a local politician and mayor of his village. He saw a vision of the cross at one of the events that Christians hosted. I asked him if he had seen visions before. He said that he had. When I asked him about his visions in the past he said, "In my dream, I saw Buddha on my left shoulder and other gods on my right shoulder." I asked what that meant to him. He said, "I thought that my life is going to be all right."

Then we asked him to describe the latest vision he saw.

> As I was watching a pastor speak at this event, all of a sudden, I saw two groups of clouds. They caught my attention and I kept looking. I noticed there were two crosses in the clouds. I started shouting, 'Look! Cross!

Cross!' The pastor on the stage did not know what I was talking about. I thought that everyone else was seeing the same thing, but the other people thought that I had gone crazy. Finally, I climbed up on the stage and tried to grab the crosses, but then they disappeared.

We asked him why he tried to grab the crosses. He thought that they would bless him. After this he was given a concise Bible, and he now reads it every day, ponders on it, and writes down what he has learned in his notebook. When he leads a town business meeting, he speaks from the Bible. "There is so much good stuff in it!" he says. No one has taught him to do a "devotional," and no one has taught him to share his faith, but he does it naturally because he simply loves it. Those who come to faith through a direct experience of God still need encouragement and training in how to read the Bible and to share their testimonies of how God has met with them. At the same time, they have a greater than usual enthusiasm to discover more about the God that has met with them.

And because their experience of Jesus is so real, these people are not shy to talk about it. They take it for granted that Jesus gets involved with our lives. This is definitely contagious. The people around will naturally want to experience the same wonderful Person. When they are in need, they will think of speaking to Jesus, because of what they heard from their friend. So before long there is a fellowship of believers of a new paradigm.

After Mr. M's vision of the cross, we went back to his past vision and asked him how he interprets it now that he has seen this recent one. He said, "I still have Buddha on my left shoulder and the other gods on my right, but now Jesus is on top."

In his traditional Japanese house, he has a big Buddhist altar, and statues and pictures of other gods. Ebisu, the god of fishermen, is prominent. A Western, modernist approach would be to convince this man to renounce all his idols, break his connection with the temple and shrine, and destroy his religious past. Doing so would cut him off from his family, his communities, and the culture of his nation, which would make it very difficult for him to reach outwards with his new-found faith. It also often requires a forceful act of persuasion on the part of the Christian worker. In the end, it is unclear whether he would be taking these steps to please God or to please the person witnessing to him.

In the case of Mr. M, however, it seemed like we didn't have to force anything on him. He and his wife started talking to Jesus about everything after the vision. They now talk to Jesus when they get in a car to drive and when they are not feeling well. When they worry about something, they talk to Jesus. Jesus has started to displace the other gods in a gentle and natural way.

CONCLUSION

God has begun a new season in Japan, where people start walking with Jesus in totally different ways than we have known or taught in the past. He is at work in mission, in ways that we cannot anticipate and where we can only strive to catch up. For these people who are experiencing God directly, evangelism may not necessarily be a matter of sharing a doctrine of salvation or explaining a set of beliefs. Instead, it is a matter of proclaiming to them the "unknown god" that they may already be worshiping (Acts 17:23). Their experience of conversion may not necessarily involve praying a sinner's prayer—it may involve hearing the voice of Jesus and choosing to obey.

These people will not renounce their idols because a missionary has persuaded them to do so; they will do so because God has won their hearts and fulfilled their needs to the point that old practices are no longer needed. They will not share their faith with others out of a sense of obedience to the Great Commission; they will do so because their experience of Jesus is so real to them that they would dearly love for those around them to partake in it. They will not read the Bible because they know that this is what Christians are expected to do; they will do so simply because the Person they have met is so wonderful that they want to get to know him more.

REFERENCES

Braun, N. 1971. *Laity mobilized: Reflections on church growth in Japan and other lands.* Grand Rapids: Eerdmans.

Fukuda, M. 2012. *Upwards, outwards, inwards: Passing on the baton of discipleship.* Gloucester, England: Wide Margin Books.

Furuya, Y. 2011. *Nihon no kirisutokyō wa honmono ka?* [Is Japanese Christianity real?]. Tokyo: Kyōbunkan.

Hastings, T. J., and M. R. Mullins. 2006. The congregational leadership crisis facing the Japanese church. *International Bulletin of Missionary Research* 30, no. 1: 18–23.

Hiebert, P. G. 1982. The flaw of the excluded middle. *Missiology: An InterNational Review* 10, no. 1: 35–47.

Kawano, S. 2005. *Ritual practice in modern Japan: Ordering place, people, and action.* Honolulu: University of Hawaii Press.

Lewis, D. 2013. *The unseen face of Japan.* 2nd ed. Gloucester, England: Wide Margin Books.

CHAPTER 11

SPIRITUAL REALITIES IN THE FOLK BUDDHIST WORLDVIEW OF SRI LANKA

RAVIN CALDERA

Each civilization has its own ways of dealing with the supernatural and unexplainable phenomena interrelated with the human-life and life-cycle events. In this quest, a metaphysical explanation of the fundamental nature of things and the cosmos leads to paranormal experiences. Such mystical encounters espouse narratives forming the communal worldview; in turn, the adopted worldview forms the community's collective memory, which is handed down over generations. Communities are captivated by their worldviews; their collective memories and narratives often imprisoned the community in fear. Muller observes this reality in nineteenth-century Sri Lanka:

> The Sinhalese, living in such a beautiful country, supplied with everything needful for human wants, should enjoy great happiness. There is, however, one great hindrance to this, which tends to embitter their life, and keeps them in constant terror . . . they suppose that there are numerous evil spirits constantly surrounding them, lurking in the rocks, trees, and jungles, seeking to do them harm. (1891, 1–2)

Sinhalese too were overwhelmed and captivated by natural phenomena. Their worldviews were fashioned by fear, awe, and reverence to the unknown. The great tradition of Buddhism in both cosmology and doctrine, interwoven with village institutionalized life, refracted in the traditional Sinhalese worldview; therefore, the Sinhalese worldview in turn reflected a typical microcosm of village life.

The decline of the traditional agrarian communities with its extended kinship networks and the rise of the segregated nuclear families have changed the spiritual topography of Sri Lanka (Gombrich and Obeyesekere 1988, 67–70). This plotted the path to new shrines and cultic groups. Urbanization provided a melting-pot effect to cultic and Buddhist rituals. The close encounters with the different provincial animistic traditions has evolved, intermingled, and standardized the practice of rituals. Days and times considered holy (*poya*) to the Buddhists have been modified to inauspicious cultic *kemmura* days (Wednesdays and Saturdays) for invoking gods and demons (ibid., 72).

In such a rapidly changing socioreligious terrain the Buddhist temple cult has failed to address the misfortunes befalling the individual, like illness in the family and poverty. Gombrich and Obeyesekere observed:

> In traditional communal rituals (*gammaḍuva*) the whole village is a congregation; there are no cult groups of selected individuals. In such ritual, the village assembles for a yearly ceremony of thanksgiving or first fruits and disperses after the celebrations are over. Cult groups (if that is not too strong a term) have been associated with the activities of the Buddhist temple rather than the god's shrine. (ibid., 70)

Hence, for the individual's spiritual needs, Buddhists congregated around the other alternative means of solutions, thus crafting popular folk Buddhism.

THE CONCEPTUAL NATURE OF BUDDHISM IN SRI LANKA

The Buddhists of Sri Lanka fall into two major categories: the majority of the population is Buddhist by the right of birth, and an exceptionally small number of Buddhists by conviction; namely, based on proof or logical reasons without tincture of doubt (Nanayakkara 2000, 253). "Those belonging to the first category almost exclusively share the common property of having the Sinhala language as their mother tongue" (Karunatillake 1979, 1). Therefore, Buddhist religion and Sinhala nationality are inseparably unified. "For the practical standpoint, however, a person born to a Buddhist family is considered a Buddhist. That becomes his second bias, language being the first" (ibid., 8). The typical terms of identification are *bauddaya* (Buddhist) or *baudda/ baddagam minissu* (people belong to Buddhism). Identity of the Sinhala Buddhist is intensified by the sentiment that Sri Lanka is the native place of the Sinhalese people (Sinhalaya/Sinhala *minissu*). Recent voices in the public square, especially by the extreme faction called Bodhubala Sena (Armies of Buddhist Power), advocate the notion that Sri Lanka is a monocultural country; namely, "Buddhist Sinhalese culture." The religious minorities are considered as the subcultures of the predominant Sinhalese Buddhist culture.

On the contrary, so-called "popular Buddhism" or "folk Buddhism" is highly syncretized with the mythology of Buddhistic, Vadic, Aryan Indian, Vedda, and local animism. Wijesekara notes,

Indian beliefs and superstitions have no doubt influenced the Sinhalese from the ancient times. The People of Lanka may have come under the cultural influences of the tribal cultures that prevailed before the development of the urban cultures in the Indus valley. Immigrants may have introduced at least some elements, the spirit, the way of life and beliefs and superstitions of the Vedic Aryans. (1987, 11)

The ancient people in Sri Lanka might have incorporated much of the beliefs, myths, and legends into their metanarrative.

Buddhism has assimilated and sometimes converted popular demonologies and divinities of the host country to its core worldview. As an example, in folk Buddhism in Cambodia, extremely malicious spirits of inauspicious death, like *brāy*, could be adopted by a monastery and become a guardian who dwells in the pedestal of the main statue of the temple. Assimilation of the ancestral animism of the Khmers and Buddhism is observed in the conversion of *brāy* under the care of the Buddhist cult and become a benevolent deity (*brāy brah pāramī*) (see Chouléan 1988, 36–37). As suggested, "Sri Lanka is a very clear example of a country where the folk demonology has been greatly influenced by Buddhism, Buddhism being influenced by the demonology in turn" (Jayawardhana 2000, 373).

As mentioned in Figure 5, folk Buddhism assimilates alternative worldviews, giving prominence to old cultic places. As an example, the

Kateragama shrine situated in the southern tip of the country is a center of Hindu-Buddhist syncretism (Gombrich and Obeyesekere 1988, 163–79). The rise of Kataragama, the war god in classical Hindu myth, is an intriguing phenomenon in the Sinhalese modern life (Obeyesekere 1977). The influence is great to the point that Kataragama shrines are frequently predominant in the Buddhist monasteries.

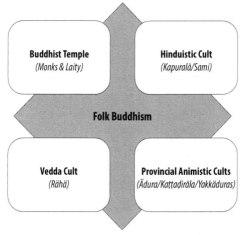

Figure 5: Sources of Sri Lankan folk Buddhism

POLAR OPPOSITES: CORE WORLDVIEW OF BUDDHISM

Buddhism is essentially a realistic analysis of the existential nature of life as suffering. Buddha's enlightenment is to understand the state of suffering in life and detach from the elements, which create existence by a process of meditative intellectualization. In this respect, Buddhism is highly intellectual and appeals to liberating knowledge (*ñāṇa dassana-patipadā*). The goal of attainment to the ultimate realization in Buddhism cannot be achieved by ritualistic worship or practices prescribed by Hinduism or any ancient religious traditions. Buddhism "does not recommend any type of worship or any other kind of *ritualistic* practices as a path leading to the attainment of ultimate reality. This has tended to make the basic Buddha dharma something that might appear sapless for the uneducated common man" (Karunatillake 1979, 2 "italics in the original"). High intellectual requirements make it difficult for a common man to comprehend and practise its core theoretical teachings (dharma). The word dharma itself is much more complex than the term "doctrinal teachings" (see Nanayakkara 2000, 438–53). Moreover, eradication of ritualistic veneration makes religion drift without an anchor.

> The Buddhist tradition arose in India against a background of alternative religious world-views, many which tend to focus the attention of the devotees on remote goals, the religio-philosophical conceptualization of which was difficult and for the most part beyond the reach of their devotees. (Karunatillake 1979, 1)

Furthermore, to an ordinary layman dharma becomes something mystical because of its complexity. For a Buddhist, the term dharma constitutes not the philosophical core of Buddhism but the ethics and moral code of principles. Hence, they are naturally oriented towards dharma through devotion and merit making. The common understanding, therefore, is the acts that make merits are *armissa* (heteropraxis) and the meditational practices are called *prethipathi* (orthopraxis). "Buddhism aims at making faith (*saddhā*) culminate in knowledge or *paññā*" (Nanayakkara 2000, 254).

The Buddhist pantheon is accommodation and systematic arrangement of the pre-Buddhist conceptions into a cosmological system. Unlike the Vedic tradition, Buddhists denied the validity of prayers and sacrifice as a means to achieve the ultimate perfection nirvana (Marasinghe 1974, 83). In the Buddhist cosmological thinking celestial beings are part of the same universe as human beings and other living beings. Marasinghe observed that the five destinies referred to in the Pali Canons are *Niraya* (purgatory), *Tiracchānayoni* (animal birth), *Pittivisaya* (realm of the Pertas), *Mannussa* (realm of human beings) and *devā* (realm of the gods) (ibid. 1974, 46).

In the ordinary Sinhalese mind, three realms constitute three planes or worlds (*loka*). The realms of happiness are the highest plane where gods dwell, followed by the intermediate world of human beings. At the very bottom of these planes lies the world of demonic hosts (*yakksaloka*), the realms of misery. This is the tripartite division in the cosmology of the folk Buddhism that prevails in Sri Lanka.

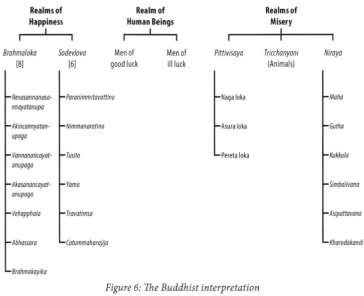

Figure 6: *The Buddhist interpretation of cosmology according to Pali Canon*
Source: Marasinghe (1974, 86)

The Buddhist deities are not immortal but enjoy the temporary refuge of blissful enjoyment. The Buddhist deities cannot attain nirvana unless they are born into the human realm (Marasinghe 1974, 86). Hence they perform charitable acts in expectation of accumulating merits from the people who have been served. There are a total of 173 visits of deities recorded in the Pali canonical texts. The purpose of the visits is to get clarification of doubt risen in their minds (ibid., 84). It is reasonable to say the association with Buddha and the *arahats* (enlightened monks) is solely beneficial for the deities only. However, when deities have close voluntary acquaintance with monks or lay-disciples, they are helpful in guiding them to truth. The role of the deities can be described as protectors of the *sāsana* (religion) as disciples of Buddha and the messengers of the doctrine (*dhammadūtas*).

All nonbenevolent spirits are not malevolent. However, Māra with his army and the *yakku* (spirits) are considered to be harmful. The belief of hells (purgatory) was similarly formed from the influence of the Vedic cosmology (for a classification, see ibid., 47).

The existence of nonempirical beings is strengthened by the concept of rebirth.

> *The acceptance of the concept of rebirth not only resulted in a more tacit acceptance of the gods, but it also largely contributed toward speeding up the process of "god making."* This idea of "god making" by no means seems to be an innovation on the part of Buddhism, but seems to fall into its place as part of a general trend that has been at work either consciously or unconsciously in the Indian religious thinking from the very earliest times. That Buddhism exploited it (almost to its maximum) for religious edification is different. (ibid., 69, italics added)

THE COSMOLOGY OF THE FOLK RELIGION

It is the belief of the Buddhists that the earth, heavens, and hells are cosmographically defined places. In classical literature each realm falls into empirical and nonempirical sets of world realms (*lōka*). The general understanding of the universe by the average Buddhist can be plotted as Karunatillake's diagram shows (1979, 12):

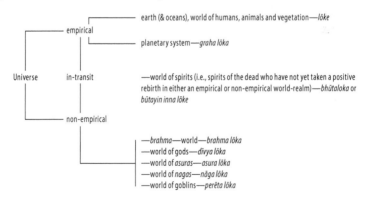

Figure 7: Folk Buddhist cosmological thinking
Source: (1979, 12)

The deities in the Sinhalese folk religion are nonhuman, rational, benevolent, and powerful: "The gods, like humans and other species, have a general attitude common to all, and specific attributes and histories differentiate them from one another" (Obeyesekere 1984, 61). The roles they play as protectors have extended to acting to bring the moral order in place. They help the men by giving help and punitively mediate in settling justice. Buddhists believe that Buddha has warranted the gods, and the gods in turn have the duty to protect the Buddha *sāsana*. In this respect Buddhists are responsible to give merits (*piṅ*) to the deities, so that they would be able sustain them for the task. However, Obeyesekere points out, "The term *dēvata* in Buddhist doctrinal texts simply meant deity. The term used in Sinhala Buddhism, it refers primarily to animistic deities of trees (*vṛkṣa dēvatā*)" (ibid., 69).

Over time, the ethical and moral nature of the Sinhalese deities becomes doubtful, and some have been renowned to be capriciously malevolent. However, Buddhists believe that Buddha has subdued and delegated the power, so that the gods necessarily have to act ethically, in justness and righteousness.

The deities in the folk religion could be divided into four categories—the guardians, the lesser gods, the deities in the intermediate state, and planetary deities.

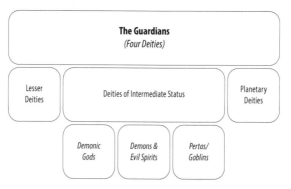

Figure 8: Four categories of deities in folk Buddhism

The Guardians

Buddhists believe that the four corners of the cosmos are guarded by four gods; namely, *Vaishravaṇa* (North), *Virūḷhaka* (South), *Dhrutharashṭa* (East), *Virūpaksha* (West). In northern and Indian Buddhism these guardians are called "The Four *Locapāla*" (see Getty 1914, 147). Scott notes,

The concept he suggests derives from the classical Buddhist concept of the guardian gods of the Four Quarters: Dhrtarāṣṭra, guardian of the East and chief of the Gāndharvas; Virudha, guardian of the South and chief of the Kumbhāṇḍas; Virupakṣa guardian of the West and the chief of the Nāgas; and Vaisravana, guardian of the North and chief of the Yakkhas. (1994, 19)

Hence, these gods were kings in the past and have been the chiefs of the respective peoples.

They were the sentinels of the secular realm, guardians of Sri Lanka, and considered the protectors of Buddhism:

> In doctrinal Buddhism the latter were the four guardians of the universe; they are formally propitiated today, but their significance, excerpt for *Vaisravana* (*Vessamuni*) or Kuvera, lord of the north and overlord of demons, is minimal. Hence, the term designating them is often given to the four gods, specially as guardians of Sri Lanka, and more generally the universe. (Obeyesekere 1984, 38)

The other equally important role they played is as the protectors of the sovereignty of the king.

Similar to canonical Buddhism, in the folk religion there is a concept of four different gods (*hathara varan deviyo*), who inhabit the four shrines (*hatara dēvāla*) in the capital. The four capital shrines (*hatara dēvāla*) of the gods had vast political significance under the Sinhalese kingdoms. At the annual procession of the tooth relic (*daḷadā perahära*) at the Kandy *māligāva*, four shrines are represented (Seneviratna 1963, 172–73). The four gods are varied from time to time. For instance, in the fifteenth and sixteenth centuries Vibishana, Vishnu, Saman, and Kataragama constituted the pantheon. However, post-eighteenth century in the Kandyan kingdom the four great gods were Nātha, Vishnu, Kataragama, and Pattini. In respect to the great gods nowadays, especially in the low country, are Vishnu, Nātha, Saman, and Kataragama or Skanda (Obeyesekere 1984, 38). Depending on the locality, the four gods may include additional gods or goddesses like Pattini, Vibhishana, and Pullear (Ganesh). The Pattini stands apart in the Central, Uva, and Sabaragamuwa provinces. Pullear is patron god for the north-central and northern provinces.

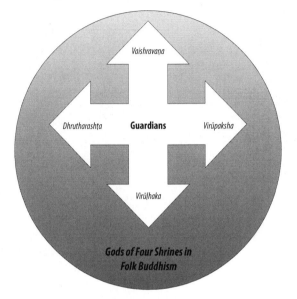

Figure 9: The evolution of traditional guardians

The Lesser Deities

The four patron gods of the four shrines are considered as the head of the pantheon. In several regions, apart from the four great gods, lesser gods are considered important. It is evident that the lesser gods (Alice Getty referred to them as "minor gods"; 1914) once were demons and then elevated to gods. At this transition these lesser gods have retained some of their demonic character. The following are considered to be the lesser gods in Sri Lanka.

Devol deviyo is a collective of seven gods (Obeyesekere 1984, 150–51), whose shrine is situated in Sinigama, in the southwest region. This shrine is popular with the Sinhalese as a place of fire-walking, cursing, and invoking harm and diseases. The *devol deviyo* is sometimes referred to as *Devol Yakku* (demons). This demon is associated with fire, and the genesis myth refers to him as quenching fire; therefore, he is named as "Gini Kuruṃba."

Dēvtā Bandara or *Dāḍmuṇda* (bear god) is considered the fearless god among the gods (ibid., 85, 215). At the Buddha's visit to Adam's peak (*Samenola* peak), which is the second highest and religiously important mountain in Sri Lanka as the folklore goes, the fearful gods ran in disarray to hide; Dāḍmuṇda hid himself behind Buddha to ridicule the fearful gods. He is renowned to mercilessly beat demons and prevent them from harming the humans (ibid., 89–90). The later mythology shows Dāḍmuṇda as the one who stood by Buddha when he was attacked by demon hosts of Mara and in turn received empowerment over demons (ibid., 57). The main shrine for Dāḍmuṇda is situated in Aluthnuwara (new city), Mawanalla, where the geographical name itself gives us a clue that the Dāḍmuṇda is a new deity.

Pattini, considered a lesser deity, was earlier known as *maṅgara* or *kiri Amma* (milk mother), probably gaining prominence later. A few ritual texts (*kōlmura*) refer to her as the "*aluth Pattini Deviyo*" (new goddess Pattini). Pattini is regarded as the goddess of charity and chastity. The protagonist of the Tamil epic *Cilapatikāram* (100–300 CE), Kannagi, was deified for her purity and chastity (Atikal 2004). The poet Ilanko Atikal wrote this epic based on the story of Kannagi taking ravenge from the Pandyan king Madurai, imposing the death penalty on her husband, Kovalan, for stealing the queen's anklet. It is stated that the city was set ablaze by virtue of Kannagi's chastity. The Sinhala Pattini corpus has incorporated part of the epic of Kannagi (Obeyesekere 1984, 25, 225, 528–29). It is a commonly held belief that the Pattini cult was introduced to Sri Lanka by King Gajabahu (113–30 CE) or Neela, a warrier who brought her anklet from South India (Wijesekara 1987, 23).

Doḷaha deviyo (twelve gods) consists of a hodgepodge of twelve deities prominent in certain parts of the low country. However, Wirz named them "*dolos deviyo*," whom Sinhalese believe to spread diseases (1954, 136–40). Some believe that seven manifestations of Pattini (*Satpattini*; namely, *gini, teda, amba, jala, orumali, mal,* and *sirimamuni*) were developed into *doḷaha deviyo* by adding various other deities. However, the twelve gods act collectively as a singular association or *samāgama* (see ibid., 160). In the low-country *gammaḍuva*, the collection is composed of *devol deviyo*, Pattini, Kataragama, Nātha, Saman, Vibhīṣana, Gini Kurumba, Vāhala, Dāḍmuṇda, Mahā Viṣṇu, and Īsvara. However, in the central province, especially in Haṅguraṇketa, the cult of twelve is called the *Baṇḍara* cult and the respective gods are completely different (see Obeyesekere 1984, 212).

The Deities of Intermediate Status

The deities in the third category are undefinable or intermediate between divine and demon. This probably has been partly influenced by Hinduism. For instance, Parvathi and Kāli are one goddess, yet act in contradictory ways—benevolently and wickedly. In Sinhala folk religion *Gambāra Deviyo* (the god in charge of the village) and *huniyam* or *Suniyam deviyo* are clear examples of gods of intermediate status. They were considered as gods and demons at the same time.

Demons and Evil Spirits

In the contemporary discourse of demons (*yakku*), there is no specific world-realm assigned to them (Karunatillake 1979, 13–14). *Yakkus* fall into two categories in the cosmological thinking of an average Buddhist. The first are the dead spirits born as *yakku* to take revenge. The second set constitutes indigenous sets of demons in folk religion, assimilated from provincial animistic beliefs.

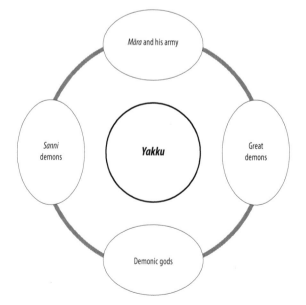

Figure 10: Folk Buddhist demonology

Demons in the Sinhalese folk religion could be divided into at least four categories. The first group is called *Sanni* demons, which is a cluster of eighteen mutilated or deformed demons, considered to cause illnesses (see Obeyesekere 1969; Halverson 1977). The second category is the great demons or chief demons. For example, *Mahasōna* (great demon of graveyards) has a mythical history of a fallen war hero who was given life by sorcery and later became the graveyard demon (see Wirz 1954, 28–30, 142). As the mythical story goes, Saman the god of the *Samanola* peak tamed the demon and was able to make people ill but not kill.

The third category falls to the intermediate gods who act sometimes as demons. As an example, *Kalu Kumara* (black prince) or *Kalu Yaka* (black demon) is the most feared demon in the village setting. It is a dark lover, whose gaze could inflict women with mysterious illnesses. The infliction is not only limited to women; it also could extend to nursing and young children (Kapferer 1983, 52, 121–22; Wirz 1954, 34–35). Mostly the demon is associated with sexual lust and is manifested as *vata kumara* (round prince) or *madana kumara yakkā* (sexual passion prince demon) (Wirz 1954, 37-38, 106–7). Kalu Kumara has a dual nature—while at the shrine he is considered as a god and outside of the shrine a demon. In respect to this demon, it is obvious that countless demonic forms constitute various refractions in the Sinhalese cosmology (Kapferer 1983, 252).

Several gods use demons as their agents to inflict punishment on the guilty. *Kurumbara* and its host of demons are the servants of the *devol deviyo* (see Obeyesekere 1984, 109, 135, 155). In the same way, *kadavara* and its associate demons in the low country are servants of the Kataragama. The Sinhalese folk religion believes demons have got their warrant from gods, which is obtained from Buddha.

The fourth is Māra or *Maruva* (the Evil One, the Harbinger of death), who is considered the chief of demon hosts. Māra with his army attacked the Buddha at the feet of the *bōdhi* tree, moments before Buddha's enlightenment, to sway him from the path (Kapferer 1983, 112). Buddha has defeated the Māra by his virtuous serenity and secured the authority over demons. Māra is a personification of death, and his daughters represent greed (*tṅna*), lust (*rati*), and hatred (*raga*).

In Buddhism, Māra is considered as the tempter; therefore, one's duty is to attack him with the weapons of knowledge and when conquered watch him without rest (*Dammapada* 3:40). Other stanzas in the *Dammapada* referring to Māra can be found in 1:8; 8:105; and 13:175. It is the common belief that "one should always be on guard against Mara, the demon of death. No sick person should be left unattended because Mara is hovering round the bed of a patient" (Wijesekara 1987, 17–18).

Pertas

The departed ancestors, who do not have immediate afterlife, are believed to become spirits. This ideology has been adopted by the Sinhalese from the indigenous aboriginal people (Veddas): "The spirit of the dead are recognized as the *Nae Yahu*, but they are certainly thought of as far less important than a number of other spiritual beings to be immediately considered" (Seligmann and Seligmann 1911, 173).

The Seligmanns observe that the Veddas have a system of ancestor worship. Those who depart in death turn into *Nae Yahu* (kin deities). The old great deities referred to as the *mahā yakini* are animistic spirits. These malevolent spirits are thought to be departed elderly women (Obeyesekere 1984, 295). Perhaps the Tamil influence has given rise to less dangerous and benevolent spirits like *kiriamma* among sophisticated Veddas (Seligmann and Seligmann 1911, 140). Popular belief holds that a deceased person could remain in the form of a homeless spirit (*mala preta*), if the funeral almsgiving (dana) is not offered (see ibid., 141). It is noteworthy that these spirits have no authority to inflict humans without the permission of the higher gods.

> It appears that the dead have no power to interfere in human affairs and take offerings until permission has been obtained from one or more high gods, of whom the chief is the Kataragam God. How the spirit obtains this permission was not clear, but the early signs of the power of the deceased were always in some way connected with the Kataragam God. (ibid., 143)

The Saligmanns further state that the Veddas believe the spirit of the dead has to report to and obtain permission from *Kande Yaka* (chief mountain demon) to help the living and accept offerings (ibid., 151). Here we see a rich example of the intermingling of cultic beliefs. Pertas are inferior spirits in orthodox Buddhism. These creatures are frequently in a state of craving because they cannot satisfy their hunger. Pertas are thought to be greedy ancestors born in domestic households. Pertas are known to bring disease, poverty, and demon possession. The other similar terms given to them are Pisas (Sanskrit: *piśāca*) and Kumbānda, who were evil spirits in early Buddhism.

Planetary Deities

The mythical planetary deities come from astrology. The sun, moon, and other various planets are considered as the divine celestial beings in henotheism. Nine planetary gods who influence the living beings are Sun (*Ravi*), Moon (*Candra*), Mars (*Kuja*), Mercury (*Buda*), Jupiter (*Guru*), Venus (*Kivi*), Saturn (*Säni*), Dragon's head (*Rāhu*), and Dragon's tail (*Kētu*). *Rāhu* causes solar and lunar eclipses. The planetary influences can be detected by reading the horoscope. However, planetary movements are irrevocable because they indicate one's karma. The planetary configurations merely chart a person's karma (see Obeyesekere 1968).

The Vedic astrological deity *Rāhu* has infiltrated into Vedda cult as *Rāhu yakka*. The *yakku* are also associated with the planetary deities. For instance, Kalu Kumara (the black prince) can assume the form of a planetary demon (*raksa*), the lowly and terrible Kalu Yaka, a woman, a dog, and a cow (Kapferer 1983, 117).

CONCEPT OF DŌSA IN FOLK BUDDHISM

Afflictions are believed to have arisen from *dōsa*. The concept of *dōsa* Obeyesekere defines as "faults" or, to be more exact, "misfortunes" (1984, 44). The etymology probably derived from the Sanskrit medicinal *Ayurvedic* terms as a fault of the organism. In Buddhism the word *dōsa* (Sanskrit: *dveṣa*) connotes hatred, an actual immoral mental factor of volition and conscious thought (Van Zeyst 2000, 665). It is considered as one of three unwholesome roots (*ahusala-mūla*); namely, greed (*lobha*), hatred (*dōsa*), and delusion (*mōha*). In contrast to the doctrinal position, medicinal usage also subdivides into three informatives in the humoural makeup. *Ayurvedic* medicinal aetiology has close similarity with exorcism practices, and they are frequently intertwined with each other. *Ayurvedic* physicians and exorcists use similar methods in diagnosis of illness. "A healthy person is seen to have a balance in the three basic body humours of phlegm (*sema*), bile (*pitta*) and wind (*vata*) and become ill when this equilibrium is disturbed by excess of any one of these humors" (Kapferer 1975, 19). The primary factor of differentiation is that *Ayurveda* perceives that imbalance is caused due to dietary and living irregularities, but the exorcists attribute it to disease with nonhumans (*amanussa dōa*). The imbalance is present in traditional exorcism as the notion that when demons attack, the whole cosmos is thrown out of joint—the natural order is in disarray. Hence, the duty of the exorcist is to bring back the proper order (Wijesekara 1987, 16–17). A helpful clarification of *dosa* has been given by Obeyesekere (1984, 45–46). Following is a summary of that discussion:

Pita pantiya dōsa is considered to be misfortunes caused by the ill gaze (*disti*) of the primitive noncorporal or nocturnal beings. Similarly, *yakṣa dōsa* is caused by demonic (*yakṣa*/*yakka*) influence. The prominent illness-causing demons are *Kalukumara* (black prince), *Mahasona* (graveyard demon), and *Huniyam* (witchcraft demon). Their ill gazes are frequent at twilight. The fear of the demonic stare is so prevalent among the Sinhalese that they avoid consuming oily foods or fried meats outside of the homes.

Deviyannē is caused by the gods of the Sinhala Buddhist pantheon. The reason for the inflictions is the wrath of the particular god. The wrath may fall on a person who failed to fulfill vows (*bāra*) made to the gods. In time of trouble, Sinhalese make vows promising offerings for a god's assistance. The vows are made by tying a few coins (*paṇḍurū*) in a white cloth onto the shrine fixtures or laid on the altar. Secondly, gods inflict misfortune for the failure to perform customary rituals.

Misfortunes or disaster inflicted by sorcery is *Avol dōsa*. The Sinhalese use the sorcerer's malice against their enemies to impose illness, disrupt family life, and to cause loss of life, wealth, and property. The poems composed to inflict a curse are called *Vas kavi dōsa*. The *dōsa* arising from cursing poems is much milder than from sorcery (*kodivina*).

Vas dōsa are caused by violating taboos (*kili*), omitting or incorrect performing of ritual, witchcraft, evil eye (*äsvaha*), evil mouth (*katava-*

ha), and evil thought (*hōvaha*). Most of these are warded off by burning chilies and salt or hanging limes in a prominent place or by minor charms. The serious types are dealt with through use of a *garā nätum* (dance of *garā*) at the conclusion section of the *gammaḍuva*.

Graha dōsa / Graha apala is caused by inauspicious planetary conjunctions or influences. The Sinhalese consult astrologers to determine the extent of the influence. The astrologers give necessary advice to remedy the effects. The *bali santti* ritual is performed to minimize bad planetary influences.

THE RITUALS PRACTISED IN FOLK BUDDHISM

Folk Buddhism is concerned with the alleviation of current suffering; however, theoretically Buddhism's goal is to attain nirvana, which is ultimate liberation.

The remedial ritual process of *dōsa* falls into two categories; namely, (1) Buddhist rituals and (2) animistic rituals. In spite of the contradictory nature with the orthodoxy, both rituals are accepted and often promoted by the temple of that particular village. Contemporary urban dwellers prefer Buddhist rituals, but the southerners favour the animistic and cultic rituals. Many of the rituals could be traced back to the early indigenous inhabitants or the Hindu rituals, rather than canonical Buddhist practices. Kapferer observed that the sorcery and ritualistic concepts pertaining to demons have come into the Sinhala repertoire from the Veddas (1992, 308). The Seligmanns attest to the intercourse between Sinhalese and Veddas from the Middle Ages, which perhaps interpollinated the cultic beliefs of these communities (1911, 142, 149).

Buddhist Rituals

The Buddhist rituals seem to have risen out of syncretistic blending with the partial animistic healing rituals. The following are four popular means of relieving *dōsa*.

Bōdhi Pūjā Rituals

Traditionally *bōdhi pūjā* have been performed to "avert the evil influence of inauspicious planetary conjunctions" (Kariyawasam 1995, 20). However, it is the popular contemporary practice to alleviate all sorts of misfortunes. In the times of war in Sri Lanka, *bōdhi pūjā* was the most commonly used means to evoke blessings or protection for the soldiers. The *bōdhi* tree (*ficus religiosa*) is considered to be the place where Buddha attended enlightenment. Hence, it is one of the three sacred objects (*paribhogika*; namely, *Buddha* shrine, *Dagabe*, and *bōdhi* tree) of worship in the temple complex of Sri Lanka. From the early times, worship of the *bōdhi* tree, especially in Anuradhapura has been practised (Kariyawasam 1995, 16–20). The tree in Anuradhapura was brought from India by Sanghamitta and planted by King Devanampiya Tissa in the third century BCE. Present-day *bōdhi pūjā* ritual has been a recent innovation by Bhikkhu Ariyadhamma (Gombrich and Obeyesekere 1988, 384–410). The elaborate chanting like singing developed in the 1970s became very popular. Harvey notes, "Centered on the Bodhi-tree, it uses chanting that is more like singing, so as to be more emotional in nature than traditional chanting, as well as involving more active participation by laypeople" (2013, 380). The ritual practices could be varied from hanging flags, tying coins (*panduru*), lighting oil lamps, offering flowers, burning incense, circumambulating (*padakkhina*) thrice, reciting stanzas, and bathing the tree with scented water. Popular Sinhalese liturgies are used for *bōdhi pūjā* rituals (see Gombrich 1981, 54, 67–68, 72; Harvey 2013, 245).

Buddha Pūjā / Aṭavisi Buddha Pūjā Rituals

Buddha *pūjā* is a daily ritual performed by devout Buddhists. It could be performed in their house or in a Buddhist temple. On the full-moon days (*poya*) communal observances could be held at the temple. The goal of the Buddha *pūjā* is to accumulate merit and transfer merit to all other beings, including the dead. At the ritual, Buddhists offer food, water, flowers, burning incense, and oil lamps placed on the altar in front of the Buddha's statue or *dagaba*. The offering is made by reciting Pali stanzas. The flowers constitute the minimum requirement at any form of Buddhist worship (Kariyawasam 1995, 5). The ritual could be performed individually or corporately, under the guidance of a monk.

The young monk Pānadurē Ariyadhamma has composed a liturgy called *Aṭavisi Buddha pūjā* (worship of twenty-eight Buddhas) or simply a *Buddha pūjā* (Gombrich 1981, 47). At the *Aṭavisi Buddha pūjā* twenty-eight pictures or statues of Buddha are placed in a flowered altar. The pictures or the statutes are named according to the Buddhas recognized in the Pali tradition. Before the ritual, devotees offer flowers, food, drink, and other offerings. Devotees are guided to offer sweets, betel leaves, medicines, puffed rice, mustard seeds, arrow-grass, broken rice, and jasmine buds as a mark of devotion. At the end monks will evoke blessings and protection. As an example, observe the ending stanzas of the *Aṭavisi Buddha pūjā* service:

> May there be every blessing; may all the deities afford protection; by the power of all the Buddhas may you always fare well . . . By checking evil influences of constellations, devils and ghosts by the power of protective texts, may they lay low your misfortunes. May all living creatures who are ill be free from illness, who are fearful be free from fear, who are giving be free from grief. (Gombrich 1981, 70)

Buddhists commonly believe merit accumulated by *Buddha pūjā* could be transferred (*pattidana*) to the dead and thereby relieve them from any unfortunate realm of existence due to their own demerits (see also Kariyawasam 1995, 13; Gombrich 1971, 208–10). Sinhalese Buddhists use *Buddha pūjā* or *Aṭavisi Buddha pūjā* to propitiate the dead by merit transferring, thus alleviating their ill gaze.

Pirit Chanting Ceremonies and Almsgiving

A popular ceremony among the Buddhists of Sri Lanka is *pirit* chanting: "In the domestic and social life of the Sri Lankan Buddhist no important function can be considered complete without this ceremony" (Kariyawasam 1995, 30). It was used in "the opening of a new house or public building, the start of a new business venture, before or after a wedding, to aid an ill or disturbed person, or at a funeral" (Harvey 2013, 316). The term *piritta* means protection; therefore, this ritual is commonly used as a safety covering. Buddhists believe that *pirits* are sanctioned by Buddha as means of protection to both laity and monks. The commonest *pirit* are three stanzas called *thun-sutra* (*Karaniyamettha*, *Ratanana*, and *Mangala*), which the Buddha himself prescribed for protection (see also Kariyawasam 1995, 31). These three stanzas are used by the laity as protective means when they are faced with supernatural encounters.

In this respect, ceremonial chanting is capable of evading all forms of evil and dangers. It is used for warding off wild animals, human attackers, disease, evil influences of planets, evil spirits, safeguarding of persons or property, and attainment of general success (see Kariyawasam 1995, 30; Harvey 2013, 249). The *pirit* is commonly used during the child-bearing period:

> During the latter weeks of her pregnancy, two or three Buddhist monks are invited to the house to chant *pirith* (recital of benedictory stanzas from Pali Buddhist canon) to expel unfortunate occurrences, evil spirits or any other bad effects brought about by the planetary deities on the pregnant woman. (Paranavitana 2008, 38)

The *pirit* ceremony consists of ritualistic, monotonous chanting of Pali texts from the *Piruvana pothvahanse* or *pirit pota*. The ceremony is usually held at night and followed by almsgiving on the following day. The simplest form is limited to a portion of the day, and the elaborate *pirit* rituals may last one week or longer according to the requirements. Kariyawasam expressed the essence of power in chanting *pirits* as manipulating sound waves: "The power of the sound waves resulting from the sonorous and rhythmic recitation and also from particular combination of certain letters and syllables also play a part in exercising this beneficial influence" (1995, 31). However, Harvey gives psycho-physiological reasons for healings (2013, 249–50). At the end of the ceremony a piece of sacred thread (*pirit-nula*) is tied to the wrist or the arm, and the *pirit*-water (*pirit-pan*) is drunk by the devotees or sprinkled over them or the property as a protective measure.

Buddhists believe that departed spirits or *pretas* are expecting merits due to the inability of performing meritorious deeds on their own (Kariyawasam 1995, 40). Hence, the *pirit* ceremonies are conducted for transferring merits to the departed loved ones.

It is common practice in the third month after a funeral to organize a *pirit* ceremony or an almsgiving to assist the deceased to attain a good existence in the next birth. If it is ignored, the relatives might face the danger of harassment by the departed. King Bimbisara was instructed by Buddha when he was harassed by departed kinsmen to give alms to Buddha; after fulfilling the request the king was alleviated from the harassment (ibid., 45). It is a general practice to perform a *pirit* ceremony once a year for the purpose of merit giving to the dead and for the purpose of protection.

Amulet and Talisman

In popular Buddhism, monks are requested to bless the protective amulets (Harvey 2013, 316). Those amulets are crafted as a *bōdhi* tree leaf or the symbol of a wheel. However, unlike in northern and eastern Buddhism, Buddhists in Sri Lanka do not wear amulets of a miniature Buddha.

It is a custom within the Sinhalese society to wear protective amulets for good luck or to repel evil:

> A small medallion called *panchayudha* or the symbols of divine weapons, which is made of either silver or gold is worn around the neck of the child. These symbols of five divine weapons include a sword, a spear, a bow, a battle axe and a shield engraved on it. This medallion is worn for the purpose of providing protection to the child and as a repellant against evil spirits generated as a result of evil eye, evil mouth and evil ear (*es waha*, *katavaha*, and *ho waha*). (Paranavitana 2008, 39)

The amulets containing a copper leaf inscribed with carved diagrams are called *yantras*. The sorcery experts or the monks use *mantras* (organized sounds and words into stanzas) or *pirits* and also inscribe those words and sounds into powerful, magical diagrams (*yantras*). They recognized that sounds and words become verbal actions; therefore, the words and sounds are both the instrument and the effect (see Kapferer 1992, 32, 40). The magical diagram itself has no power; it has to be emblazoned with its own spells.

> Yantras do not have force in themselves. They must have life (*jiva*) breathed into them. This is the force of mantras that are uttered in relation to them. Yantras

and mantras comprise an inseparable unity, the mantra giving the life which the yantra then holds and
further materializes. (Kapferer 1992, 99)

According to the purpose, *yantras* are made and worn around the neck
or fastened on the arms or waist of the patient (*āturayā*).

As funeral houses are considered to be spiritually polluted, Buddhists remove amulets before entering a funeral house. "Yantras and
amulets are supposed to lose their power and should be left at home
and put back on only after one has had a bath on return from the funeral house" (Langer 2007, 70).

Some Animistic Rituals Incorporated into Folk Buddhism

Animistic rituals blended with Buddhism are practised by sorcery experts (*anavina karuva*), exorcists (*āduras*), demon priests (*kaṭṭaḍirāla/
yakkäduras*), and shrine priests (*kapurālas*). The rituals may be simplistic (as for an hour) and elaborately complex (to be performed for
several days) in Sri Lanka.

Boiling Milk (Kiri Itiravīma)

The rite is performed by boiling coconut milk in a pot until it over-
flows. *Kiri itiravīma* is done symbolizing abundance and is regularly
performed when starting a new enterprise, always at an auspicious
time (*neketa*). In the farming community, it is the convention to tie a
coconut on a tree, and at the harvest people boil milk to prepare milk
rice as a thank offering for gods. In some parts of Sri Lanka, at the ceremonial entering, the pot in which the milk was boiled is hung on the
main beam of the house.

Sēt Kavi / Vas Kavi

The most simplistic form of warding off evil is by reciting poems. It
is usually used in the inauspicious planetary conjunctions and in the
Vas dōsa. The *Äduras* used to compose a set of poems and instruct
the patients to recite them in a manner prescribed for the occasion.
Similarly, cursing verses of a poem (*vas kavi*) has the power to inflict
harm to the person to whom it is addressed. The *Set kavi* are used to
protect and minimize the negative power of the curses. The *set kavi* is
composed focusing on the virtues of Buddha and his achievements.

The verbal attention is given in a manner that produces a mental and physical equilibrium in the patient.

Set-santi

The *set-santi* (*yatukarma/yagakarma*) are rites used to smother the demonic powers. The word *santi* in Sanskrit derives from the meaning of "extinguishing" fire. Hence, the various rites are performed to repress the evil heat from the provoked demons.

The first most common rite is called *nūlmatirima*, where a seven- or nine-stringed thread (*äpa-nūla*) is energized by chanting spells and worn around the neck or around the arm and waist. This thread will protect the victim from misfortune and any *dōs*. At the end of any *set-santi* rite, *äpa-nūla* will be tied to the patient. Apart from the above, water or oil is chanted over and given to drink or to apply on the body of the victim. In the *Aryurvada/Sidharurveda* medicinal system, medications are applied after casting spells on them.

The second common method of warding off *dōs* is lime cutting (*dehi-käppīla*). Magical spells are chanted over twenty-one limes, and the exorcists cut them using an areca-nut cutter on the patient's head. While cutting each lime, he pronounces exorcising words to ward off the evil influences that have been cast upon the victim. The whole ritual will last for an hour or so. At the end of the ritual the exorcist utters benedictory incantations and ties a protective thread (*äpa-nūla*) on the patient.

The rituals for the treatment of illness in children are twofold. The rarest rite performed by exorcists is for the *bala-giri* female demons (Kapferer 1983, 249; see also Wirz 1954, 96–102). The second common treatment is almsgiving for nursing mothers (*kiri-amma danaya*). This is an elaborate almsgiving for seven mothers, given before the first light of the day (see Marzano 2002, 88,90). After receiving the alms, the women in turn bless the child invoking the goddess Pattini to guard the child against diseases and various kinds of evil influence of ill-willed people.

At the minor rituals as referred to above, it is customary to advise the patient to wear an amulet with a protective *yantra*. The *yantra* will be designed, empowered, and given by the astrologers or the cult priests.

Balitovil and Yaktovil

In the case of a person under bad planetary influence, the astrologer would recommend a specific kind of bali ceremony (see Kariyawasam 1995, 49–52). The bali is a clay representation of the planetary deities on a framework of bamboo or banana leaf and trunk. At the ceremony, the exorcist dances and recites propitiatory incantations of protection in front of the bali and the patient. A live cock is placed near the bali as a scapegoat. The bird is released on the following morning, while the bali figures and the altar with offerings are placed at a crossroad.

Sinhala village society believes that the demon's gaze (*bālma/distiya*) could result in illness (*yak dōsa*), misfortune, or at a worst case result in demon possession. Eva Ambos describes two rituals associating with possession (2011, 199) as follows: In the south and southwest of the country, *yaktovilya* healing ritual, where the drummers and dancers perform the ritual. The second is *kohoba kankariya*, a propitiatory ritual in the central province to get rid of misfortunes and evil eye (*vas dōs*). Kandyan dancers with *ves* costume dance to invoke gods, while women who act as mediums go into a trance.

Any person being alone or travelling at odd times may be at risk of sicknesses by the ill gaze (*tanikam*). In such cases a ritualist or *kapurāla* (priest) conducts minor *set-santi* and, if it is a possession, traditionally *yaktovil*, an overnight healing ritual, is performed.

In the context of *yaktovil*, the ritual is performed in a public open-air arena with the participation of neighbours, friends, and relatives (see Kapferer 1975; 1983, 42–43). There are five exorcism rituals under the category of *yaktovil*: *Suniyama* (sorcery demon), *Sanni yakuma* (disease-spreading demons), *Mahasona Samayama* (graveyard demon), *Rata Yakuma* (sicknesses of women and children by Kalu Kukara), and *Iramudun Samayama* (midday demon, the blood demon) (see Kapferer and Papigny 2005, 17,30–145). In a village setting such healing rituals could be extravagant and have many components like drumming, masked dances, dramatic performance, comic dialogues, chanting poems and uttering spells, offering handouts to gods and demons, etc. At the height of the healing phase, the chief specialist becomes possessed (*āvēsa*), generally followed by possession of the patient, with violent and sporadic shaking of the body. In such instances, the specialist offers appeasements to the demon/god and appeals to it to leave the patient. At the final phase, the specialist throws resin powder (*dummala*) onto a fire torch (*pandama*), to burn and cast away the malevolent spirit. The patient's healing is visible after, he or she awakes from the possession. The ritual transfers the reenactment to the patient; if the ceremony is successful, the patient is healed and the cause of the affliction is removed. The *yaktovil* is generally used to rid women and their children of the lustful blight of Kalu Kumara demon (Kapferer 1992, 318).

Communal Rituals

The most common practice in villages is boiling milk and offering rice cooked in the milk at the sacred tree or shrine (*sanhida*). This appeasement ritual is generally performed for the village guardian deities (*gambara deviyo*) to secure the well-being of the community. The whole village is expected to participate in the corporate offering. As a symbol of belongingness to the community, they share the consecrated rice (*pē bat*) as a communal meal.

The next common rituals are *gammaḍuva* and *devolmaḍuva*. The *gammaḍuva* ceremony is practised as a post-harvest thanksgiving ritual for the goddess Pattini. In some parts of the country, as a communal rite they practise *devolmaḍuva* for the twelve *devol* deities or for the village deity. A variation of the *devolmaḍuva* is exorcistic rituals known as *Rata Yakuma* and *Sanni Yakuma*, used to purge the sufferer of the inflictions and incurable diseases caused by numerous demons. The *gammaḍuva* is for propitiating Pattini, for the purpose of obtaining a good harvest or to ward off evil and infectious diseases. These ceremonies are often practised in the wider community of interconnected villages and have a natural inclination to promote the *status quo*. Kapferer acknowledged Obeyesekere's notion that these communal rites are part of the political hierarchies: "The *gammaḍuvas* in his observations, and in my own experience of these ceremonies, are community rites that give vital expression to local political hierarchies: a function of the rites that can be traced well into Sri Lanka's precolonial history" (1992, 129).

In the central highland of the country is practised a purification ritual named *kohom̆bāyak kaṅkāriya*. The overnight ceremony includes several deities; namely, *kohomba deviyo* and *doḷaha deviyo* (twelve gods). The purpose of this communal ritual is to cleanse the people from the afflictions of sorcery attacks (ibid., 31) or communal calamities. The ritual-drama is the ancient mythical story of Vijaya and Kuveni and uses a leopard-cursing pot to resemble the curses placed on the people. However, *kohom̄bāyak kaṅkāriya* is also used in honour of the *kohomba* trinity (*Aluth, Paran, and Maha Kohomba* deities) for the support of the good rice harvest. Similarly, Vedda tradition has a *kirikoraha* dance, where they use a coconut milk bowl as a center to appease the *yakku* and in turn make good merit (see Seligmann and Seligmann 1911, 229–30).

Finally, ancient villages play *aṅkeliya* (horn game) to honour the Pattini goddess (see Obeyesekere 1984, 383–423). The ritual horn game is played in the auspicious time after the harvest in the month of May. Two wooden hooks made from strong tree roots are interlocked. One horn is tied to a tree, and the other is tied to a pole, which pivots in a hole in the ground. Two tug ropes are tied to the pole, and the two teams (upper team and the lower team) take turns until one horn snaps. Obeyesekere notes, "The horn that snaps is the loser; the winning team expresses its jubilation and humiliates the losing team" (ibid., 383). The *aṅkeliya* ceremony lasts for about fifteen days. The festival ends with carrying the deities around the village at night, and the next morning they perform water sports. The *aṅkeliya* is played to thank and honour Pattini and to prevent epidemics in the village.

Vow Making and Fulfilling Vows
Buddhists fulfill their vows (*bāra*) in a manner sometimes very costly and painful. The simplest manner is to offer fruits, foods, and other valuable objects. Certain vows need to boil milk and prepare milk rice for the deity as an offering. Other ways of fulfilling vows are dancing in a procession dedicated to that particular deity, fire-walking on burning charcoal, releasing a life (*rupeta rupe*), and extreme self-infliction. In Kataragama, devotees vow to be hung on hooks. They hang on eight hooks (for different vows like healing, victory at court cases, protection from dangers, etc. (Sarath Mohotti, interview with author, February 22, 2014). Fire-walking is another classic example of how the

Buddhists have absorbed the *bakti* (devotion) religiosity of the Hindu Tamils (Gombrich and Obeyesekere 1988, 411–44).

The Concept of Time and Divination

The Buddhist concept of impermanence gives value to time. The cosmic time referred to in the canonical texts is counted in *kalpa* (epoch/aeon). There is an infinite number of *kalpas*. At the end of each *kalpal*, the dissolution of the world system and the starting of another happens. The *kalpa*, which is blessed with the birth of Buddha, is considered the *sāsana* of that particular Buddha being prevalent. The *sāsana* will end at the extinction of relics of the Buddha (*dhatu parinirvāṇa*) (Karunatillake 1979, 11).

The popular belief that the Gotama Buddha's *sāsana* will remain five thousand years gives precedence to the notion of Buddha's existence after his *painibāna*. Karunatillake writes, "The belief is that although Gotama Buddha is physically dead, he will remain spiritually alive throughout this time span of the five thousand years" (ibid. 11–12). Hence, the practitioners of folk Buddhism invoke the virtues of spiritual powers to ward off ill influences and bless success or health.

Astrology is an inseparable component of the ancient South Asian civilization. Therefore, astrology is part of the traditional learning in Sri Lanka, and the Sinhalese life is imbedded in it. The traditional society calculation of auspicious time and moments are part and parcel of the way of life. The first thing a family does at the birth of a child is to cast a horoscope. At an important juncture in life or at a life crisis, it is common to consult horoscopes to determine the causes and then plausible solutions.

For enterprises that require auspicious beginnings, astrologers predict the auspicious times and days. Inauspicious *kemmura* days (Wednesdays and Saturdays) and the *poya*, the Buddhist holy day, are considered as not suitable for any new beginnings. The life-cycle events, agricultural cycle, and individual or communal rituals need a suitable moment to initiate the work. Nothing could start on Tuesdays, and business people avoid Wednesdays. No ritual is held for gods on full-moon days (*poya*). Marriages are held on Thursdays. Certain Catholics avoid Fridays, the day that Christ was crucified, which has also influenced the Sinhalese Buddhists. The terms *suba* (good/auspicious) and *asuba* (bad/inauspicious) are generally used in connection with days and precise moments of time. It is the astrological belief that Marā inhabits certain direction at various times; therefore, Sinhalese avoid starting a journey in the direction that Marā resides.

Gombrich and Obeyesekere observe the concept of omens in agrarian society:

> Village society was also much concerned with omens. A bad omen, or obstacle (*bādā*), encountered for example as one left home, caused one to turn back and postpone the enterprise. There were texts (called *bādāvali*) that listed such bad omens: inauspicious people and animals one might meet and sounds one might hear. (1988, 310)

Divination in the Sinhalese society is a complex exertion. People use a variety of means like horoscopes, oracles, soothsayers, interpreters of dreams and visions, astrologers, and other mechanical methods. At marriages it is the custom to consult the horoscope of both parties. Even important political decisions are timed by consulting astrologers (ibid.).

Dreams are a significant part of divination. Some ancients believed that dreams are real and formulated a traditional system of interpretation. Some cultures believed that dreaming is the roaming of the spirit in the body. Others believe that certain dreams indicate omens or predict coming events. Dreams are the means of communication with the dead and spirits. Mohini (female phantom of beauty) and Kalukumara (an irresistibly handsome prince) are two evil spirits that use dreams as a means to inflict illnesses. The appeasement of these demons will prevent their ill effects. There are numerous prescribed ritual practices to divulge a bad dream averting its evil effects.

People are superstitious about giving another eggs, salt, and fire after sunset. Until recently, even the boutiques in towns will not sell those commodities after dusk (Wijesekara 1987, 17).

THE CHRISTIAN ALTERNATIVE PRACTICES

Life-cycle events are closely linked with spiritual realities. The rites along the path leading each human from his birth to the end guard him from unforeseen adversities and misfortunes and set him on a path of success and well-being.

The birth of a child marks an important phase of a family—joy, hopes, and fears are emotionally intermingled in such period. The customs set for evading evil spiritual attacks in the Sinhalese culture are elaborate. The application of milk mixed with gold dust on the tongue (*Ran kiri kata gaema*), consulting the horoscope, naming the child, dressing with bangles and amulets, placing a large black dot (*tilaka*) on the middle of the forehead, cutting hair, giving of solid foods, reading of the alphabet. If it is girl, certain rituals are performed upon the child up to the age of puberty to ward off ill influences (Paranavitana 2008, 37–39).

These life events offer participation with critical points in both the shared life of the community and the individual life cycle from birth to death (see Williams 1996, 249). The Christians in Sri Lanka share the same life-cycle junctures with prayer meetings and celebrations with the family and the community. Apart from prayer meetings, Christian parents take solace in performing rites like infant baptism, or in the Pentecostal tradition, dedication of the child to God. They believe that the dedication ritual has embedded power to ward off all ill influences which might harm the child. Catholics use protective amulets of the Virgin Mary or other blessed ornaments to prevent possible evil spiritual attacks.

The intention of performing rites in the Buddhist culture is the fear of misfortune. One such fear-driven rite is the puberty rite. It is the common belief that women who are menstruating are liable to demonic possession (Winslow 1980, 614). This is due to the pollution caused by the issue of blood. Hence, at the time of menstruation, women (especially young girls) are under strict dietary regulations and taboo to travel at dusk. The puberty ceremony symbolically removes the pollution and restores purity to a girl (Kim 2006, 183). Mantae Kim has documented the complex process of the ritual (ibid., 99–115; also see Winslow 1980, 607–10, 612). However, in his survey it is intriguing to understand that the Sinhalese Christians almost abandoned the Sinhalese Buddhist's appreciation, importance, and spiritual concerns of the puberty ritual (see Kim 2006, 116–60). In the event of puberty, Sinhalese

Catholics and Christians usually kept the girl for three days, bathed her, and asked a clergy to pray over the girl. Some Catholics performed the Buddhist rituals mildly (Winslow 1980, 604, 606, 608, 610–11). Nevertheless, Catholics do not consult astrology.

Marriage is another location where spiritual realities are present. Purity and correct observance of the marriage rituals secures the woman's offspring (Good 1991, 1, 5). In Sinhalese culture, barrenness is cause of anxiety due to the notion of birth as a sign of a successful marriage (ibid., 244–56). The childless women are considered as a bad omen. Hence, subfertility in the early years calls for vow making, *pirit* blessings, *bōdhi pūjā*, and other cultic rituals to help with conception. At the event of pregnancy it is customary to vow to perform *kiri-amma danaya* and *Ratrayakuma* rituals (Paranavitana 2008, 35–36). Catholics follows similar rituals like vow making and services for blessings. Other Christians in Sri Lanka mostly rely on prayer meetings and fasting.

The Christians arrange prayer meetings at the foundation laying, fixing the front doorframe, or on the dedication of a new house. This has a close resemblance to the Buddhist practices observed by Kapferer:

> Commonly, new houses have their foundations laid at an astrologically auspicious time, and in some instances a *pirit* ceremony will be performed by Buddhist monks to ensure the well-being of the household. In many houses pictures of the deities will be prominently displayed, often above the entrance to the house. (1983, 107)

The Buddhist converts occasionally emulate the Buddhist custom of consulting for astrologically auspicious times.

Farmers and the herdsmen believe offering part of the produce to God will protect their farms. Post-harvest thanksgiving is offered to the church, traditionally at the set day of the firstfruits service. In Pentecostal churches part of the harvest is brought to the church altar and dedicated to God. This practice very much resembles the harvest dedication (*asvanu-maṅgalaya*) or *kiri-itiravima* in the Buddhist context. In rural settings farmers dedicate a few animals from their herd and bring them to the church, or sell the animal and the money is placed in the offertory.

Pentecostals are renowned for the exorcism (deliverance) and healing ministry, notably similar to folk Buddhist practices. Not to underplay the contributions of Catholics and other Christian traditions in the practice of exorcism, but Pentecostals have perfected it to build a ministry around it. Many converts from other religions are attracted to such kinds of deliverance ministries, increasing the number of evangelical churches. In such services, the clergy becomes the proxy of God, and demons are considered to be agents of evil. In the Buddhist ritual both the demons and human parties hold to their end of the bargain— the exorcist propitiates with ritual and offering, and the demons cure and leave. The Christian exorcists never enter into bargains but cast out demons. Folk religious exorcism rituals take at least half a day, but the Christian exorcism, at times, lasts not more than an hour.

The Christian response to the folk Buddhist rituals and practices is traditional. Catholics in Sri Lanka have imported the usage of holy water, sprinkling salt, anointing oil over the sick, and special prayers for initiation of new ventures or dedication of places. Pentecostals have assimilated much of the practices, except for sprinkling salt, and sporadically engage in unconventional practices like praying and giving coconut juice for curing illness or praying over handkerchiefs and keeping them under the pillow of the sick person.

In a culture submerged in the practices of divination it is a natural tendency to gravitate towards astrologers and soothsayers. Mostly in Pentecostal churches this felt tendency is met by the so-called prophets or anointed servants of God, who occasionally act as medians or harbingers of God. In folk Buddhist culture, practitioners go into a trance with sporadic shakes while the message is delivered. Similar trance-like behaviour and vocabulary adapted to the Christian context or vocabulary close to the Sinhala Bible (1938 version) is used by these clergy and laity while they deliver the messages of God. It is the general practice to have special programs and prayer meetings for divination and to deal with a life crisis. Some churches and clergy arrange open-air deliverance meetings to assist the spiritual needs of the general public.

Finally, it is a recent trend of several evangelical churches to have meetings or set times of prayer for spiritual warfare. It is customary to conduct all-night prayer services at homes with evil demonic influence, believed to be the reason for domestic misfortune. At the end of the service, the practitioner sprinkles water as a sign of dedicating the house to God.

The Christian church has much more work to do towards acculturation and inculturation into the Buddhist folk religion for greater witness to the folk Buddhists of Sri Lanka (Kraft 1996, 367; Grunlan and Mayers 1979, 282).

REFERENCES

Ambos, Eva. 2011. The obsolescence of the demons? Modernity and possession in Sri Lanka. In *Health and religious rituals in South Asia: Disease, possession and healing*, ed. Fabrizio M. Ferrari, 199–212. Oxen, NY: Routledge.

Atikal, Ilanko. 2004. *Cilappatikaram: The tale of an anklet*. Trans. Rajagopal Parthasarathy. New Delhi: Penguin Books.

Chouléan, Ang. 1988. The place of animism within popular Buddhism in Cambodia: The example of the monastery. *Asian Folklore Studies* 47: 35–41.

Getty, Alice. 1914. *The gods of northern Buddhism*. Oxford: Clarendon.

Gombrich, Richard F. 1971. Merit transference in the Sinhalese Buddhism: A case study of the interaction between doctrine and practice. *History of Religions* 11, no. 2: 203–19.

———. 1981. A new Theravādin liturgy. *Journal of the Pali Text Society* 9: 47–73.

———, and Gananath Obeyesekere. 1988. *Buddhism transformed: Religious change in Sri Lanka*. Princeton, NJ: Princeton University Press.

Good, A. 1991. *The female bridegroom: A comparative study of life-crisis rituals in south India and Sri Lanka*. New York: Oxford University Press.

Grunlan, Stephan, and Marvin Mayers. 1979. *Cultural anthropology: A Christian perspective*. Grand Rapids: Zondervan.

Halverson, John. 1977. Dynamics of exorcism: The Sinhalese Sanniyakuma. *History of Religions* 10, no. 4: 334–59.

Harvey, Peter. 2013. *An introduction to Buddhism: Teachings, history and practices.* 2nd ed. Cambridge: Cambridge University Press.

Jayawardhana, Bandula. 2000. Demonology. In *Encyclopaedia of Buddhism.* Colombo: Government of Sri Lanka.

Kapferer, Bruce. 1975. Entertaining demons: Comedy, interaction and meaning in a Sinhalese healing ritual. *Modern Ceylon Studies* 6, no. 1: 16–63.

———. 1983. *A celebration of demons: Exorcism and the aesthetics of healing in Sri Lanka.* Bloomington: Indiana University Press.

———. 1992. *The feast of the sorcerer: Practice of consciousness and power.* Chicago: University of Chicago Press.

———, and Georges Papigny. 2005. *Tovil: Exorcism and healing rites.* Colombo: Viator.

Kariyawasam, A. G. S. 1995. *Buddhist ceremonies and rituals of Sri Lanka.* Kandy, Sri Lanka: Buddhist Publication Society.

Karunatillake, W. S. 1979. The religiousness of Buddhists in Sri Lanka through belief and practice. In *Religiousness in Sri Lanka,* ed. John Ross Carter, 1–34. Colombo: Marga Institute.

Kim, Mantae. 2006. The Sinhalese perception and attitude regarding the puberty ritual: Toward a relevant missiological response. PhD diss., Fuller Theological Seminary.

Kraft, Charles. 1996. *Anthropology for Christian witness.* Maryknoll, NY: Orbis Books.

Langer, Rita. 2007. *Buddhist rituals of death and rebirth: Contemporary Sri Lankan practice and its origins.* New York: Routledge.

Marasinghe, M. M. J. 1974. *Gods in early Buddhism: A study in their social and mythological milieu as depicted in the Nikāya of the Pāli Canon.* Kelaniya, Sri Lanka: Vidyalankara Campus Press.

Marzano, Mariella. 2002. Sowing new ideas: An investigation of anthropology's contribution to rural development in S. E. Sri Lanka. PhD diss., Durham University.

Muller, M. 1891. *Demon worship and other superstitions in Ceylon.* New Delhi: Asian Educational Services.

Nanayakkara, S. K. 2000. Dharma (1). In *Encyclopaedia of Buddhism.* Colombo: Government of Sri Lanka.

Obeyesekere, Gananath. 1968. Theodicy, sin and salvation in a sociology of Buddhism. In *Dialectic in practical religion*, ed. E. R. Leach, 7–40. Cambridge: Cambridge University Press.

———. 1969. The ritual drama of the Sanni demons: Collective representations of disease in Ceylon. *Comparative Studies in Society and History* 11, no. 2: 174–216.

———. 1977. Social change and the deities: The rise of the Kataragama cult in modern Sri Lanka. *Man*, new series, 12 (December): 377–96.

———. 1984. *The cult of the goddess Pattini*. Chicago: University of Chicago Press.

Paranavitana, Rohini. 2008. Some customs and superstitions associated with the childbirth in Sri Lankan Sinhalese society. *Folklore and Folklorists* 1, no. 1: 35–39.

Scott, David. 1994. *Formations of ritual: Colonial and anthropological discourses on the Sinhala Yaktovil*. Minneapolis: University of Minnesota Press.

Seligmann, C. G., and Brenda Z. Seligmann. 1911. *The Veddas*. Cambridge: Cambridge University Press.

Seneviratna, H. L. 1963. The Äsala Perahära in Kandy. *Ceylon Journal of Historical and Social Studies* 6: 169–80.

Van Zeyst, H. G. A. 2000. Dosa. In *Encyclopaedia of Buddhism*. Colombo: Government of Sri Lanka.

Wijesekara, Nandadeva. 1987. *Deities and demons, magic and masks*. Colombo: Gunasena.

Williams, Paul. 1996. The ritual reason why: Towards an evangelical theology of ritual within pastoral care. *Anvil* 13, no. 3: 225–54.

Winslow, Deborah. 1980. Rituals of first menstruation in Sri Lanka. *Man*, new series, 15, no. 4: 603–25.

Wirz, Paul. 1954. *Exorcism and the art of healing in Ceylon*. Leiden: Brill.

CHAPTER 12

SIGNS AND WONDERS:
NECESSARY BUT NOT SUFFICIENT

ALAN R. JOHNSON

There is a popular assumption in many Pentecostal circles that if something powerful happens in Jesus' name—a healing, dramatic answered prayer, dream—conversion to Jesus will immediately follow. Signs and wonders are seen as the answer to the mission problem of a slow response to the gospel. My thesis in this essay is that among the great world religions with their vibrant folk religious practices "signs and wonders" acquire a much more ambiguous status. While works of power are necessary to bring people to faith in such environments, they are generally not sufficient in and of themselves to create a robust commitment to Jesus. I begin by defining "signs and wonders" and then offer a definition of the notion of "necessary but not sufficient" as it relates to encountering God's power. In this section I narrate some of my experiences with people in the Thai setting where the manifestation of God's power was not a fast track to conversion and which caused me to start investigating this subject. In the second part I theorize as to why works of power are not always sufficient to produce faith in the context of a world religion like Buddhism and then in the third section look at the biblical evidence for a mixed response to miracles. Finally, I examine some of the implications for ministry on the ground among people with worldviews where signs and wonders are not likely to lead to immediate allegiance to Jesus Christ.

DEFINING "NECESSARY BUT NOT SUFFICIENT"

When we look at the idea of miracles in the Bible there is a diversity of terms in Hebrew, Aramaic and Greek that in general can be categorized into three distinct emphases. There are discrete sets of words that carry the notions of distinctive and wonderful, mighty and powerful, and meaningful or significant (Cressey 1996, 771). These terms are expressed in English translations by a variety of words like "miracles," "wonders," "signs," "might acts," and "powers" (1996, 771; Hofus 1971, 620–35). In missiology the idea of "power encounter" is often used as a broad cover term for the miraculous but as developed by mission theorists it actually has a very specific meaning as a kind of experience of God's power.

In this essay I take the definition of signs and wonders given by Greig who examines the lexical field of power in the New Testament and concludes that signs, wonders and miracles denote healing, deliverance from evil spirits and spiritual gifts (1993, 137–38). Similarly Grudem notes that "signs and wonders" can be used as a stock expression for miracles (such as Ex 7:3, Deut 6:22, Ps 135:9, Acts 4:30 Rom 15:19) and that three times signs, wonders and miracles appear in combination (Acts 2:22, 2 Cor 12:12 and Heb 2:4) (1994, 356). For my purposes here Grudem's definition of miracle fits well with this broader coverage: "A miracle is a less common kind of God's activity in which he arouses people's awe and wonder and bears witness to himself" (1994, 355). Thus the kinds of events that I am speaking of are encounters with God's power in a broad sense with the divine activity pointing to God and arousing wonder.

The missiological concept of "power encounter" had a very specific original setting in the South Pacific islands when it was coined by Alan Tippett and was later broadened by current theorists to include healing and deliverance from demons (Kraft 2000, 775). Kraft sees power encounter in a rubric of spiritual warfare as dealing with ground level issues of inner healing, deliverance, and inter-generational curses and a host of other power related practices that both enslave people and are manipulated by them (Ma 2010, 186; Kraft 2005, 361). In his model of the three encounters of truth, power and allegiance, power deals with the affective or feeling realm and the normal routing would be that power encounters move people to a greater appreciation of truth and on to allegiance (Shaw 2003, 179, 191).

In my reflections here on signs and wonders and their relationship to conversion the idea of encounters with power includes this more specific use of power encounter but goes beyond it to include things that point people beyond the natural realm and create a sense of wonder. This can include things like dreams or visions, more obvious miraculous answers to prayer such as a dramatic healing for oneself or another, or even an answer to prayer of a seemingly small event but which has sign value for the person who prayed. In such a case the "supernatural" part is the juxtaposition of the answer experrienced to the timing of the prayer.

In order to set up my definition of the notion of signs and wonders being necessary but not sufficient to bring people to faith, I will begin by narrating some specific events that caused me to question my original assumptions. I came to Thailand with the baseline understanding from my Pentecostal background that once Thai people experienced the power of God it would set them on the sure road to becoming a follower of Jesus Christ. This has turned out to be true, but in a more qualified sense, and not nearly as "automatic" as I first thought. Over my years of listening to Thai people tell their stories of how they came to faith in Jesus Christ, there is an unmistakable theme —the frequent demonstration of God's power particularly in healing and unusual answers to prayer. Relatively few come to faith just through someone sharing the Gospel verbally or reading Scripture. Convert narratives are peppered with experiences of the supernatural. However, I also began to accumulate a great deal of evidence first from my own ministry experiences and later through hearing similar stories from others that forced me to rethink the signs and wonders/conversion relationship.

One of the first incidents happened when we were showing the JESUS film in a village on the edge of a major city and praying for the sick. We discovered that a woman had been healed of back pain and sent her son to the gathering the next night to also be prayed for. We found out where this woman lived and went to visit her a few days later. Her living area was filled with all kinds of Buddha images. We sat down, telling her we heard from her son that her back pain had been healed. When we asked how she was feeling, she surprised us by saying "horrible," because her back pain was back. We asked her what happened and she said she came home from our gathering and bowed before her images and gave thanks to Buddha for healing her. Soon after that her back pain returned. When we offered to pray for her, she put up her hands and refused saying, "These are two different powers that don't get along." This was the first time I had met an instance of a person receiving prayer in Jesus name but giving thanks to Buddha.

Another time a small house group that I had started in a slum was told that a man who lived in their community was dying. So we went to pray for him; he was unable to rise, and doctors told him they could not help him. We prayed. Several weeks later I ran into him. He was walking and looking healthy and I asked him what happened. He said he got better. So I told him I would visit him. When I met him I went over how we had prayed in Jesus' name and he got better and would he like to follow Jesus? He said no. So I reviewed everything again and asked the same question. He said no again. When I asked him why not, he told me that he had previously done what Thai's call *rap ong*, which is to invite a spirit to indwell you generally for the purpose of being healed from some ailment. They are taught that if you deny this spirit and do not make its annual offering it will drive you insane or kill you. Since in the past he had done this he was unable to follow Jesus, even though that particular spirit had been unable to heal his nearly fatal ailment.

More recently a local Thai church that I work with developed a relationship with a family that has a child with Down's syndrome. He also had a hole in his heart and the parents were told that it would require surgery one day. This church was actively helping the family, who were quite poor, taking them to the doctor when the child was sick as well as bringing them to church and praying for the little boy's healing. At one point the doctor said it was time to do the surgery but when they did another test before prepping for the surgery, they discovered the hole was closed and the boy was totally healed. The local Thai pastor was very upset after all of this prayer and help in Jesus' name that upon his next visit to the family he discovered the mother had put a Buddhist amulet around her son's neck. He was dumbfounded. The mother continues to remain friendly and to talk about faith with us but has not become a Christian.

In addition to my own personal experiences and the things that I have heard from others, I found supportive empirical evidence in the work of Marten Visser on Protestant conversion patterns in Thailand (2008).

Visser developed a hypothesis based on the work of Edwin Zehner who found in the convert narratives he collected the themes of love and power. Visser tested to see whether or not perceived miracles are as important in bringing people to a decision to become Christians as experiences within social relationships. He found that only 21 percent of respondents listed a miracle as the most significant factor in their conversion and concluded that "perceived miracles play a decisive role for a significant minority, but experiences directly set in social relationships are decisive for four times as many people." (ibid, 137).

Experiences like this set me on the path to try and understand what is happening around the nexus of supernatural power and moving towards or away from Jesus. I began to formalize my interviews with converts and to question their experiences of God's power and its role in their decision to become a Christ follower. What I began to see more clearly was that for people who came to faith the supernatural was embedded in a set of relationships with believers and other experiences. This fit well with what Visser found in his research. In trying to find a way to explain this I landed upon the idea of signs and wonders being necessary but not sufficient in and of themselves to bring people to faith. Thus by "necessary but not sufficient" I mean that powerful manifestations alone generally do not result in robust faith unless they are happening in a set of conditions that facilitate turning to Jesus.

With this definitional work as background, I will now offer some possible explanations as to why signs and wonders alone are often insufficient to bring people to faith by looking at Buddhism and how it is practiced in Thailand. I then proceed to examine the biblical data to see if there is a mixed response to miracles there.

IMPACT OF LOCAL RELIGIOUS CONTEXT ON INSUFFICIENCY OF SIGNS AND WONDERS

In the folk Buddhist world it is not hard to see that miracles, healings, dreams, visions and remarkable answers to prayer are vitally important to people coming to faith in Jesus. It does not take long to realize that you can talk about religion, compare religions, and point out the excellencies of Jesus, yet it will make very little sense to those listening. Local people are convinced of the superiority of the belief system they were born into and are aware of the difficulties that will accrue to them if they leave it. Works of power grab the attention of people; they shake up and destabilize worldviews, opening people to new options. I have heard over and over again in Thai conversion testimonies how a person had a problem and "tried everything" they knew—visits to temples, shrines, ceremonies to reverse bad luck and misfortune, meditation, making extra merit all to no avail. Then someone told them that Jesus can help, and prayer in his name brought results.

It is a bit harder to understand why powerful supernatural manifestations might not always be sufficient to bring people to faith or keep them in it. Practical experience from people working in the Hindu, Muslim, and Buddhist worlds shows that it is not just a straight linear movement from a power encounter to following Jesus. In trying to shape a more nuanced view of the signs and wonders / conversion relationship I have found it fruitful to look in two different directions. The first, which I will deal with in this section, examines how the local religious context impacts the person who experiences God's power. At the individual level this concerns their interpretive framework and then at the social level the religious context provides filters for making sense of the kind of experiences I have narrated above. The second, which I will examine in the section below, looks at Scripture and shows that in biblical history works of power and signs and wonders were no guarantee of a faithful response to Yahweh in the Old Testament or to Jesus in the New Testament.

Andrew Walls talks about the three great intakes of peoples into the Christian faith, each of which has shifted the center of gravity of the faith. The first was when Jewish Christians proclaimed the good news to Greeks and brought Hellenistic civilization to faith in Christ, the second was when the barbarian peoples, who were seen as the destroyers of Christian civilization, turned to the God of the Christians; and the third has been the "massive movement towards Christian faith in all the southern continents" that is still happening today (1996, 68). Walls notes that "the obvious feature which these three great intakes of Christians have in common is that each has consisted overwhelmingly of adherents of the primal religions; by comparison, converts from the other religious tradition have been few" (ibid.). In trying to account for why this is the case Walls introduces the idea that while taking on the Christian faith caused great social change, it also "was often part of the mechanism of adjustment to social change" (ibid., 68–69). Primal religions under the impact of social change found tools for coping with this change particularly in the areas of values, hierarchy of leadership and the provision of a universal point of reference, "linking the society with its traditionally local and kin-related focus to a universal order" (ibid., 69).

I think that Walls' observations here can be turned around to provide a useful perspective on why the great religious traditions such as Hinduism, Buddhism and Islam have proven less susceptible to the Christian faith. Not only do their religious systems give them tools to deal with social change, but the interpretive schemas of people raised in these religious worldview provide a powerful force that is constantly pulling all experiences back into their frames of reference and plausibility structures. This makes the woman's experience I narrated above more understandable. While we prayed for her back to be healed in Jesus' name, her Buddhist worldview provided her a more compelling explanation of why she got better.

In folk Buddhist worldview Jesus is just one of many power options. Jesus is inside the boundaries of *samsara* and is on par with the many kinds of demi-gods and powerful beings who have enormous stores of merit but who at the end of the day are still subject to the law of karma and are in need of enlightenment. Others have achieved enlightenment but choose to remain as *bodhisattva* in order to help other sentient beings. Practically, what can happen is that people will turn to Jesus initially but with the internal caveat that if things do not work out they will seek out other power sources. So you can see people make a profession of faith, come to church, read the Bible, and even bear witness, but all the time keep their options open should Jesus not "deliver" what they need. This leads to people becoming disappointed when prayer does not "work" and a shift to engage other powerful beings for help. What I have observed is not so much a syncretistic playing of both sides as the end result but rather that people in these circumstances move away from faith and the church on their own.

In one church I worked in a couple who had a business failure and were in great financial straits began to attend the local church. They experienced divine provision, mediated in part by a dream with very specific instructions. They attended church services regularly and were studying the Bible. However, when they had recovered and started a new business it required that they bid on projects. After the loss of a crucial bid they began to go to a local shrine to ask for help, while initially attending church. As time went on, rather than continuing along in a dual state, it was not long before they simply stopped attending church and moved away from their faith.

Local religion also provides a powerful social system that dampens response to miracles. In many societies religion is woven warp and woof into everything and is central to personal and national identity formation. When a person comes to faith in Jesus it places them outside of the group and in the eyes of others; they are no longer seen as an insider. Thus the compulsion to conform can overcome the worldview destabilization that an answer to prayer or miracle creates. Social pressure is often combined with the pull of the interpretive framework when a convert goes through difficult times. They are told that the reason for their current problem is that they have left the ancestral ways. This kind of constant pressure can wear down those who have experienced signs and wonders in the past and yet have troubles in the present that do not seem to resolve easily with prayer.

Another source for insights into why encounters with God's power may not be enough to move people to religious change comes from the work of Horton and Fisher who proposed conflicting theories in the 1970s and 1980s on the conversion of African's practicing traditional religion to Islam and Christianity. Horton saw the pre-Islamic or pre-Christian cosmologies and the socio-economic matrix as the source of change linked with Islam or Christianity acting as catalysts (1975, 219–21). Fisher disagreed and saw the religion (either Islam or Christianity) as having the momentum and unleashing new forces (1985, 153, 156). The insight that seems relevant to our discussion here is Fisher's observation that what begins to break down conditions and creates the space for change either in the traditional religion cosmology (Horton's view) or in the initial stage Fisher calls quarantine, before new local converts actually come in, is "fundamentally compatible" (1985, 156). The key here seems to be conditions creating an environment open to change. If this is the case in the move from traditional religion to Islam or Christianity, it would seem to be just as likely to apply to a change from Islam to the Christian faith. The difference however would be that where an encounter with power is itself an agent of change in the traditional worldview, challenging the superiority of their gods, it does not have the same effect in a great tradition religion. This is because great tradition religions not only create and reinforce identity but have ultimates, whether liberation from *samsara* in Buddhism or Hinduism or paradise in Islam, that are not destabilized by an encounter with power in the same way as a traditional religion. They are true no matter what kinds of situations prevail. By contrast, traditional religion needs to deliver results and a power encounter in Tippett's sense (see Kraft 2000), or miracles that show the superiority of God's power provide a direct challenge. This then links back to my observation above about the reinterpretive power of great tradition religions. An encounter with the living God's supernatural power can be reabsorbed much easier under religious concepts found in the great tradition religions

THE BIBLICAL EVIDENCE OF
MIXED RESPONSE TO MIRACLES

Biblically we also find that mighty works are insufficient to draw out faith and obedience. In the Pentateuch, from the Exodus to the renewing of the covenant before crossing the Jordan to take possession of the land in Deuteronomy, there is arguably no cohort of people who has ever seen mightier works. Yet they continually forgot Yahweh (see the prophetic testimony in Amos 5:25–27, cited by Stephen in Acts 7:42–43), and they actually worshipped other gods in the sojourn in the desert even after seeing all of Yahweh's mighty works.

Jesus himself upbraids Chorazin and Bethsaida for their hard hearted rejection of the mighty works he did there that did not lead them to repentance (Matt 11:20–24; Luke 10:13–15). Early in Jesus' ministry his healing, rather than stimulating faith, draws a reaction against him for breaking Sabbath laws (Matt 12:1–14; Mark 3:1–6; Luke 6:6–11).

Only one of the ten lepers healed in Luke 17 returns to give thanks to Jesus, the raising of Lazarus in John 11 gets a very mixed response, and the healing of the ear of the high priest's servant after Peter cuts it off during Jesus' arrest does nothing to inspire faith in those who have come to arrest him (Luke 22:49–51).

John's Gospel goes even further than the Synoptics and develops the idea of the inadequacy of a faith based on signs. Keener points out that while John shares with the Synoptic tradition the idea that signs-faith is inadequate in such texts as Matthew 12:38,39; 16:1–4; Mark 8: 11,12; 15:32; Luke 11:16, 29, signs "perform a more ambiguous function in the fourth Gospel, which emphasizes the potential hiddenness of God's revelation to those who may not prove to be persevering disciples" (2003, 275). Keener says that while the synoptics use signs to authenticate Jesus' missions, John places them in a Christological context and uses them and their connected discourses to interpret Jesus' identity and call for faith (ibid.).

Keener observes that, while John frequently mentions that many "believed" in Jesus (2:23; 7:31; 10:42; 11:45; 12:11, 42),

> at least in many of these cases this faith proves inadequate to preserve for salvation. John here echoes earlier biblical portraits of human nature in general and perhaps of recipients of God's revelations in particular; for instance, the Israelites believed when they saw Moses' signs (Exod 4:31), but their faith collapsed when it was challenged (Exod 5:21–23). (ibid., 746)

Signs are not unimportant in John. The story of Thomas shows how signs-faith, while seen as inadequate is still valid faith (ibid, 275). "If they would not believe Jesus' words and identity directly, Jesus invites them to believe by means of his works (10:38; cf. 14:11); these were his Father's works (10:37; cf. 5:17), hence revealed his origin" (ibid., 830). Keener affirms that signs serve a revelatory purpose but "they do not control one's response, and response to the Spirit's testimony in the word is a higher stage of faith, they are among Jesus' works which testify to his identity (10:32, 37–38; 14:10–11; 20:29–3" (ibid., 275). He concludes that signs are not negative, just inadequate:

Thomas's unwillingness to believe without seeing reflects a thread that runs throughout the Gospel: many respond to signs with faith (1:50; 10:38; 11:15, 40: 14:11) and refuse faith without signs (4:48; 6:30), but unless this faith matures into discipleship, it must prove inadequate in the end (8:30–31). (ibid., 1208)

Thinking about signs-faith in this way has helped me to understand the phenomena of partial healings I have seen over my years in Thailand. It used to puzzle me how some people would receive a great measure of healing and yet be left with a specific physical problem. I have now come to see such partial healings as having a kind of parabolic function where people can either choose to seek more light and go deeper or to turn away. It is Jesus' role to reveal his glory (John 2:11) but there is an inherent ambiguity that allows for varying understandings. The sign invites to faith, but the ongoing physical problem can serve as a reminder that a relationship with Jesus will not be predicated solely on benefits conveyed.

SOME MISSIOLOGICAL IMPLICATIONS OF MIXED RESPONSE TO SIGNS AND WONDERS

In this section I discuss briefly four implications for cross-cultural ministry that follow from the thesis that signs and wonders are necessary but not sufficient to bring people to faith. My hope is that the reflections here can provide grist for the development of ministry methods that incorporate signs and wonders as a part of a larger strategy for evangelism and discipleship.

Let me begin by saying that I am not intimating here that there are people who would pray for miracles to happen for people and then simply leave them on their own. People who believe God for signs and wonders to confirm the proclamation of the Gospel are very interested in people becoming Christians. What is problematic is when people feel like the hard work is done when a work of power happens and push for a "profession of faith" without much concern for ongoing discipleship. People often wonder why converts do not "stick" or will not come to church. To rely on works of power without engaging worldview issues can short circuit the process of rooting people in faith.

A reductionist approach that sees signs and wonders as the silver bullet of missionary strategy, the single answer to bring people to faith, can discourage cross-cultural workers from doing the kind of labor intensive cultural homework that will help to deal with the worldview issues of the potential convert.

In what follows I develop four areas that can help start us on the road to ministry approaches that will help provide the environment where encounters with God's power can more easily facilitate the movement to conversion and discipleship.

1. A key first step is to prepare specifically to deal with worldview issues that are related to understanding signs and wonders. If we know that people can reinterpret what has happened through prayer in Jesus' name in terms of their own religion, we can prepare the ground for understanding by teaching that Jesus is not bound by the worldview they hold. Helping people to see that Jesus is outside of *samsara* and not subject to it means Jesus is qualitatively different than all beings that are bound by karma.

2. We need to begin to develop field-based research on the three encounters of power, truth and allegiance (Kraft 2005, 364). Knowing their order and timing before and after their conversion could enable us to build grids for helping people navigate their current encounters and prepare for those that are to come. Since so many Thai experience something supernatural in their journey to faith, learning how they made meaning from their encounter with God's power could be extremely helpful to those working in discipling seekers and new converts. It also helps us to know how to pray when we understand better where a person is in their journey.

Thai conversion narratives I have listened to show that most of the people who persevere and become solid Christians had all three of these encounters, but not in the same order. Power is the most common because it awakens interest. However there are people who will begin with a tentative allegiance to Jesus by committing to his people and later on strengthening that through encounters with truth and power. Others are confronted with truth, through studying Scripture or some exposure to the Christian message, and then often it is power that moves them to full commitment to Jesus. I am wondering if more research on this would not reveal a kind of developmental sequence or set of pathways that could be similar to what J. Robert Clinton did with leadership development in *The Making of a Leader*. If it turns out there are discernible patterns this could guide us in the evangelism and discipleship process to know what kind of experiences and biblical content to insert and in what appropriate sequence.

3. If signs and wonders are necessary but not sufficient I believe it also means we should be more intentional about setting up strategies that go beyond only exposing people to God's power and include assessing the claims of the gospel. We can let people know that the Jesus who can heal their body or deliver them from evil spirits or provide for financial needs can also help them come to know the living God personally and free them from the cycle of rebirth to live in his eternal family. Chris Wright in his article "Salvation Belongs to Our God" looks at the breadth of the idea of salvation in both Testaments:

> Since the experience of salvation lies within the historical covenant relationship, it has a very broad and comprehensive range of significance—in both Old and New Testaments. "God saves" covers a huge range of realities precisely because of the immense variety of circumstances in which God's saving engagement with people takes place through the great sweep of biblical history . . . So in both Testaments, then, God saves people in a wide variety of physical, material, and temporal ways from all kinds of need, danger, and threat. But of course, and also in both Testaments, God's saving action goes much further. The Bible recognizes that all those proximate evils from which God saves his people are manifestations of the far deeper disorder in human life. Enemies, lies, disease, oppression, false accusation, violence, death—all of these things from which we pray to be saved are the *results of rebellion and sin in the human heart*. That is where the deepest source of the problem lies". (2010, 4, italics in the original)

Signs and wonders are very often salvation from what Wright calls proximate evils and as such can serve as signposts to a more ultimate salvation from the source of all such evils. Framing works of powers in this way has important methodological implications as we share our faith. It is tempting to make Jesus into the one who can solve all of our problems, giving a nod to sin and brokenness with God. In a folk Buddhist world people will seek help but do not have a notion of being broken in a broken relationship with their creator. Telling more of the story of God's salvation from proximate and ultimate evil can help provide interpretive grist for them as they experience God's power in their lives.

4. Finally, helping Thai people deal with the disappointment of unanswered prayer is needed. The Thai worldview that looks to powerful spiritual beings of great merit who are still in *samsara* and can be supplicated for help with life's problems can set them up for disappointment when God does not answer prayer. When people with desperate problems hear about Jesus and their prayers are answered it starts their process towards faith. The back side of this is that there are also many people who experience the same thing and begin to move towards faith or make a full profession of faith, but upon experiencing unanswered prayer they begin to seek help from other spirit beings.

It is a spiritual version of what happens in social relations with patrons and clients; when the flow of benefits diminishes clients will seek new patrons. Developing theological resources to help people understand biblical prayer as based in relationship rather than the tit-for-tat of a transactional relationship where promises are made and fulfilled is critical. If the Christian faith is presented only in patron and client terms where Jesus becomes the big patron dispensing benefits, then it is too easy for new believers to simply move on when the benefits stop.

CONCLUSION

Signs and wonders are absolutely necessary in the process of drawing people to faith in the Buddhist world but not sufficient in every case to bring people to a robust faith. When we understand the inherent ambiguity of works of power among people in the world religions like Hinduism, Buddhism and Islam we can begin to add appropriate content and experiences to our evangelism and discipleship that will facilitate people to become Christ followers for the long haul.

REFERENCES

Clinton, J. Robert. 1988. *The making of a leader: Recognizing the lessons and stages of leadership development*. Colorado Springs, CO: Navpress.

Cressey, M. H. 1996. "Miracles." In *The new Bible dictionary*, edited by J. D. Douglas, N. Hillyer, D. R. W. Wood, I. Howard Marshall, A. R. Millard, J. I. Packer, and D. J. Wiseman, 771–73. Downers Grove, IL: IVP Academic.

Fisher, Humphrey J. 1985. "The juggernaut's apologia: Conversion to Islam in black Africa." *Africa: Journal of the Africa Institute* 55, no. 2, 153–73.

Greig, Gary S. 1993. "The purpose of signs and wonders in the New Testament: What terms for miraculous power denote and their relationship to the Gospel." In *The Kingdom and the power*, edited by Gary S. Greig and Kevin N. Springer, 131–74. Ventura, CA: Regal Books.

Grudem, Wayne A. 1994. *Systematic theology: An introduction to Biblical doctrine*. Nottingham, England: Inter-Varsity Press.

Hofus, O. 1971. *The new international dictionary of New Testament theology*. Vol. 2, 3 vols. Grand Rapids, MI: Zondervan.

Horton, Robin. 1975. "On the rationality of conversion." *Africa: Journal of the Africa institute* 45, no. 3, 219-35, 373–99.

Keener, Craig S. 2003. *The Gospel of John: A commentary*, 2 vols. Peabody, MA: Hendricksen.

Kraft, Charles H. 1992 "Allegiance, truth and power encounters in Christian witness." In *Pentecost, mission and ecumenism: Essay on intercultural theology: Festschrift in honour of professor Walter J. Hollenweger*, edited by Jan. A. B. Jongeneel, 215-30. Frankfurt am Main: Peter Lang.

———. 2000. "Power encounter." In *Evangelical dictionary of world missions*, edited by A. Scott Moreau, Harold Netland, and Charles Van Engen, 774-75. Grand Rapids, MI: BakerBooks.

————. 2005."Spiritual power: A missiological issue." In *Appropriate Christianity*, ed. Charles Kraft, 361–74. Pasadena, CA: William Carey Library.

Ma, Julie C., and Wonsuk Ma. 2010. *Mission in the Spirit towards a pentecostal/charismatic missiology.* Oxford: Oxford Centre for Mission Studies.

Visser, Marten. 2008. Conversion growth of Protestant churches in Thailand. Unpublished dissertation.

Missiological research in the Netherlands, vol. 47, ed. G. J. van Butselaar, T. van den End, M. T. Frederiks, M. M. Jansen, J. A. B. Jongeneel, A. M. Kool, and J. J. Visser. Zoetermeer, Netherlands: Uitgeverij Boekencentrum.

Shaw, R. Daniel, and Charles E. Van Engen. 2003. *Communicating God's word in a complex world: God's truth or hocus pocus?* New York: Rowman and Littlefield Publishers.

Walls, Andrew F. 1996. *The missionary movement in Christian history: Studies in the transmission of faith.* Maryknoll, NY: Orbis Books.

Wright, Christopher. 2010. "Salvation belongs to our God." *Evangelical interfaith dialogue.* http://cms.fuller.edu/EIFD/issuesFall_2010/Salvation_Belongs_to_Our_God.

CHAPTER 13

CHRISTIAN RESPONSE TO BURMESE
NAT WORSHIP IN MYANMAR

PETER THEIN NYUNT

Christian mission to Burmese Buddhists in Myanmar can be traced back to two Italian Catholic priests in 1720. Protestant missions began with the arrival of American Baptist missionary Adoniram Judson in July 1813 (Sangermano 1893, 277), but the gospel to the Burmese remains alien today. In addressing the problems confronting Christians communicating the gospel to Burmese Buddhists in particular, there may be many possible reasons. But one remarkable factor is that the message the missionaries and Christians in Myanmar communicate does not meet the needs of the spiritual quest of Burmese Buddhists. In other words, the churches in Myanmar till today do not give much attention to the predominance of worship (K. Nyunt 2005, 111; see also Khan En 2012, 65–66), which is linked with the Burmese worldview, beliefs, spirituality, culture, and lifestyle.

In this chapter I will discuss some concepts related to *Nat* worship in Myanmar,; the human practitioners who are *Nat-kadaw* (spirit mediums); *Badin-saya* and *Yadayar*; witch masters (*Bodaw* or *Weikza*), functioning as professional mediums or intermediaries with the spirit world; the variegated methods they employ to deal with the spiritual realities of Burmese Buddhists; and some other superstitious practices which are highly influenced by them. I will then respond to Buddhist spiritual realities from a Christian perspective.

Nat is a derivative form of a Pali word *Natha*, which means a resplendent being worthy of veneration. Generally the term *Nat* refers to any of a host of animistic spirits, including the spirits of the ancestors, national heroes, and those who died tragic or violent deaths: former royal figures; spirits in fields, trees, and rivers; and regional, territorial overlords. *Nat* worship in Myanmar is the belief in all spiritual beings in the most inclusive form. It also involves finding the way to deal with those spiritual beings. The deep-rootedness of *Nat* worship with the same general background is found in the ethnic groups of Myanmar, but it appears in different form. In this chapter, however, I will deal with the *Nat* worship among the Burmese Buddhists. There are two reasons for making this selection: one is that, significantly, there is no animal sacrifice in Burmese *Nat* worship like in other ethnic groups; secondly, the images of the *Nats* are made side by side with the images of Buddha and worshiped.

BURMESE FOLK SPIRITUALITY IN THE CONTEXT OF NAT WORSHIP

Buddhism in Myanmar was introduced by the beginning of the Christian era, and today it is known as Theravada Buddhism or Philosophical Buddhism (Lubeigt 2004, 236–37). In reality, however, it is mixed with *Nat* worship. For Maung Htin Aung, "the worship of *Nats* was purely native in origin and developed out of that form of animism which still prevails among some of the hill peoples of the country" (1962, 1). Min Si Thu and Taw Sein Ko believe *Nat* worship was imported from India through Hinduism, but according to Melford Spiro it was imported from India through Buddhism (Si Thu 1992, 32; Sein Ko 1913, 167; Spiro 1970, 70–71). Despite having different views on its origin, *Nat* worship has been penetrating into the hearts of people in Myanmar as a primal religion since before the adoption of Theravada Buddhism. Khan En states,

> When Theravada Buddhism was introduced to Bagan by the great Primate Shin Arahan and promoted by the King Anawrahta (a.d. 1044–77), he began to replace *Nat* worship with Theravada Buddhism. He ordered the seizure of all the images of the gods of the planets, the Hindu gods, put them in a former Vishnu temple, which was renamed, *Nat-hlaung kyaung*, meaning the monastery where all the *Nats* are kept

as prisoners. The temple stands at present day. As to the other indigenous *Nats*, Anawrahta set up images of them on the platform of the Shwezigone pagoda that he built, and he let the people come to discover by themselves the truth that Theravada Buddhism is better than *Nat* worship. In so doing, Anawrahta centralized *Nat* worship so that he might control it for he discovered it would die a natural death in the course of time. The opposite of King Anawrahta's expectation became the case; however, *Nat* worship still survives today. Rather, Anawrahta's setting up of *Nat* images at the Shwezigone pagoda became an example to the people to amalgamate Buddhism with *Nat* worship, as many *Nat* images are found on the premises of famous pagodas like Shwedagon, Sule, and Shwemawdaw, with inscriptions on the images which are worshipped by the adherents side-by-side with the images of Buddha. (2012, 60)

In addition, in regard to the prevalence of *Nat* worship over Buddhism, Temple also rightly states,

In Burma, Buddhism has certainly not succeeded in destroying the Animism of the people, for all observers agree that the Burman [Burmese], despite his now ancient official adoption, after a long fight, of the purest form of Buddhism, is at heart an Animist, his professed faith being little more than "a thin veneer of philosophy laid over the main structure of Animistic belief." (1906, 1)

Despite the Theravadic form of Buddhism being declared the national religion, why is *Nat* worship so prevalent within the Burmese Buddhist communities? On the other hand, why is the gospel to them still alien? Significantly, Theravada Buddhism and Christianity in Myanmar tend to provide solutions for the major issues of life or the ultimate realities, such as the issues of salvation, or life after death, but both religions seem to have no answer for the issues of people's everyday lives. Meanwhile, *Nat* worship seeks more the welfare of intramundane life than for the supramundane. In addition, due to socioeconomic situations, for Burmese folk Buddhists, meeting the immediate needs in daily lives seems more important than life after death. They need a lord who can solve their problems faced in their daily lives. Let's review the spiritual realities of their Buddhist context.

POPULAR SPIRITUALITY OF BURMESE BUDDHISTS

Nat worship in Myanmar is connected to the belief in all spiritual beings in the most inclusive form. Thus Burmese Buddhists believe in all spirits, and their concern is primarily with devotions, rituals, ethics, and all kinds of protection from dangers, and a source of blessings for the present days and future. Critically speaking, these popular Burmese spirit beliefs are poles apart from the authentic teaching of Theravada Buddhism that "faith is taken without a sense of fear, or a hope for a reward, or status" (Htay and Tin 2002, 17). Examining Burmese spirituality, however, reveals that fear is dominant. The greatest fear comes from the danger of the harmful spirits or evil spirits such as devil attacks, bad spirit beings, curses, or being harmed by the popular earthbound *Nats*. It leads them to seek liberation from other dependable beings (M. Nyunt 2010, 34).

As pointed out, Burmese spirituality is derived from fear of *Nats*. In this section, in regard with spiritual realities, I will briefly discuss how Burmese folk Buddhists relate to household *Nats* (*Eindwin Nat* in Burmese) in their daily life. They believe that there will be sickness and social problems among the family members if any member of the household or a devotee lacks in the paying of offering and respect. As a contrast, if they give proper propitiations and do not rebel against their will, household *Nat* will bless the devotee's family. Nyunt says,

> There is a Burmese saying that, nevertheless, *kyar kyauk lo shin gyi ko; shin gyi kyar htet so*. That means "worship *Nat shin gyi* if you are afraid of a tiger; *Nat shin gyi* is more dangerous than a tiger." That is why Burmese always make solicitations of favour to be protected by the house *Nat* but they still fear the anger of *Nats*. It is said that these *Nats* provide their followers with protection from their enemies; give

blessings; and solutions to their problems (social, financial, business, etc.) if they do proper propitiation. (M. Nyunt 2010, 35)

It shows that the *Nats* stand as friends or helpers to their devotees in times of trouble when they are given regular offerings correctly but harming them when they are not provided adequate offerings or given proper respect. Spiro also observes that fear is the more prominent Burmese attitude toward the *Nat* (1978, 94). That is why whenever Burmese Buddhists are in crisis they go to the *Nats* and ask for help. It seems that they take refuge in *Nats* for all kinds of fear. They might assume that *Nats* will stand in front of them and solve all kinds of problems they face in this world. This has become traditional belief.

To the Burmese Buddhists, their spiritual realities totally depend on self-reliance in seeking betterment of life after death. In contrast, they practice *Nat* worship in their daily lives, and their spirituality entirely depends on their traditional beliefs of *Nat*. Myint mentions,

> People have practiced *Nat*-worship since the beginning of time; they have always relied on the spirits when they are in need. They have experiences of receiving blessings and goodness and have shared their experiences with their fellows. Finally, *Nat*-worship became *mi-yo-pa-la* or *yo-ya* [tradition or custom]. (n.d., 22)

Myint's statement seemingly is true that the peoples in Myanmar have worshiped *Nats* ever since they settled in Myanmar and thus it became the indigenous religion of the people. It is remarkable that for king after king and even till the present government Buddhism is being promoted as the national religion. In reality, however, most Burmese have more interest in the reality of spirit beings, good spirits or gods, bad spirits or demons, terrestrial gods, or earthly spirits from Hindu-Buddhist cosmology rather than the authentic Buddha's teachings. To perceive the spiritual realities of the Burmese Buddhists in daily life, Nyunt states,

> Animistic ideas and belief in the existence of the supernatural power has influenced every phase, every story, every festival, every artistic performance, and

the everyday life of the Burmese up till now. Every construction of a new building is necessarily preceded by giving homage to *Nats* with an offertory tray. Every dramatic troupe opens each performance with a *Nat*-dance. Most Burmese consult with *Nats* or fortune-tellers before they start their business. (M. Nyunt 2010, 38–39)

As *Nat* worship dominates in every aspect of Burmese Buddhists' lives, the numbers of professional practitioners of Burmese *Nat* worship are also enlarged. Below I will be briefly investigating the *Nat-kadaw*, *Badin-saya*, *Yadayar*, and witch masters, whose professions are related to the communication with *Nats*.

Nat-kadaw

The most important reason Burmese people believe in *Nats* is mainly related with overcoming their practical problems such as illness, hardships and oppression, poverty, natural disasters, and so on. Due to the economic crisis, the Burmese Buddhists, over 65 percent of the country population, try to find the *Nats* to help their present welfare. To appease the *Nats* they offer food, go to the *Nat* festivals, pay annual homage to them, and make vows. *Nat*-believers can encounter *Nats* through possessed *Nat-kadaws* (spirit mediums; literally meaning "wife of *Nat*"), "an oracle, a medium, a diviner and a cult officiant" (Spiro 1978, 94), as they take a mediator's role in relationship between the *Nats* and their followers. Burmese *Nat*-believers can discuss their problems and hardships with *Nats*; they can also make vows to receive good luck and solutions to their problems, and can make other requests for any future problems through a *Nat-kadaw*. Burmese Buddhists go to a *Nat-kadaw* to meet especially their spiritual, social, and economic needs.

Burmese popular spiritual practices are concerned with their daily and personal difficulties so that they seek to encounter the power that helps solve their day-to-day problems. Let's see how the current Burmese popular superstitious beliefs and practices such as *Badin-saya* and *Yadayar*, witch masters (*Bodaw* or *Weikza*), and other popular superstitious practices are related to communicating with *Nats*.

Badin-saya and Yadayar

The term *Badin* in Burmese is used for astrology. For the Burmese, astrology means "not only the methods of tracing the courses of the planets and their influence on morals, but also the ritual by which the planets are appeased and made to withdraw their baneful influence" (Aung 1962, 1). The one who predicts the fortune of people through *Badin* is called a *Badin-saya* (astrologer). Accordingly, he or she advises people to solve their current problems through *Yadayar*.

The term *Yadayar* means "a kind of art that applies to the present life" (Fink 2001, 227), whereas Aung Zaw interprets it as "the Burmese form of voodoo" (2008, 1). Actually, it is the power of prevention of a misfortune and the power which brings good luck prescribed by *Badin-saya*. It is a belief that *Yadayar* can shield one from misfortunes. Although the practice of *Yadayar* cannot be found in the Buddha's teaching, most Burmese in Myanmar including country leaders, apply it. Even many monks and nuns who follow Theravada Buddhism in Myanmar engage in it. According to Myo, most of the present popular Burmese Buddhists practice *koe-na-win Yadayar* to solve their life struggles. Burmese *koe* in English is the number nine. For their success, they are suggested to offer nine kinds of tendrils or nine candles and the like to Buddha's statue (Myo 2009, 9). Burmese are practicing many kinds of *koe-na-win Yadayar* to get back credit, to be successful in their business, to reconcile a fragile family, and so on. The most popular superstitious practice of the Burmese military generals and the majority of politicians is also related to the auspicious number nine. It is believed that nine is their lucky number, which is strongly associated with power. Actually it is the special number of *Nats* (in Myanmar the name of the ninth month of the year is *Nat-taw*). In reality, superstitious practices are still very strong in Myanmar, and all these popular spiritual beliefs and practices are directly or indirectly linked with *Nat* worship.

Witch Masters (Bodaw or Weikza)

In Myanmar a witch master is called *Nat saya*, which means master or teacher. Anybody can become a witch master if they desire and practice communicating with the *Nats*. There are two types of witch masters, known as *athet-lan saya* (*weikza*) and *aut-lan saya*. Spiro understands *athet-lan saya* as "a member of many quasi-Buddhist sects (*Bodaw* groups), all of which share the common aim of acquiring magico-religious power" (1970, 230). Presently, many military officers and well-educated Burmese still retain a strong interest in *weikza* matters. The *ah-thet-lan saya*

> practices good things and is resorted to by people in times of crisis like sickness, and loss of property, he chiefly depends upon Buddhism to influence *Nats* and to overcome evil powers. But the *aut-lan saya* practices evil things like killing others by *mandras*, which are magical utterances. (Khan En 2012, 400–401)

In general, their practices relate to the communication with *Nats*.

SUMMARY

Burmese popular spiritual practices are concerned with their daily and personal difficulties so that they seek to encounter the powerful beings and powers that can protect them from danger and bring blessings to them. They look for power that can demonstrate the ability to respond to their practical needs. Of course, they deal with *Nat-kadaw*, *Badin-saya*, *Yadayar*, witch masters, and some other superstitious practices. For the *Nat*-worshipers, however, there is no feeling of indebtedness to the *Nats*, because they repay the *Nats* for any help they receive. On the other hand, it doesn't seem that all the *Nat*-worshipers fulfill their vows nor do the *Nats* always fulfill their needs. They still need someone who can give ultimate answers for their daily lives and who welcomes them with grace and peace. Let's see how the Christian message will answer the issues of spiritual realities of Burmese Buddhist *Nat* worshippers.

CHRISTIAN RESPONSE TO BURMESE NAT WORSHIP

In this section, a brief investigation will be made of how the belief in *Nats* has prepared the people in Myanmar for a better understanding of the Holy Spirit. There will be an attempt to understand how the belief in the spirits, the *Nats*, helps towards an understanding of the existence, nature, and the work of the Spirit. The theological challenge for the church in Myanmar today is how to relate the functions of *Nats* in the religio-culture, to the Spirit in Christianity.

Pneumatological Response

In responding to the *Nat* worship from the pneumatological perspective, out of having different functions, I would select two functions which will be compared with the work of the Holy Spirit. The works of the *Nats* can be analogous to the works of the Holy Spirit, making the work of the Holy Spirit more intelligible to the Christians in Myanmar. Michael Green has mentioned three characteristics of the Spirit in the Old Testament: restricted to special people, fitful, and perceived as sub-personal (Green 1993, 203–20). By careful investigation it can be said that the works of the Holy Spirit are more spectacular in the Old Testament; however, in the New Testament the Spirit enters into the lives of all believers. One function of the Holy Spirit, then, is the indwelling or possession of the believers' lives. In spite of many discrepancies, I would like to draw a comparison between two possessions in the first place, that of the Holy Spirit and that of the *Nats*.

One of Paul's metaphors to express the believer's relationship with the Holy Spirit is that he dwells in the person, as he said: "But you are not in the flesh; you are in the Spirit, since the Spirit of God dwells in you" (Rom 8:9 NRSV). It can be claimed that the Holy Spirit possesses the believers. This concept is very helpful to grasp for the people of Myanmar who have already had the experience in *Nat* worship. The nature of the function, however, is different. The function of the indwelling Holy Spirit in humans is always transformative and constructive (Gal 5:22,23), whereas the work of the *Nat* in possessing humans is sometimes destructive and becomes the cause of misery. The characteristic of *Nat* possession is more similar to that work of the Holy Spirit in the Old Testament, which is spectacular, than the work of the Holy Spirit in the New Testament, which is more transformative inwardly.

The second function is prophecy. One of the remarkable signs for the inauguration of the Holy Spirit is prophecy, as foretold by the prophet Joel (Acts 2:18). In the Bible, prophecy is foretelling as well as forth-telling. But it is hard to divide these two functions explicitly. Michael Green spells out the difficulty of division:

> It is not easy to be clear precisely what early Christian
> prophecy was. It could vary from the predictions of a

man like Agabus, the mysteries of the Book of Revelation (a remarkable example of early prophecy, see
Revelation 1:3), to the induction of a Christian for a
particular office (1 Timothy 4:14), testimony to Jesus
(Revelation 19:10), and use in evangelism, edification,
consolation or teaching. (1975, 169–70)

The prophets or prophetesses in *Nat* worship are soothsayers, in the
true sense of the word, who can predict what will happen in the future
and can discern the mysteries, but biblical prophecy is not only futurist
but also contextual.

The existence of the spirits, the *Nats*, has been real in the experiences of the people in Myanmar for many ages and thus has become
part of their culture. When Christianity came and taught about the
Holy Spirit, the people juxtaposed the two beliefs side by side. There
are times when the *Nats* disguise themselves as the Holy Spirit, and
John's warning to the churches, to have the wisdom of discernment, is
vitally significant (1 John 4:1). In the same manner, two beliefs should
not be seen as *dualistic* but *interconnected*. The Burmese Buddhists
can comprehend the Holy Spirit only with reference to the powerful
being, which is deeply grounded in the experience of the people and
expressed in terms of indigenous religio-culture, which is *Nat* worship.

Christological Response

In responding to *Nat* worship from the Christological perspective,
churches have to confront the living question of Jesus Christ, "Who
do you say I am?" (Matt 16:15). There are different levels of approach to
answer this existential question of Jesus Christ. In this section I will be
responding to *Nat* worship from a Christian approach that views Jesus
Christ as the Ancestor and as the Liberator. These topics will be dealt
with separately.

Jesus Christ, the Ancestor

In Revelation 1:17,18 we see Christ claiming to be the First and Last,
and the Living One. It is clear that he is the Ancestor par excellence
through his divinity and humanity. Jesus qualified himself to be an
Ancestor by his incarnation, by his death and resurrection, and by
his ascension. The concept of incarnation by identifying himself as a

human being makes sense to Burmese folk Buddhists, as God in Christ has taken the form of a human being in order to become the Ancestor. Jesus' kenotic nature of taking upon himself our condition can be regarded as the inauguration of his Ancestorship, for an Ancestor could never be a perfect Ancestor if he did not become a perfect human being. In regard with the requirements of the Ancestorship of Jesus Christ in the Burmese Buddhist context, Khan En points out:

> During his lifetime on earth, the Ancestor was supposed to achieve the trust and confidence of his clan both in conduct and leadership. He would be the person to whom the clan members resorted to in times of crisis, and he would also be a peace-maker with the clan. He was thus a promoter of security for the members of the clan. Jesus meets the requirements for Ancestorship as he is depicted as the good Shepherd (John 10:11–18), a Way to the Father (14:6) and a peace-giver (16:33). These are some of the life requirements for Ancestor, which Jesus perfectly met and even went beyond, during his life time. To sum up briefly, the incarnation and the earthly ministry of Jesus Christ was the process whereby Jesus became the Ancestor for the new clan he would create—the church. All the virtues and more, of the Ancestors in *Nat* worship, are fully embodied in Jesus Christ and therefore he is regarded as an Ancestor par excellence. (2012, 226)

The process of Jesus Christ's Ancestorship is most clearly seen in the Cross and the aftermath of the cross event. The Cross is the culmination of the earthly ministry whereby God himself was involved in suffering for the sake of justice. From this perspective, the uniqueness of his death on the Cross has a sociopolitical dimension. How can this concept of the Ancestorship of Jesus Christ be applied and integrated into the context of Burmese folk Buddhists? It is by the Cross and the Resurrection that Jesus created a new clan and thus became a true Ancestor for that new clan which will live under a new order of life. In other words, the Cross became an instrument and even a catalyst for the new clan. Paul articulated this concept when he said, "For as all die in Adam, so all will be made alive in Christ. But each in his own order: Christ the first fruits, then at his coming those who belong to Christ" (1 Cor 15:22,23 NRSV). Thus Jesus has become the new Ancestor of all the members of the new clan. The Cross thus has a specific, significant role between ancestor-clan relationships in *Nat* worship.

The ascension of Jesus Christ was the fulfillment and the glorification of his earthly ministry. By this act he entered Ancestorship, which was not confined to only one particular clan but extended to the whole universe and thus promoted him as the cosmic and universal Ancestor. By this ascension, Jesus surpassed all the human ancestors and thus become the proto-Ancestor, the unique Ancestor, the source of life, and Lord of all other *Nats*. This belief has a vital significance for the lives of the people in Myanmar, for he subdued all the diabolical powers which threaten their daily lives. The lordship of Jesus Christ after he attained Ancestorship was also extended to the spirits of the deceased who live in the abode of the dead (1 Pet 3:18,19). He thus became Lord over the universe and all creatures, visible and invisible. As a proto-Ancestor, Christ has the prerogative to give the desired blessings to the new clan, such as health and prosperity and also spiritual security. In addition, to portray Jesus as a proto-Ancestor, in the Myanmar context has several significances. Three significances should be mentioned here briefly.

Presenting Christ as an ancestor shows that he is still part of the human family and does not live in a far-distant heaven unrelated to clan members. He protects, guards, and guides the clan members. It is from this proto-Ancestor that the new clan, the whole tribe of God, has taken the inward name—Christians. Thus the clan members can have an inward soteriological experience.

The portrait of Jesus Christ as proto-Ancestor also has an ecclesiological significance. To become a Christian means to join the new clan, which the proto-Ancestor Jesus Christ created through his blood. This concept of accepting Jesus Christ as proto-Ancestor, and becoming a member of the new clan, is much more profound than the current concept of church membership by faith. This consolidated relationship between the pro-Ancestor, Jesus Christ, and the church—the new clan—is the solid foundation for a living church for which Paul used different metaphors like the head and the body (Eph 5:23) and husband and wife (Rom 4:2–6).

The portrait of Jesus Christ as proto-Ancestor has also an ethical significance for the church, or the new clan. The ancestors were the persons who during their lifetime achieved credibility among all the clan members by their exemplary conduct, selfless concern, and leadership in a particular clan. They were not forgotten after they died but remembered and venerated or even worshiped by the clan members for generations. Besides, the ancestors were regarded as custodians of the morality of the family or the clan, and were infuriated when the clan members did something wrong. People have to appease the ancestors. If the ancestors are offended, they will punish them. To sum up, the deceased ancestors were generally regarded as archetypes of conduct whom the clan members needed to look up to. As proto-Ancestor, Jesus Christ stressed his guardianship of morality by demanding a deeper and a more serious response from the new clan member.

Jesus as Liberator

In the Burmese Buddhist context, it is very important to portray Jesus Christ as the Liberator. Christ can be a Liberator from the circle of rebirths (*samsara*), which is caused by the deeds of human beings in their past existence (*kamma* in Pali). Because life or existence is suffering (*dukkha*) caused by ignorance (*avijja*) and rebellion (*moha*), human beings are pursuing liberation from existence. The stage of these liberations is called nirvana, meaning cessation from all existence. To present Jesus Christ as Liberator at this level, the Christians in Myanmar have to engage in dialogue with the Buddhists and make an attempt to articulate how Jesus ends those series of existence (*samsara*) by carrying vicariously all the suffering (*dukkha*) caused by deeds (*kamma*) in the series of existence (*samsara*). Thein Nyunt points out,

> Buddhists are pursuing liberation through self-effort. He or she remains bound to samsara (thirty-one planes of existence: four woeful states, one human plane, six planes of deva and twenty planes of Brahma). It clearly shows that salvation is impossible

through human efforts but only through the One who
comes from outside of samsara. And those who take
refuge in him have the chance to obtain the "nirvana,"
the liberation of samsara. (Thein Nyunt 2014, 106)

This will open new ways of introducing Jesus Christ to Burmese
Buddhists and open new ways in which Buddhists can find their liberation and express their faith in Christ. As pointed out, the lives of
Nat worshipers were constantly fearful and under menace because they
were threatened by the *Nats* who haunted every object and every place.
All misfortunes, natural calamities, diseases, and deaths were believed
to be caused by the malevolent *Nats*. Briefly, life in its totality was subject to constant fear and insecurity due to the belief in *Nats*, and there
was no hope in life. When Christ was accepted as the Liberator, first
of all he liberated people from the power of evil *Nats*, and he imparted
hope to the people in their hopeless lives. What Vincent J. Donovan
stated as the purpose of his missionary work with the Masai people is
true of the situation in Myanmar.

> I believe this is what lies at the heart of the urgency
> and necessity of missionary work and evangelization.
> This is what I, and others like me, are trying to do
> *out there*. Not to bring salvation and goodness and
> holiness and grace and God, which were there before
> we got there. But to bring these people the only thing
> they did not have before we came—hope—a hope
> imbedded in the meaning of the life and death and
> resurrection of Christ. It is a cleansing and humbling
> thought to see your whole life and work reduced to
> being simply a channel of hope, and yourself merely
> a herald of hope, for those who do not have it. (1982,
> 143, italics in the original)

When Christ became the Liberator of the people, fear and despair
subsided at the personal level and life was filled with hope. All those
places once regarded as ruled by the *Nats* and regarded as taboo were
no longer avoided but cultivated and turned into productive farms.

Christ as the Liberator can also be seen at the cultural level. Many
of the cultural elements have their origin in *Nat* worship, as already

stated. When the *Nat* worshipers accepted Christ as their Liberator, they started to study their culture from the perspective of the gospel and transformed those cultural evils which dehumanize people. In this sense Christ became the Liberator, as cultural evils were challenged and transformed in the light of the gospel.

Summary

The pre-Buddhist Burmese belief in the relevance of supernatural spirit beings to daily life is close to the biblical teaching regarding the works of the Holy Spirit in daily life and the salvation which includes intra-mundane and supramundane. Traditional Western Christianity and missionaries to Myanmar religions have failed to address this belief in spiritual power which interconnects with daily life. For all the followers of Christ who want to proclaim the good news of Jesus Christ to the Burmese Buddhists, they should convince them that the true freedom can be found only in Jesus Christ through the conviction of the works of the Holy Spirit.

MISSIOLOGICAL REFLECTIONS

If *Nat* worship has been beneficial for the people for generations past, it is because it gave them some relief from their predicaments. The people in Myanmar believed that every place and every object was haunted by the *Nats*, and therefore felt threatened by those *Nats* who could revenge them for conscious or unconscious mistreatment. Most of the trouble from these *Nats* was physical and terrestrial such as sickness, which is the most common predicament, and also injures, failure of crops, and tensions in the family. On the other hand, those who are in good terms with the *Nats*, specifically the tutelary *Nats*, called *siam*, are showered with the earthly blessings, such as bountiful crops in times of harvest, success in hunting, good health, and prosperity. It is thus essential that the people try to get in good terms with the *Nats* by making appeasement and reconciliation with the baneful *Nats*. From this, one can say that the concept of relief or salvation, as it exists in *Nat* worship, has to do with physical aspects and has nothing to do with spiritual salvation. Maung Htin Aung has aptly remarked on this concept:

> The Burmese who resort to astrology, alchemy, or *Nat*
> worship do so for safety and success in their mundane

life, and the same Burmese will observe the Buddhist religious days and perform deeds of merit in preparation for the countless existences that they must undergo in the whirlpool of rebirth. (Aung 1962, 4–5)

This statement shows clearly that *Nat* worship is meant solely for the intramundane life, while Buddhism is meant for the supramundane, the next life. The emphasis on physical salvation can be constructive in helping the Christians in Myanmar to extend their scope of Christian salvation to embrace all aspects of human life. The biblical concept of salvation includes the physical and the spiritual in its wholeness, so that human beings will enjoy salvation in this life, here and now, and in the next life, hereafter. Paul S. Fiddes has encapsulated this idea:

"Salvation" is an idea which has the widest scope, including the healing of individuals and social groups and even the conserving of a natural world ravaged and polluted by human greed. The quest for salvation is the search for authentic life, and many people hope for it beyond death as well as here and now. (1989, 3)

The integration of these two components should be stressed in the churches of Myanmar to help the gospel to permeate among the people. Tracing the history, with the arrival of Christianity the missionaries in Myanmar introduced comprehensive and holistic salvation, embracing both the spiritual and the physical aspects. They promoted social works such as schools, hospitals, orphanages, and other philanthropic works, but theologically the emphasis upon the future became more dominant among the churches. It is at this point that the present-oriented *Nat* worship can make a contribution to the Christians; namely, that salvation is never salvation out of this world but salvation in the context of human society en route to a whole and healed world (Bosch 1991, 399).

In *Nat* worship, though there is a vertical dimension as regards relationship with the deceased ancestors, the prevailing concept is rather the horizontal that is communal and social rather than personal and individualistic. The biblical concept of salvation is both vertical and horizontal as well. However, due to the influence of the stated factors, the popular understanding of salvation in Myanmar is vertical rather than horizontal, meaning it is more individualistic and personal than social and communal.

The two are soteriological complementary, and both are necessary to form a comprehensive and holistic salvation. The biblical concept of salvation is the past event, the present experience, and the future hope (McGrath 1994, 337–68). It is essential for the Christian to experience salvation at the present time and exercise the power of salvation in the present world. Khan En states,

> One of the major contributions of *Nat* worship to Christian theology is its primal worldview. A worldview seeks to answer the fundamental questions of human beings, their relationship with God and the universe . . . *Nat* worship in Myanmar provides a basic and crude concept of worldview for the Christians to be redefined by the gospel. From the beginning the *Nat* worshipers in Myanmar have had a unified and an integrated worldview. They perceive things in one unit as they have no dualistic worldview concept. Life is not divided into secular and religious, but everything is seen as one unit under the control of the *Nats* ... sometimes *Nats* influence human beings, and sometimes vice-versa. There can be no rigid separation between the material and spiritual world, the temporal and the non-temporal, time and eternity, the cosmic and meta-cosmic, the "here-and-now" and "here-after." Even the life after death, which is a salient characteristic of *Nat* worship, is viewed as part and parcel of the whole existence, in continuity. This original worldview of *Nat* worship is very fundamental to the right understanding of the Christian concept of salvation. Unfortunately, however, both Buddhism and the Graeco-western oriented soteriological concept have distorted it and original worldview of *Nat* worship with its concept of cosmic (*lokka*) and meta-cosmic (*lokkutra*), while Graeco-western oriented and now and hereafter, or time and eternity. Time, in most

archaic form of *Nat* worship, is equated with eternity. To sum up, the worldview of *Nat* worship is not only inter-dependent or inter-penetrated as one cosmic unit, but it is also contemporaneous. They do not conceive history as a succession of events, as everything is contemporaneous to them. This is very close to the theological worldview which holds the presence of God's kingdom in both here-and-now and here-after not as separated but in continuity. (2012, 119–20)

RECOMMENDATIONS AND CONCLUSIONS

Many Christians in Myanmar have been introduced to Christianity at an ideological level since they have been influenced by traditional Western theology for a long time: they do not believe in the supernatural at the level of practice. In reality, they perceived Burmese spirituality as the high plane of spirituality. It is remarkable that today the Spirit of God reveals himself to these religious Burmese grassroots in paranormal ways and they directly encounter him. When they initiate relationship with him, he reveals himself through different ways. Here I would like to recommend four channels of spiritual connections.

Prayer

The most important channel of spiritual connection that fits with Burmese spirituality is practicing prayers. Folk religious Burmese usually pray to Buddha statues, *Bodaw*, and earthbound *Nat* for their felt needs and real needs and for their spiritual fulfillment. They also go to *Ba-din-saya* and *Nat-kadaw*, from whom they receive some kind of aid. Additionally, the present reality of Myanmar forces grassroots Burmese to turn to prayer, and prayer becomes a vital practice for them. Due to economic crisis, for the Burmese prayer is a daily hope for freedom from poverty, hardships, and illness. Although missionaries introduced the Burmese to hope for life hereafter, for the Burmese their hope and prayers are very practical and for this real life. In this sense, Burmese folk belief, unlike Buddha's teaching which has no place for prayer, is similar to Christianity. Our Lord Jesus Christ taught his disciples to pray (Mark 11:24). The Apostle Paul also taught us to pray without ceasing (1 Thess 5:17). Having interviewed with some Buddhist converts and one *Nat-kadaw* convert, the results show that most of them experience directly God's presence. According to a *Nat-kadaw* convert, the protection from the Holy Spirit and liberation in Christ cannot be compared with any powerful beings from her former *Nats*.

Dreams

Another spiritual channel between God and people which is also a focus for Burmese people is dreams and the interpretation of dreams. In general, Burmese believe that they can meet with *Deva-Nats*, *Bodaw*, earthbound *Nats*, and other powerful beings in a dream. It is their belief that *Nats* usually use dreams when they communicate with *Nat-kadaws* and some of the *Nat*-worshipers. It seems that dreams and interpreting dreams are quite serious for the Burmese.

Scripture

One more spiritual channel from the divine Spirit to charismatic and evangelical Christians which can create a center for Burmese attention is through the Scripture as a guide. As pointed out, Burmese folk Buddhists and some traditional Christians alike go to *Badin-saya* and *Nat-kadaw* for their fortune, to receive advice before decision making, to get assistance in some way so that they can overcome their daily problems. Burmese Christians are keen to encounter and consult with the *Nats*, other powerful beings, and extraordinary powers in times of crisis.

Need for Discernment

Even though extraordinary spiritual experiences have been effective in communicating the gospel to the Burmese Buddhists, the issues of revelation and discernment are questionable. The private revelations should be tested against Scripture to see if the content of the revelations is esoteric or trite. Despite the fact that the Spirit has promised to guide his children (Ps 23:4; 25:8,9), and the Spirit, as a Counselor, can give divine suggestions, advice, and revelation to the believers, we need to be aware that a human's inner guidance is often obscure, confusing, or completely nonapparent to his or her consciousness. One thing we need to know is that all the gifts of the Holy Spirit, including abilities to teach and guide, lead to the edification of the individual and of the church for God's glory, not for our own glory.

As stated earlier, the Burmese Buddhists are over half of the total population, and the main religion of Myanmar is Theravada Buddhism. But their spiritual realities are influenced by the practices of *Nat* worship. *Nat* images are found on the premises of thousands of golden pagodas, Buddhist shrines, temples, and monasteries. Their belief in the existence of a spirit world has different levels and kinds of supernatural powers and spirit beings. Their faith is, furthermore, centered in the persons who became spirit-*Nats* who were killed unjustly and prematurely and became spirit-*Nats*. It is believed that the experiences of their tragic lives have led the *Nats* to hate the unjust society, help their followers out of difficult situations caused by socioeconomic forces, protect them from devils, and enable them to have peaceful lives as long as they are given respect and offerings. We have also learned that prayer, dreams, and Scripture are vital practices for the Burmese. In fact, belief in the existence of spiritual beings, their powers, and traditional experiences are points of contact that Jesus Christ is the only Liberator, and the true freedom can be found only in him.

REFERENCES

Aung, Maung Htin. 1962. *Folk elements in Burmese Buddhism.* London: Oxford University Press.

Bosch, David J. 1991. *Transforming mission: Paradigm shifts in theology of mission.* Maryknoll, NY: Orbis Books.

Donovan, Vincent J. 1982. *Christianity rediscovered.* London: SCM.

Fiddes, Paul S. 1989. *Past event and present salvation: The Christian idea of atonement.* London: Darton, Longmand & Todd.

Fink, Christian. 2001. *Living silence: Burma under military rule.* Bangkok: White House.

Green, Michael. 1975. *I believe in the Holy Spirit.* London: Hodder & Stoughton.

———. 1993. *Acts for today: First century Christianity for twentieth century Christians.* London: Hodder & Stoughton.

Htay, U Han, and Saya U Chit Tin. 2002. *How to live as a good Buddhist.* Vol. 1. Yangon: Department of the Promotion and Propagation of the Sasana.

Khan En, Simon Pau. 2012. *Nat worship: A paradigm for doing contextual theology in Myanmar.* Yangon: Judson Research Center of the Myanmar Institute of Theology.

Sein Ko, Taw. 1913. *Burmese sketches.* Vol. 1. Rangoon: British Burma Press.

Lubeigt, Guy. 2004. Myanmar: A country modeled by Buddhist traditions. In *Traditions of knowledge in Southeast Asia*, part 2, ed. Myanmar Historical Commission. Yangon: University Press.

McGrath, Alister E. 1994. *Christian theology: An introduction.* Oxford: Blackwell.

Myint, Saya. n.d. *Nat-Paung-Sone.* Yangon: San Taw Win.

Myo, Gambiya Saya Hla. 2009. *Ah-swan-Htet yadayar saung-par-myar.* Yangon: Cho-Te-Than Sarpay.

Nyunt, Khin Maung. 2005. *Myanmar traditional monthly festival.* Yangon: Inwa.

Nyunt, Moe Moe. 2010. *A pneumatological response to the Burmese Nat-worship.* Yangon: Myanmar Institute of Theology.

Sangermano, Vicentious. 1893. *The Burmese Empire a hundred years ago.* Philadelphia: Wesminster.

Si Thu, Min. 1992. *The history of Nat worship in Myanmar.* Yangon: NIlah Kaba Sa-oh Saing.

Spiro, Melford E. 1970. *Buddhism and society: A great tradition and its Burmese vicissitudes.* London: University of California Press.

———. 1978. *Burmese supernaturalism.* Philadelphia: Institute for the Study of Human Issues.

Temple, R. C. 1906. *Thirty-seven Nats: A phase of spirit-worship prevailing in Burma.* London: W. Griggs.

Thein Nyunt, Peter. 2014. *Missions amidst pagodas: Contextual communication of the gospel in the Burmese Buddhist context.* Carlisle, UK: Langham Monographs.

Zaw, Aung. 2008. Than Shwe, voodoo, and the number 11. The Irrawaddy, December 25. http://www2.irrawaddy.org/opinion_story.php?art_id=14844 (accessed January 1, 2015).

CHAPTER 14

PEOPLE OF POWER:
BECOMING AN "ALONGSIDER"
IN THAILAND AND BEYOND

JOHN P. LAMBERT

Although they have not yet been widely accepted, advances in understanding culture and contextualization of the Gospel for Thai peoples have made some new headway over the past few decades (Petchsongkram 1975, Prometta 2000, DeNeui 2002, Gustafson 2009, Wetchgama 2014). Though recorded case studies are sparse at this point, advances in understanding the organic nature of the New Testament church and the methodology of house church planting have also helped the growth of the movement to Christ in Thailand for those who have learned from it (Garrison 2004, Serithai 2014). The introduction of a powerful Christianity through the Pentecostal-Charismatic movement has also brought a greater measure of breakthrough for those who practice this expression of the faith (Hosack 2001, Swanson 2003, Visser 2008). All of these recent movements are good, but I propose that none of them alone has been or will be enough to see a major breakthrough of the Gospel among the Thai.

Something foundational is needed. I would argue that a new movement of every day people—empowered, equipped, and released as people of power to serve within their own socio-cultural communities in the name and authority of the Lord Jesus Christ. These "people of power" will move beyond the artificial boundaries of the clergy-laity divide (often a distortion) in order to share the good news of Jesus in a way that makes sense to their own people. Their words will be accompanied by signs, miracles, and wonders following (Mark 16:20). The first step is their having a Biblical understanding what it means to have the Spirit of God living in them empowering them for the work of ministry God has prepared in advance for them to do (Eph 2:10).

In this paper I examine some of the historical, Biblical, and cultural perspectives related to what it means to be a person of power, rooted in a Biblical identity, equipped and released, within the Thai culture. I draw from Western and Asian mission thinkers and practitioners for the purpose of gleaning insights into what it may take to see greater breakthrough of the Gospel among the Thai and other similar cultural contexts. Although there are many other potential issues that may be obstacles to greater breakthrough, including cultural identity issues, I have sought to only briefly mention some of them in relationship to the main issue of Biblical identity.

Finally, I will suggest some practical approaches that may be used to help influence the work towards the aim of empowering the majority of non-professional servants (ministers) of the Gospel. My ultimate hope is that the reader will take these insights and join the work as an "alongsider" (Travis 2013) in order to empower every believer to make other empowered disciples. This is especially true for leaders, it is my hope that they would work to retool their ministry and begin to measure their success by the number of empowered disciples they equip and release into their own God-given sphere of service.

HISTORICAL CONTEXT

For almost 150 years, the name of Jesus Christ has had some representation in Thailand. During this time, very few Thai people have become Christians. It has been estimated that only 0.3 percent of the ethnic Thai people identify as Protestant Christians (Visser 2008, 77). However, within the last forty years, great advances have been taking place to the point where the annual conversion rate of people in Thailand, 3.5 percent (Visser 2008, 104), is now greater than the annual population growth rate of 0.1 percent for the years 2012–2030 (Unicef). These statistics represent great potential for momentum for the growth of the faith in the Thai context and among other similar nations.

In 1567, the first Portuguese speaking Catholic emissaries arrived in Siam. Five years later, in 1662, French-speaking Jesuits made their home in the capital of Ayutthaya (Chumsriphan, 2002). In 1828,

Karl Gutzlaff & Jacob Tomlin became the first Protestants to arrive in Thailand. A few years later in 1831, David Abeel began work as representative of the American Board of Commissioners for Foreign Missions. For the last 448 years, the name of Jesus Christ has had some form of representation in Thailand (Thai Church, Chaiwan 1975: 19). So much effort has been made in the work of the Gospel in Thailand, but why has there been so little visible fruit? Many authors have asked the same question over the years (Petchsongkram 1975, Davies 1998, Johnson 2002, Saiyasak 2007, Boon-Itt 2011). The early history shows that both Catholics and Protestant missionaries were ethnocentric and westernizing in their approach to Christianize, importing the only forms of ministry they knew (Thai Church). These forms of ministry included the clergy-laity model of leadership and outreach devoid of the supernatural gifts and power of the Holy Spirit.

The Clergy-Laity Obstacle

The idea of laypersons versus a special clerical class of ministers has continued to be a hindrance to the growth of the Gospel in Thailand, not to mention many other places in the world. This distinction distorts New Testament teaching on the relationship between Biblical eldership and the average every day follower of Jesus. (I Peter 2:9) I believe distortion has negatively influenced of the majority of Thai believers to impact others around them for Jesus, both today and over the last 450 years.

In contrast to that distinction, a study done in 2008, discovered that seventy percent of all Thai converts said the main influence in their conversion was not a church leader, but a layperson. The study also found that relatives of (Thai) Christians are seven hundred times more likely to become Christians than those who have no Christian relatives (Visser 2008, 138). It is evident that the largest untapped potential in reaching Thailand with the gospel is the pool of everyday empowered "lay people" reaching out within their family and social networks.

Instead of ministering out of the Holy Spirit's grace and power to whomever they have opportunity, Thai believers have been confined to simply inviting their friends and relatives to Sunday morning services or special outreach events, such as are commonly held during the Christmas season. If a person has any questions or needs, the Thai believers will, most often, direct them to their priest or pastor who they believe is the religious specialist. This is a crucial issue now to break-through in the Thai context, especially since now the Thai church is growing stronger than it ever has been in its history.

A once famous high-ranking monk turned Christian minister once observed,

> One of the problems of the church in Thailand is that when someone comes to ask about the Christian faith first of all they look to see if the missionary is there. If the missionary isn't there, they say, 'Too bad, if the missionary (or Pastor) were here you could ask any-thing you wanted and he could answer you. I am a Christian. Christianity is good, but I can't tell you why. (Petchsongkram 1972, 9)

Although the doctrine of the "priesthood of all believers" is known to be a key doctrine of the Protestant reformation, it has been lost in practice in many Protestant denominations. Even Luther failed at this—reformers came chiding him for transgressing his own origi-nal teaching. Further reaction to the ecclesiastical system of Roman Catholicism came from the Anabaptists who rejected a hierarchical structure of leadership and emphasized that ministry was the respon-sibility of the entire congregation (Hyatt 1996, 80).

"Puritanism emphasized the importance of preaching with the focus on the pulpit, while Catholicism emphasized sacraments where the focus was on the altar. In Puritanism, therefore, salvation required hearing sermons" (Emerson 1990, 14). In this author's opinion, both the altar and the pulpit have to be dismantled in the Thai context in order to see greater Gospel breakthrough. It is the day of the saints, the every day people of God (Eph 4:11–12). However, this does not mean that we become leaderless people who do not value the New Testament gift of teaching or cease taking the Lord's Supper or Communion. These are all Biblical and essential, in their proper place.

Unfortunately, both Catholic and the majority of all Protestant workers have perpetuated the clergy-laity distinction in their mis-sion efforts in Thailand, even up until the present day. In his book,

Poles Apart, John Davies has a whole chapter on this issue (1993, 237–266). One thought he gives which we should ponder, especially where the population of followers of Jesus still numbers less than 2% of the total population:

> I would like to suggest that millions of members (potential), are either never won to Christ, or when they are, are harnessed and hindered from effectiveness within the body of Christ because of a stubborn unwillingness to be prepared for new forms and functions to appear. Of course, I accept that no structure as such can produce a spiritual church, but given other necessary spiritual qualifications, they can certainly either effectively accelerate church growth or hinder it. (Davies 1993, 263)

Beyond the historical and theological insights and from a simply pragmatic point of view, Thai and expat church planters should be mindful of the kinds of churches that they are attempting to plant in Thailand. Visser's research also found that "traditional churches with a lot of rules and emphasis on the role of the clergy are less likely to grow" (Visser 2008, 163). Traditional models of churches can tend to disempower and frustrate those who would otherwise be useful in the work of ministry.

The Patron-Client System and Thai Leadership

Steve Taylor has worked for the Evangelical Fellowship of Thailand for thirty years and is on staff at the Bangkok Bible Seminary. He gives some great insight into how this system can clash with Biblical values.

> Hierarchy and inequality, fundamental to the patron-client system, bring benefits, but the system could be seen on some fronts as not biblical. Christian doctrine allows for: equality of all believers, who have one Lord; leaders who listen, sometimes receive instruction; members who understand God can speak to them, not just to leaders; leaders who do menial tasks; providers of help and their recipients are equals,

including society's poor and weak who are disqualified as patrons and clients.

Indebtedness, also fundamental to patron-client relationships, in some ways can be viewed as contrary to Christ's teaching to give and expect nothing in return (Mat 6:3; Mat 10:8; Luke 14:12). A better model would be grace (*prakhun*), in which favors are dispensed freely for the sake of God's kingdom, without thought of personal gain. (Taylor, 2014)

If Gospel breakthrough is going to be accelerated in Thailand, the Biblical teaching of the priesthood of all believers needs to be recovered and strongly emphasized to every new follower of Jesus within the existing patron-client system. Every new believer should understand what the Bible says about their identity in Christ and the reality of Christ in them. New structures and forms of discipleship should be created that make it possible for every follower of Jesus to be equipped, empowered, and released into mission with God, wherever they are.

At a minimum, it should be emphasized that each believer:

- has a unique story that they can and should share that with others of how the Holy Spirit has been working in and through their lives
- has a right to read, understand and share God's Word
- has a responsibility to take the grace gifts that have been given to them through the Holy Spirit and serve others (minister) in the power and might of the Spirit as much as they have opportunity.

The Cessationist Obstacle

It has been recently verified that the growing edge of the Protestant Church in Thailand is found in the charismatic/Pentecostal wing. Again Visser's 2008 study found that although the majority of all Protestant Christians are non-Charismatic, among the ethnic Thai charismatic churches are growing faster than non charismatic ones and the large majority of this growth is internally generated (2008, 75, 81, 83, 163).

Missiologist Allan Anderson gives some insight as to why these forms of church may be growing in Thailand:

> Most forms of Pentecostalism teach that every member is a minister and should be involved in mission and evangelism wherever they find themselves. Although increasing institutionalism often causes a reappearance of the clergy/laity divide the mass involvement of the 'laity' in the Pentecostal movement was one of the reasons for its success . . . Pentecostals and Charismatics emphasize a spontaneous liturgy, which is mainly oral and narrative with an emphasis on direct experience of God through his Spirit, which has been contrasted with rationalistic and written liturgies presided over by a clergy that is the main feature of most other forms of Christianity. (2006, 184)

Visser goes on to point out, in contrast, that growth among Calvinistic Presbyterians in Thailand, generally known to be cessationist, is slow." In fact, the Christian Churches in Thailand (CCT) have the lowest average annual church growth rate in Thailand (Visser 2008, 83, 145). The CCT churches are a part of the World Council of Churches and are a mixture of Presbyterian, Disciples of Christ, and some Baptist denominational groups.

Cessationists are those who believe that the miraculous gifts of the Holy Spirit ceased at the close of the apostolic era and are not normative for today. Yet, according to Prof. Thomas Schreiner, a top New Testament scholar and cessationist, " . . . it should be acknowledged that the arguments for a cessationist reading aren't open and shut. Nowhere does the New Testament clearly teach that the supernatural gifts have ceased" (Brown, 2014, 170). Even prominent Western Mainline Evangelicals, such as Eric Metaxas, are going further and embracing the miraculous (Mextaxas 2014).

Speaking to Westerners, mission consultant Paul Borthwick writes, "Our worldviews are so influenced by the Enlightenment that we really don't comprehend the miracle-driven, spirit-aware world of the Bible . . . My advice: if you want to be a cessationist, don't travel! The church in the Majority world did not get the memo" (Borthwick 2012, 45).

Concerning the necessity of the gifts of the Spirit for missions and evangelism, Pentecostal pioneer Donald Gee remarked that the gifts of the spirit are "divine equipment for the work of world evangelization. They are not a hobby to play with; but tools to work with and weapons to fight with" (McClung, 2006, 108).

In this author's opinion, if we are working in spiritual work with a severely limited use of the Spirit's tools, then we are at a distinct disadvantage. Thai believers, pastors, and even expat workers may be able to survive in their faith without use of the Spirit's gifts, but will they be able to really thrive so that great blessing flows to others.

ADDRESSING FELT NEEDS FOR SUPERNATURAL POWER

Chuck Kraft brings perspective on how our spiritual impotence can affect real people's lives.

> When spiritual power issues are not addressed, large segments of believers—many of whom have a genuine relationship with Christ-remain captive to the enemy in various degrees. People who call themselves Christians faithfully attend church on Sundays but also seek the help of healers and diviners who operate under satanic power when they need healing, guidance, or other power related assistance. (Kraft 2005, 9)

He goes on to conclude, "We cannot be either biblical or relevant to most of the peoples of the world without a solid approach to spiritual power" (Kraft 2005, 362).

Speaking from his unique vantage point in the world of Northeast Thailand among the Thai-Isan people, Chansamone Saiyasak writes,

> The animistic belief systems provide the Isan people with consistent ways of dealing with their present felt needs for survival, safety, security, and prosperity. In addition, Buddhism reinforces these felt needs. Up until now, Christianity has presented itself as an alternative religion, but, it has not clearly and effectively addressed the people's felt need for survival, safety and security, and prosperity.
>
> Although the historical veracity of a religious faith is important, the Isan people take less notice of the historical truthfulness of a religious faith and instead

focus on its effects, especially on one's present life. If Christianity is going to replace animistic beliefs, it has to clearly, specifically, and effectively show its effects in responding to the present-life situations of the Isan people. (Saiyasak 2007, 275)

In contrast he remarks,

Historically, Protestant Christianity as represented by the Christian & Missionary Alliance (C&MA) in the Isan area has focused on the "doctrinal" Christ instead of the "supernatural" Christ. Christianity has not been able to address the supernatural tendencies of the Isan people. (Saiyasak 2007, 278)

Saiyasak's conclusion is,

The Isan believes in auspicious time, ill omens, amulets, and magic and primarily focuses on the matter of avoiding misfortune or calamity and of acquiring power, protection, and prosperity . . . Consequently, the matter of power encounter or any teaching which centers on the power of Christ over other supernatural powers or beings will have a huge appeal amongst the Isan people. (Saiyasak 2007, 278)

How can we address the supernatural concerns of the Thai and others like them if we ourselves are not prepared to walk in the supernatural gifts and graces that have been freely given to us by the Holy Spirit?

Throughout Thailand animistic practices within Folk Buddhism address some of the heart issues of Thai people by providing them with a source of power they believe will assist them in life. A careful study of what is actually happening will show that much of what is being "offered" is a very clever counterfeit to what is actually found in Jesus Christ. (DeNeui 2002, 11–12)

So another burning question for me is, "Are we offering the Gospel with power or are we simply offering religious speeches and dialogues?" Even if our communications are contextual and "bridge-building," are they enough, especially in the Southeast Asian context? We may be doing well with truth encounters, but how are we doing in regards to power encounters that demonstrate the power of Jesus Christ, in very real and practical life situations? These life situations may include the need for supernatural physical healing, deliverance from demonic spirits, and prayers for God's blessing and protection over life cycles and every day needs.

Our neglect of the Holy Spirit in the Western evangelical world has gotten so bad that one popular Western Evangelical author could get away with a book entitled *Forgotten God: Reversing Our Tragic Neglect of the Holy Spirit* (Chan 2009). Since many of the existing Thai churches and ministries were influenced by Western cessationist background missionaries, could it be possible that they too are just as bad in their tragic neglect of the doctrines of the Holy Spirit?

I believe one of the reasons the Charismatic and Pentecostal churches in Thailand have been growing is because of their emphasis on the supernatural aspects of their faith and the relationship of the supernatural to the average believer's life. This Biblical emphasis meets a real felt need of the Thai people, including the Isan.

Miracles Within Social Relationships

Christian anthropologist Edwin Zehner found that miracles were as important in bringing people to a decision to become Christians as experiences within social relationships (Zehner 2003, 152–245). Though Visser rejects Zehner's hypothesis in his 2008 study, he nevertheless discovered that the "data reveals that miracles were the most important experience for 21 percent of all people who became Christian" (Visser 2008, 137).

Though miracles were not everything, Visser found that "perceived miracles play a decisive role for a significant minority. But experiences directly set in social relationships were decisive for four times as many people" (Ibid.). These social relationships included personal testimony, life example, and Bible study.

Given these realities, what would it look like to combine personal testimony of God working powerfully in one's life with the life example of what it means to live an empowered life through the Holy Spirit, as well as a serious reverence for understanding and living out the Word of God?

Charismatic Counterexamples vs. Cultural Fit

Even the Charismatic ministry emphasis won over previously staunch pro-contextualization leaders, such as former monk turned Thai Charismatic pastor, Wan Petchsongkram. Wan wrote *Talk in the Shade of the Bo Tree,* which was a highly contextual approach to communicating the Gospel in Thailand to Buddhist background people. However, he became a charismatic pastor in 1978 and totally abandoned the contextualized approach he advocated in his book (Visser 2008, 99). I am not asserting that we automatically follow his example and give up our contextualized approaches, but rather that we look more deeply into counterexamples having to do with spiritual power issues that ultimately affect conversion and church growth rates.

The fastest growing churches in Thailand, the Hope Churches, were started by, Kriengsak Charoenwongsak, who is said to have led the movement with a strongly charismatic theology with emphasis on the miraculous gifts of the Holy Spirit (Visser 2008, 100).

In dealing with what he calls "counterexamples" that override cultural fit, in this case the culture of the Buddhist world, Kraft asks the question, "Are there factors that override cultural fit (and church planting strategies)? If so, what are they? Are we missing something in commitment to our theory?" He goes on to say,

> A start toward dealing with the counterexamples would be to look at the relationship of spiritual power to the growth of these large, uncontextualized churches. I venture to suggest that most of them are healing churches, churches that regularly pray for healing and deliverance. Though these churches many be very Western in most features and even in some cases quite anti-traditional culture, they would be speaking to a major felt need of most of the peoples of the world by involving themselves in demonstrating the power of God to heal and deliver. Perhaps the exercise of spiritual power is more important to peo-

ple than cultural appropriateness. Should this be true,
we ought to be aware of it. (Kraft 2005, 13)

Being Charismatic Is Not Enough

Though, I myself am a Charismatic background believer, and have attempted to demonstrate why the Charismatic form of Christianity has
been the most effective in conversion and church growth in Thailand,
I must admit that I am not convinced that the current forms of Char-
ismatic-Pentecostal devotion, discipleship, outreach, and ecclesiology
will be enough to accelerate breakthrough in Thailand in the decades
to come.

Unless a broader understanding of the power and gifts of the Spirit
are emphasized along with a focus on planting culturally appropriate
and organically reproducible ecclesia within the Thai socio-cultural
context, greater breakthrough of the Gospel in Thailand will continue
to remain leashed and hindered. Kraft writes,

> Pentecostal and charismatic Christianity have often
> been more relevant to the peoples of the nonwestern
> world through their emphasis on spiritual power,
> but have often compromised their strength through
> an overemphasis on tongues and emotion and/or a
> negative attitude toward the cultures of the receptor
> peoples. (2005, 364)

Charismatics have often been guilty over emphasizing the anointed preacher or evangelist to the exclusion of the other gifts and graces
of the Holy Spirit. They have often been known to emphasize the person on the stage over the man on the street and the anointed religious
specialist over the average believer, who is called to live a naturally supernatural life.

The current set up of most Charismatic churches in Thailand, modeled many times by the Western missionaries who first introduced the
Charismatic paradigm of ministry, has lent itself to abuse of authority
and misuse of power. This is especially true when proper checks and
balances are not in place or heeded by founding leaders. Many Charismatic churches have been known to emphasize a carnal prosperity
message that, at the very least, has been a distraction to many followers

of Jesus who have given their focus to believing God and praying for wealth to the exclusion of serving others sacrificially.

Research shows that the current groups of Charismatics in Thailand have been most effective in the urban areas of Thailand rather than rural areas (Visser 2008, 167). The rural areas represent a slight majority of Thailand and the core people of the nation. According to the World Bank, in 2010, 66 percent of Thai people lived in rural areas (Trading Economics). Rural Thai people not only have concerns related to spiritual power, as was observed by Saiyasak, but also that of socio-cultural identity and cohesion. Those working in and among rural populations must become by emphasizing the empowerment of every new believer in addition to dealing with socio-cultural concerns through the work of critical contextualization.

The greatest need is to empower, equip, and release the vast majority of non-professional ministers into Spirit empowered service, within their own socio-cultural contexts. Rather than extracting them out of their communities, workers need to help Thai people discover living for Jesus within their own naturally formed and existing communities, helping them to discover for themselves what it means to "come out from among them" while remaining within as much as possible (2 Cor 6:17, 1 Cor 7:24).

The Holy Spirit Makes The Difference

In looking at what is means to be a Spirit empowered follower of Jesus, we must first start with a Biblical understanding of what it means for the Holy Spirit to take up residence in each believer and endow them with different gifts and graces (*charis*). The indwelling and empowerment of the Holy Spirit distinguishes the followers of Jesus from all other people on the face of the earth. This subject transcends the Charismatic vs. non-Charismatic divide.

> A very important first step in contextualizing spiritual power, therefore, is to help people know who they are scripturally and how this is to be expressed culturally. Scripturally, we are the children of God, made in his image, redeemed by Jesus Christ to be heirs of God and joint heirs with him (Rom 8:17). This gives

us all the power and authority Jesus gave his followers to cast out demons and cure diseases (Luke 9:1), to do the works Jesus himself did (John 14:12), to be in the world what Jesus was (John 20:21) and to crush the enemy under our feet (Rom 16:20). Scripturally then, we need to follow Jesus' example, always using his power to show his love. (Kraft 2005, 378)

We will touch on the contextualizing of spiritual power in the next section, but we will start building out the identity of every follower of Jesus below.

The Spirit of His Son In The Heart of Every Believer

The Bible clearly portrays the intrinsic worth and glory of each and every disciple of Jesus. We are brought from a position of slaves to that of sons and daughters. Each and every true follower of Jesus, God has made him a joint heir together with Christ. "And because we are his children, God has sent the Spirit of his Son into our hearts, prompting us to call out, 'Abba, Father.' Now you are no longer a slave but God's own child. And since you are his child, God has made you his heir" (Galatians 4:6–7). "Now if we are children, then we are heirs—heirs of God and co-heirs with Christ, if indeed we share in his sufferings in order that we may also share in his glory" (Rom 8:17).

A Kingdom of Priests for God

The Bible clearly portrays that each and every disciple of Jesus is a priest. The special clerical class seen in denominations is a carry over from the Old Testament model of the High Priest. However, Jesus has become our final high priest and has made us a kingdom of priests that offer up spiritual sacrifices that are acceptable to God. "And you are living stones that God is building into his spiritual temple. What's more, you are his holy priests. Through the mediation of Jesus Christ, you offer spiritual sacrifices that please God" (1 Peter 2:5 NIV). "But our High Priest offered himself to God as a single sacrifice for sins, good for all time. Then he sat down in the place of honor at God's right hand" (Heb 10:12 NLT). "He has made us a Kingdom of priests for God his Father. All glory and power to him forever and ever! Amen"

(Rev 1:6 NLT). "And you have caused them to become a Kingdom of priests for our God. And they will reign on the earth" (Rev 6:10 NLT).

Signs Accompanying the Proclamation of the Believers

"And the disciples went everywhere and preached, and the Lord worked through them, confirming what they said by many miraculous signs (Mark 16:20 NLT). These miraculous signs will accompany those who believe: They will cast out demons in my name, and they will speak in new languages. They will be able to handle snakes with safety, and if they drink anything poisonous, it won't hurt them. They will be able to place their hands on the sick, and they will be healed (Mark 16:17–18 NLT).

For those who may be getting a little worried at this point, the "snake handling" mentioned in the verse above does not refer to the antics of some rural minority American Pentecostal groups who test the Lord by handling venomous snakes, but its veracity is seen in the context of real ministry when the Apostle Paul is bitten by a viper and suffers no ill effects while serving the Lord on the island of Malta. The protection from poison also falls under this very practical example (Acts 28:3–5). It should be noted that miraculous signs in this verse include casting out demons and healing the sick as normative for the broad category of "believers."

Stephen and Philip: Powerful "Laymen"

The New Testament example of Stephen is one of how God used an average man, not an Apostle, to work in signs, miracles, and wonders. Stephen was said to be "a man full of faith and of the Holy Spirit." (Acts 6:5 NIV) The Bible says, "Now Stephen, a man full of God's grace and power, performed great wonders and signs among the people" (Acts 6:8 NIV).

After Stephen, we find another non-Apostle, Philip, performing signs such as casting out evil spirits. "When the crowds heard Philip and saw the signs he performed, they all paid close attention to what he said. For with shrieks, impure spirits came out of many, and many who were paralyzed or lame were healed" (Acts 8:6–7). Philip, another "layman" baptized a sorcerer who was impressed with the signs and wonders that followed him. "He followed Philip everywhere, astonished by the great signs and miracles he saw" (Acts 8:13).

"When Simon saw that the Spirit was given at the laying on of the apostles' hands (Peter and John), he offered them money and said, 'Give me also this ability so that everyone on whom I lay my hands may receive the Holy Spirit'" (Acts 8:18–19). Something was physically happening to those who received the Holy Spirit, so much so that Simon reverted to his sorcerer ways and attempted to buy the gift of God with money. Peter demonstrated that a person of power in God's economy does not minister in the supernatural to become wealthy (2 Peter 2).

You May All Prophesy

Philip had four unmarried daughters who prophesied (Acts 21:8–9). This passage is a great example of how the New Testament affirms ministry in regards to both age and gender, especially those without any official titles or positions. These girls were simply young daughters operating out of Joel 2:28–29, which I believe is still normative for today. "And afterward, I will pour out my Spirit on all people. Your sons and daughters will prophesy, your old men will dream dreams. Your young men will see visions. Even on my servants, both men and women, I will pour out my Spirit in those days."

This verse even goes beyond age and gender to include social status. Zehner points out that "we are missing out on a lot of potential power, creativity, and insight in mission by overlooking the wisdom of those who are deemed to be 'poor' and of 'low estate' in terms of their financial resources, social ranking, formal education, or international visibility" (2010, 85). The Holy Spirit's empowerment in the life of the believer is what makes the difference and levels the ministry playing field.

Prophecy in the New Testament was seen as normative for all believers and was to be used for edification, exhortation, and comfort. "But the one who prophesies speaks to people for their strengthening, encouraging and comfort" (I Cor 14:3). All believers were encouraged to earnestly desire and seek after spiritual gifts. "Follow the way of love and eagerly desire gifts of the Spirit, especially prophecy" (I Cor 14:1). The instruction to all believers gathering together then was that they could all prophesy. "For you can all prophesy in turn so that everyone may be instructed and encouraged."

New Testament prophecy, combined with what seems to be a word of knowledge, served an evangelistic purpose in house church gatherings. "But if an unbeliever or an inquirer comes in while everyone is prophesying, they are convicted of sin and are brought under judgment by all, as the secrets of their hearts are laid bare. So they will fall down and worship God, exclaiming, "God is really among you!" (1 Cor 14:24–25). All of this New Testament evidence points to the supernatural ministry potential of each and every believer and is essential for work in supernaturally oriented cultures like the Thai.

Power and Authority As Fruits of Redemption

The Scriptures demonstrate that every believer in Jesus has access to Christ's power and authority by faith, just as we have been granted justification by faith.

> Colossians 2:15 includes the triumph of Christ over the powers of darkness among the fruits of redemption, and the New Testament makes clear that our union with Christ gives us authority to execute the judgment he accomplished by displacing the powers of darkness from our lives and from the field of our ministry, just as justification, sanctification and the indwelling Spirit helps us to displace sin."
>
> These four benefits of redemption-justification, sanctification, the indwelling of the Spirit and authority in spiritual conflict-are normally encompassed in theological treatments of the atonement, and they might be called primary elements in the dynamics of spiritual life." (Lovelace 1979, 77)

Many Protestant workers in Thailand emphasize the doctrine of justification by faith through the atonement, but here Lovelace points out that the indwelling of the Spirit and authority in spiritual conflict are also included in treatments of the atonement and are called "primary elements in the dynamics of spiritual life." I would add that they are primary elements in the dynamics of every day spiritual life, for each and every believer!

Meekness in Thai Culture and Spiritual Power

When we talk about Spiritual power within the Southeast Asian context, especially among the Thai, some may be concerned that the exercise of spiritual power is antithetical to the Thai culture, which values coolness and meekness as primary virtues (O'Sullivan, K. and Tajaroensuk, S. 1997). However this does not have to be the case.

The nine-fold gifts of the Holy Spirit mentioned in 1 Cor 12:8–10 are balanced by the nine-fold fruits of the Holy Spirit outlined in Gal 5:22–23. These fruits include "agape" love as outlined in 1 Cor 13 as well as gentleness and meekness. 1 Cor 13 speaks of love not being proud or puffed up. In Matt 11:28–30, Jesus describes himself as meek. In Matt 5:5, he calls his followers to meekness. Even teachers are called to be meek and gentle when correcting those who are in opposition (2 Tim 2:25).

However, some mistakenly understand meekness as weakness. Though they sound similar in the English language, they are not the same. Jesus demonstrated power through his meekness. He healed the sick, raised the dead, cast out demons and called his followers to do the same (Matt 10:8). He was on a mission to destroy the works of the devil (I John 3:8) and sent out his followers to do the same (John 14:12).

I believe the proper balance of the call to walk in power and meekness can be seen in the passage Luke 10:17–20,

> The seventy-two returned with joy and said, "Lord, even the demons submit to us in your name." He replied, "I saw Satan fall like lightning from heaven. I have given you authority to trample on snakes and scorpions and to overcome all the power of the enemy; nothing will harm you. *However,* do not rejoice that the spirits submit to you, but rejoice that your names are written in heaven.

It is important that we understand that Biblical power demonstrated within the Thai context should not be loud and brash, but rather it should coincide with the nine-fold fruits of the Spirit, which includes Biblical love (I Cor 13), gentleness, and meekness. I agree with Nantachai Mejudhon's assessment, "A meek approach is not a 'weak' approach. It is rather a biblical approach" (Mejudhon 2005, 176).

Examples of abuses of spiritual power have been cited when followers of Jesus have uncritically used the methods of shamans and have sought to bring about healing and deliverance by using dramatic displays, loudness, manipulation, and even violence (Kraft, 2005: 376).

True power does not require a loud voice or shouting. It does not have to call attention to itself. It can be demonstrated in joy, with laughter, and in a spirit of gentleness and still remain just as supernatural. Shouting or manipulation demonstrates that we believe that the power is from us. The power is not of us, but rather it is available to us. The Apostle Paul says, "But we have this treasure in jars of clay to show that this all-surpassing power is from God and not from us" (2 Cor 4:7). If there is any power demonstrated through the believer, it is imperative that we understand and humbly acknowledge that the power is from God, not us, taking no glory for ourselves (Acts 3:12–13).

Humility is seen then when we are absolutely dependent on God, but still confident enough to serve others through supernatural ministry such as revelation (word of wisdom, word of knowledge, discerning of spirits), power (faith, gifts of healing, working of miracles), or vocal (prophecy, tongues, interpretation of tongues) (1 Cor 12:8–10).

Thai Women As Spiritual Power Brokers

The spiritual "power brokers" of the Thai culture are the Brahmins, mediums, and fortunetellers. Some special Buddhist monks are also sought for their spiritual powers. The uniqueness of the mediums and fortunetellers in Thai culture is that they can be male or female, young or old, wealthy or poor.

The incoming of a "spirit" levels the playing field when it comes to being a "power broker" in the Thai culture. This is especially true for women.

> "Popular Buddhism in Thailand is a large-scale, cross-social spectrum of beliefs and practices–incorporating the supernatural power of spirit, deity, and magic–that have emerged out of the interplay between animism, supernaturalism, folk Brahmanism, the worship of Chinese deities, and state-sponsored

Theravada Buddhism," with its boundaries extending as far as it can be commercialized. (Kitiarsa 2012, 2)

Mediums who act as mouthpieces for deities are often popularized in mass media, as are magic monks who use mantras, magic, and amulets (Kitiarsa, 2012, 40). While both men and women may go to magic monks for assistance, spirit-medium cults, according to Kitiarsa, have become a refuge for many women. As monkhood offers social mobility to men, mediumship offers a type of mobility for women. Further, Kitiarsa writes,

> urban spirit-medium cults, rather than positioning themselves as an alternative to mainstream Buddhist practices, have emerged as a moral and psychological refuge for an urban population, primarily women, who are disoriented, frustrated, and often struggling to survive on the margins of poverty and battling the hardships of urban life. (2012, 146)

The potential model of Holy Spirit empowered women on mission with God can be both an answer to the needs of the Thai woman's heart as well as those she serves. By making space for Thai women to receive confidence in God as well as Spiritual empowerment and release for service, a mighty harvest force can be released into every village and home throughout the country.

The potential for massive impact through the mobilization and empowering of Thai women can be seen through the work of Victor and Bindu Choudhrie's house church network in India. They teach that the recognition and valuation of women—in anything and everything that is done by the men, from apostolic leadership to the baptism of new believers—is vital to the rapid spread of Jesus' Kingdom in India and many other nations around the world (Butler 2011). It is these kind of foundational assumptions and practices of empowerment, I believe, that either unleashes or hinders a movement. The movement in Thailand is still far behind in this area, but I have seen encouraging signs from the field.

I want to share just a couple of recent stories to emphasize what I have been saying so far. This first testimony, which I received by a Thai friend via email, is from a Thai lady named Kanchana.

Kanchana: I used to be a spirit medium, and God freed me from the evil spirit that had authority over my life.

Interviewer: Before you came to know Jesus, you would've experienced supernatural powers. How was the power of Jesus different than the power that is in you before?

Kanchana: When I had an experience with the power of God and the Holy Spirit, it made me happy, it gave me peace, and I wasn't afraid anymore. I felt warm, and it's like a spirit that is pure unlike the spirit I had when I was a spirit medium. Those spirits, I was afraid of. I didn't want them to control me, because once they control me, I would do the things that I didn't want to do. So I thought "How can I be free from this power?" Once I found God's power and God's authority, His spirit is clean, and there's no fear in it at all. It helped me to know that God's power is great. It is true, it is pure, and the closer and nearer I draw, the happier I become. For the other spirits, the closer I get, the worse it feels. It is something that is horrible, and I was living in constant fear.

This story demonstrates how a Thai woman experienced the power of the Holy Spirit and how that experience contrasted with her former experience as a spirit medium. Her experience moved her from fear to faith, from an unclean to pure, and from Satan's power and authority to God's power and authority.

I have personally experienced firsthand the testimonies of what some traditions may consider "laymen" Thai believers who have been empowered by the Holy Spirit. From the story of the poor Thai pig farmer who raised his neighbor from the dead in Jesus' name to the divorced woman down the street who raised her friend's baby from the dead through fervent prayer offered in Jesus' name, each incident bears witness that Jesus is still alive and working powerfully through common every day people who dare to take him at his Word. There are many other less dramatic testimonies of farmers and housewives praying for the sick and seeing them recover and walking in Christ's authority to intercede for and bless their families and neighbors. Jesus is the same yesterday, today, and forever, (Hebrews 13:8) and he is no respecter of persons (Acts 10:34, Rom 2:11).

One Thai leader with whom I am a friend recently testified,

> We have seen the Holy Spirit moving among the believers when they read the Bible and practice daily repentance; reconciliation and mutual understanding takes place in the household, workplace, and community. They lay hands on the sick and they are healed, the dead come back to life, even animals with broken legs stand up and walk, and plants that had been eaten by bugs are mended. They stop stealing and lying, and instead tell each other the truth. They are people of faith. All of this happens because Jesus is building them to be the church and the Holy Spirit is their teacher. (Serithai 2014, 34)

Strategic Implementation

Does Thai Folk Buddhism, and other belief systems like it, have something to teach us? What are the needs that caused animistic believers to seek solutions in the first place?

> Perhaps what Thai Folk Buddhism can best teach cross-cultural workers who seek to follow and communicate Christ, is the recognition of the reality of the power found in the spirit world. I Corinthians 4:20 says, "For the kingdom of God is not just a matter of fancy talk; it is living by God's power" (NLT). It was because of a need for power that many sought out animistic practices in the first place. What is the attitude of the cross-cultural worker to be? (DeNeui 2002, 21)

What should we do in response to these realities? Have we been given the tools we need to face these obstacles and challenges? I believe so. Here are just a few summary suggestions:

- Recognize and teach all new believers the implications of the indwelling and empowerment of the Holy Spirit and what it means to them personally (Acts 1:8–9).
- Lead them to the Word and teach new believers to demonstrate power through the paradigm of love, humility, and meekness, acknowledging that the power is of God, not us (1 Cor 13, 2 Cor 4:7).
- Teach believers to earnestly desire spiritual gifts and to seek God for them (1 Cor 14:1, 1 Cor 12:31).
- Take every opportunity to exercise the power of the Spirit by praying for the sick, demonized, and oppressed and by proclaiming God's blessing in ways that are meaningful within the culture (Mk 16:17–19).
- As leaders and "patrons," take every opportunity to demonstrate the servant nature of Christ's power by serving those of perceived lower status, expecting nothing in return (Matt 20: 25–28, Acts 8:20).
- Don't grieve the Holy Spirit (Eph 4:30, 1 Tim 4:12) but lead by example in devotion, prayer, and a set apart life in the Spirit.
- Don't quench the Holy Spirit or despise prophecy but test all things and hold fast to the good (I Thess 19:20–21). Don't forbid speaking in tongues (1 Cor 14:39).
- Empower all believers, including women and youth, to baptize and lead in the Lord's Supper or Communion (1 Peter 2:5, Rev 1:6, Rev 5:10).
- Prepare believers to stand firm when they are suffering for their faith and not seeing answers to their prayers by helping them to understand the realities of faith, prayer, Spiritual warfare, and God's sovereignty. (Whole books can be written on this!)
- Finally, remember that humility releases power in others. Make it your main goal as a leader to equip the every day people of God (saints) for the work of the ministry, the good works that God has prepared in advance for them to do, and teach to be careful to maintain their ministry

and bear fruit (Eph 4:11–12, Eph 2:10, Titus 3:8, John 15:8).

CONCLUSION

As missionary scholars, practitioners, and national church leaders have surveyed the history the Gospel's progress in the Thai context, many have lamented the slow growth of the Church in Thailand. In searching for answers, some have looked to a great breakthrough that is happening in other parts of the world through what many have called "church planting movements" or "disciple making movements." These movements to Jesus are marked by great multiplication of new believers in a relatively short amount of time.

Others have sought to apply contextualization principles in order to help build bridges in communication so that the Gospel could be understood in the context of a specific worldview and culture. Some workers have blended both multiplication movement principles and various levels of contextualization and seen fruit from their endeavors. Both national leaders and missionaries have sought at various times to apply certain strategies with little to no success. These unsuccessful attempts have inoculated many to believe that certain approaches will simply "not work here."

But there is something more foundational in our efforts that we are missing when we seek to simply mimic what we see others doing in mission without understanding some of the basic assumptions and worldviews that make these movements successful. It has been demonstrated that there are some basic assumptions that are critical to seeing these movements happen emerge. If the issues related to spiritual power and identity are not understood and incorporated into discipleship, breakthrough in contexts like Thailand will be not be accelerated and will continue to be hindered.

There are key foundational issues that have to do with identity that must be addressed and incorporated into initial discipleship as foundational before we are going to see new multiplicative movements to Jesus in Thailand. The author has sought demonstrate that a majority of Thai followers of Jesus are not being empowered, but are stuck in static ecclesiastical systems build on clergy-laity distortions that hinder the ministries that have been given to each believer.

It is the will of God for each and every believer to live as a person of power, operating beyond his or her natural abilities, gender, age, and place in society. Through the supernatural gifts and graces of the indwelling Spirit, God desires for each of his people to live empowered and on mission with him.

I believe we are on the verge of a massive movement of empowering the other 98 percent of nonprofessional ministers, the every day "saints"—young and old, male and female, rich and poor, successful and marginalized. It will not be a movement that looks best from the stage, but a movement that is found in the streets and villages-in the daily lives of common people empowered by the Spirit, formed in contextual community life, and released by leaders as people of power. It is my ultimate hope that leaders be raised up who believe this and incorporate it into their own lives and ministries, for the sake of the advancement of the Kingdom among the Thai and beyond.

REFERENCES

Anderson, Allan. 2012. Towards a Pentecostal missiology for the majority world. In *Azusa Street and beyond: Missional commentary on the global Pentecostal/Charismatic movement.* Revised Edition. Ed. Grant McClung, Alachua: Bridge-Logos.

Boon-Itt, Bantoon and Mali. 2011. What is being communicated to Buddhists? In *Suffering: Christian reflections on Buddhist Dukkha,* ed. Paul H. de Neui, Pasadena: William Carey Publishers.

Borthwick, Paul. 2012. *Western Christians in global mission: What's the role of the American church?* Downers Grove: IVP Books.

Butler, Robby. 2011. Church planting movements from one Indian perspective. http://www.missionfrontiers.org/issue/article/church-planting-movements-from-one-indian-perspective

Brown, Michael L. 2014. *Authentic fire: A response to John MacArthur's strange fire.* Lake Mary: Excel.

Chan, Francis. 2009. *Forgotten God: Reversing our tragic neglect of the Holy Spirit.* Colorado Springs: David C. Cook

Chumsriphan, Surachai. 2002. "A brief history of The Catholic Church in Thailand." In Newsletter of the District of Asia.

Davies, John. 1998. *Poles apart*. Bangalore. Theological Book Trust.

De Neui, Paul H. 2002. Contextualizing with Thai folk Buddhists. http://www.thaicrc.com/collect/MIS/index/assoc/D4113.dir/4113.pdf.

Emerson, Everett H. 1990. *John Cotton* (2 ed.). New York: Twayne Publishers.

Garrison, David. 2004. *Church planting movements: How God is redeeming a lost world*. Arkadelphia: WIGTake Resources.

Gustafson, James W. 2009. Pigs, ponds, and the Gospel. In *Perspectives on the World Christian movement: a reader*, 4th edition. Eds. Winter, Ralph D., and Steven C. Hawthorne, Pasadena: William Carey Publishers.

Hyatt, Eddie L. 2002. *2000 years of charismatic Christianity*. Lake Mary: Charisma House.

Hosack, James. 2001. A history of the Pentecostal and Charismatic movements in Thailand.http://thaimissions.info/gsdl/collect/thaimiss/index/assoc/HASH4ffa.dir/doc.pdf.

Jamieson, Robert, Fausset, A. R., and Brown, David. 1871. Notes on 1 Cor 3. http://www.biblestudytools.com/commentaries/jamieson-fausset-brown/.

Johnson, Alan. 2002. Wrapping the good news for the Thai: Some suggestions for a contextualized presentation of the Gospel in Thai society. http://www.thaicrc.com/collect/MIS/index/assoc/D1783.dir/1783.pdf.

Kitiarsa, Pattana. 2012. *Mediums, Monks, and Amulets: Thai popular Buddhism today*. Chiang Mai: Silkworm Books.

Kraft, Charles H. 2005. *Appropriate Christianity*. Pasadena: William Carey Library.

Lovelace, Richard F. 1979. *Dynamics of spiritual life: An Evangelical theology of renewal*. Downer's Grove: Inter-varsity Press.

Mejudhon, Nantachai. 2005. Meekness: a new approach to Christian witness to the Thai people. In *Sharing Jesus effectively in the Buddhist world*. eds. Lim, David, Spaulding, Steve, and De Neui, Paul. Pasadena: William Carey Library.

Metaxis, Eric. 2014. *Miracles: What they are, why they happen, and how they can change your life*. New York: Penguin Group.

O'Sullivan, K. and Tajaroensuk, S. 1997. *Thailand: a handbook in intercultural communication*. Sydney: Macquarie University.

Petchsongkram, Wan . 1975. *Talk in the shade of the Bo Tree*. Bangkok http://thaicrc.com/gsdl/collect/MIS/index/assoc/D1729. dir/1729.pdf.

Prometta, Tongpan. 2000. Jesus must be reborn. DeNeui, Paul, trans. http://www.thaicov.org/resources/contextualize/reborn1_4. html.

Saiyasak, Chansamone. 2007. *A study of the belief systems and decision making of the Isan people of northeast Thailand with a view towards making use of these insights in Christian evangelism*. Evangelische Theologische Faculteit te Heverlee (Leuven), België.

Serithai, Jiraphon. 2014. God of the Thai: How one movement overcomes the perception of a foreign God. *Mission Frontiers* 36, no. 6.

Swanson, Herb. 2003. The Finnish free foreign mission and the origins of Pentecostalism in Thailand, 1946–1960. http://www.thaicrc. com/gsdl/collect/MIS/index/assoc/D4891.dir/4891.pdf.

Taylor, Steve. 2014. A challenge for the Thai church. http://www. missionfrontiers.org/issue/article/church.

Thai Church History in Global Context. An Interactive Timeline. http://interactivetimeline.com/2048/thai-church-history-in-global-context/.

Trading Economics. World Bank Statistics on Thailand. http://www. tradingeconomics.com/thailand/rural-population-percent-of-total-population-wb-data.html.

Travis, John, and Anna. 2013. Roles of "alongsiders" in insider movements: contemporary examples and biblical reflections. http://www.ijfm.org/PDFs_IJFM/30_4_PDFs/IJFM_30_4-Travis.pdf.

Unicef Statistics on Thailand. Demographic indicators. Population annual growth rate (%). http://www.unicef.org/infobycountry/ Thailand_statistics.html.

Wetchgama, Banpote. 2014. "The new Buddhists: How Buddhists can follow Christ." *Mission Frontiers* 36, no. 6.

Visser, M. 2008. Conversion growth of the Protestant churches in Thailand, Uitgeverij Boekencentrum, Zoetermeer (The Netherlands)

Zehner, Edwin. 2003. Unavoidably hybrid: Thai Buddhist conversions to Evangelical Christianity, unpublished PhD dissertation, Cornell University.

INDEX

3/11, 195
  post-3/11, 193

A

Aaron, 52–53
Abeel, David M., 279
Abraham, 51, 93, 137
Adam, 54, 116, 266
Africa, 7, 169
  African, 169, 246
  East, 168
America(n). *See* United States of
  America
ancestor, 58, 71–72, 75, 87, 91,
  124–27, 129–39, 148, 150,
  218–19, 266–67, 270
  altar, 133–35
  dead, 126
  graves, 125–26, 138
  pagan, 87
  spirits, 255
  veneration, 72, 123–31, 133–37,
    139–40
  worship, 52, 126–31, 135–36,
    138, 218

Anderson, Neil, 83
animism, 27, 37, 50, 57, 80, 92,
  123, 141, 151, 163, 206–8,
  212, 216, 218, 221, 226,
  255–57, 259
Arnold, Clinton, 30
Asia, 6, 43–44, 51, 63, 91, 93–94,
  104, 113, 132, 151
  Asian, 101, 103, 105, 108–13,
    117, 130, 139
  Central, 160
  East, 126, 132
  South, 231
  Southeast, 175
  Central, 49
assimilation, 45, 123, 128, 130,
  207
astrology, 26, 44, 57, 74, 157,
  159, 164, 219, 221, 227–28,
  231–32, 234–35, 261, 269
Aung, Maung Htin, 256, 269
Australia, 28

B

Baal, 21

Bangkok, 33
baptism, 29, 33, 37, 43–44, 74, 79, 136, 197, 233
Bavinck, J. H., 87
Bawden, C. R., 49
Beckett, Bob, 84–85
Beyer, Stephan, 157–58
biblical
  analysis, 51
  evidence, 239, 247
  faithfulness, 135–36, 138
  imagery, 3, 10, 13
  spirituality, 88
  text, 79
  truth, 27
  understanding, 30
Boyd, Gregory, 5, 37
Brahmin, 54, 143
Brazil, 43
Buddhism
  basic beliefs, 107–8
  Buddha, 44–45, 50, 54–57, 60, 73–76, 105–6, 108, 129–31, 135, 143–44, 146–47, 157–58, 174, 176–80, 182–83, 187, 200–202, 208, 210, 212, 214–15, 217, 222–23, 225–26, 231, 241–42, 256–57, 259, 261, 272
  Buddhist
    background believers, 60, 187
    jihad, 56
    monk, 43, 50, 74–76, 80, 129–30, 146, 157, 181–82,

185, 187, 224–25, 234
    view of person or self, 105, 108
    five aggregates, 105, 107
  worship, 28, 183–84, 222
  classical, 45, 56, 213
  core worldview, 208–9
  folk, 26, 29, 35, 37, 43–45, 48, 56–57, 59, 62, 64–65, 69, 90–91, 94, 143, 205–7, 209, 212, 214, 219, 221, 226, 231, 235–36, 243, 245, 252, 258, 265, 273
  theories of, 54
Burma, 77, 257
Burmese, 44, 77, 181, 255–62, 264–65, 267–70, 272–74
Buyandelger, Manduhai, 49

C
Calvin, John, 44
Calvinistic Presbyterians, 283
Cambodia, 175, 207
Cantwell, Cathy, 160
Central America, 6
cessationist, 282–84, 286
Chan, Francis, 33
Chan, Kim Kwong, 87
Charlemagne, 6
Charoenwongsak, Kriengsak, 287
China, 25, 43, 54, 74, 87, 89–91, 93, 124, 129–30, 132–33, 155–56, 161–62, 164
Chinese, 25, 54, 69–72, 74, 87, 90, 94, 110, 124, 130,

132–33, 155–56, 161–65
folk Chinese worldview, 71
Chinese Rites Controversy,
    132–33
Christ-centered communities
    (CCCs), 69–70, 80–82, 85–94
Christendom, 6–7, 93
Christianity, 6, 36, 48, 72, 78,
    87–88, 90, 93–94, 126, 128,
    130, 145, 151–52, 173, 175–
    78, 184–85, 187, 189, 197–98,
    201, 246–47, 257, 263–64,
    269–70, 272
Christology, 70, 80, 85, 94
clergy, 301
Clinton, J. Robert, 250
collectivism, 102–3
commercialism, 129
community development, 81
    and C-5 strategies, 91
Confucianism, 72, 90, 110, 124,
    130
Confucius, 89, 130, 132–33
Congo, 7
contextualization, 27, 91
conversion, 6, 9, 58, 69, 81, 86–87,
    152, 187, 203, 207, 239–42,
    244, 246, 250
    convert, 58, 60, 79, 81, 86–88,
        90, 92, 113, 135–36, 175,
        185, 198, 234–35, 241, 243–
        44, 246, 249–50, 272–73
cosmology, 44, 73, 82, 205,
    209–11, 217, 259
Cultural Revolution, 155, 162

culture
    cultural types, 103, 116
    social dimensions, 103
    Strong Community cultures,
        103–5, 108–10, 112, 117
    group harmony, 104
    Weak Community cultures,
        103–4, 117

D

Daniel, 59, 85
Daoism, 72
David, 21
Dawson, John, 84–85
de las Casas, Bartolomé, 6
De Rhodes, Alexander, 133
deities, 51, 57, 71, 74, 79, 126, 129,
    131, 143, 148, 157, 159–60,
    164, 175, 183, 210–12,
    214–16, 218–19, 223–24,
    228–30, 234
demon, evil spirit, 25–26, 29, 34,
    47, 558, 73–78, 82–84, 86, 88,
    143, 153, 159–60, 175, 197,
    205–7, 209, 212–21, 224–29,
    232–33, 235, 240, 251, 258–59
    possession, 26, 142, 197, 219,
        228–29, 233
demonology, 73–74, 78, 82, 207,
    216
dGelugpa, 157–58, 163
Dhammananda, K. Sri, 56–57
discipleship, 25, 31, 33–35, 75, 80,
    93, 249–52
divination, 45, 47–52, 54, 57,
    71–72, 159, 164, 231–32, 235

Donovan, Vincent J., 268
Driver, John, 11
dualism, 102
  nondualism, 76

E
Eastern, 101–3, 105, 11, 113, 127
  Easterner, 111–14
ecclesiology, 70, 88, 94
Egypt, 51, 58
Eightfold Path, 55, 75, 106–7, 176
Einstein, Albert, 77, 145–46
Eliade, Mircea, 167
Elijah, 21
En, Khan, 256, 265, 271
enlightenment, 51, 55, 76, 105, 129,
  157–58, 208, 217, 222, 245
Europe, 6, 44
  European, 6, 101
evangelical, 3, 19, 83, 87, 126,
  135–36, 173, 175, 235, 273
Evangelical Fellowship of
  Thailand, 281
evangelism, 33, 78, 85, 91, 138,
  176, 203, 249, 251–52, 264
  extraction, 81
  friendship. *See* friendship
    evangelism (FE)
Eve, 54
exorcism, 73–76, 78, 82, 220,
  226–29, 235
Ezra, 85

F
Fiddes, Paul S., 270
filial piety, 124
Filipino, 69, 71–72

Folk Buddhism, 285, 298
fortune-telling, 43–44, 46–48, 51,
  57, 62–64, 142, 146, 164–65,
  196, 260
Four Noble Truths, 55, 107, 174,
  176, 179
France, 6, 9
Frazer, James, 49
friendship evangelism (FE), 70,
  72, 75, 88, 94

G
Gautama, Siddhartha, 55, 174
Germany, 43
Gideon, 52
gifts of the spirit, 283
Gombrich, Richard, 206, 232
Granberg-Michaelson, Wesley, 59
Great Commandment, 89
Great Commission, 26, 203
Green, Michael, 263
Greig, Gary, 240
Grudem, Wayne, 240
gifts of the spirit, 282–88, 292

H
Haman, 53
Hare, John, 48
healing, 26, 34, 76, 82–84, 92,
  164, 221, 224, 228–30, 235,
  239–43, 247gifts of the spir-
  it49, 270
Hellenism, 244
heresy, 80, 86
Heskett, James, 7
Hiebert, Paul, 37, 45, 64, 71

Hinduism, 26, 208, 216, 245, 247, 252, 256
Hindu, 10, 19, 54, 189, 208, 221, 231, 244, 256
Holy Spirit, 283, 285–87, 291–94, 296–99
Hong Kong, 90
Hope Churches, 287
Horton, Robin, 246
Hunter, A., 87

I

identity, 35, 38, 73, 83, 86, 102, 105, 112–13, 141, 168, 173, 207, 246–48
    cultural, 30, 87
idolatry, 52, 79, 126, 131–32, 134
imperialism, 6
India, 69, 164, 209, 222, 256
    Indian, 73, 207, 211–12
    South, 215
indigenous, 46, 62–63, 72, 80, 86–87, 92, 123–24, 129, 137–38, 163, 216, 218, 221, 257
    leadership, 80
    religion, 128, 133, 137, 259, 264
individualism, 102
Indonesia, 69
injustice, 37, 73
inner-city, 62
Isaan, 26–31, 33–35, 37–38, 148
Islam, 48, 72, 245–47, 252
Israel, 5, 30, 51–52, 58, 92–93, 137
    Israelite, 21, 58, 248

J

Jacobs, Cindy, 84

Japan, 60, 91, 132–33, 193–96, 198–200
Japanese, 55, 74, 133, 195–98, 202–3
Jerusalem, 52–53, 93
Jesuit, 132
Jesus
    Ancestorship, 265–66
    Liberator, 264, 267–69, 274
    prnboto-Ancestor, 266–67
Jobson, Orville D., 4
John the Baptist, 32
Johnson, Paul, 10
Jonah, 52
Joseph, 59
Joshua, 53
Josiah, 52
Judaism, 48
    Jewish, 27, 38–39, 189, 244
Judas Iscariot, 53
Judson, Adoniram, 255
Jung, Karl, 167–68
justice, 212, 265

K

Kalachakra Tantra, 56
Kapferer, Bruce, 221, 229, 234
karma, 44–45, 54–56, 59, 73, 107–8, 110–11, 127, 131, 176, 179, 219, 245, 250
Karunatillake, W. S., 211, 231
Kateragama, 208
Keener, Craig, 248
Kellner-Rogers, Myron, 76
King of Pasenadi, 56
kingdom of God, 29, 31–32, 34, 37–39, 65, 88, 195–96, 272

Kinnison, Jack, 37
Ko, Taw Sein, 256
Korea
    Korean, 74
Kotter, John, 7
Kraft, Charles, 82, 84, 166, 240

L

lama, 43–44, 48–49, 74, 157, 159, 164
layperson, 279
Laos, 141, 175
Larson, Bruce, 35
liturgy, 89, 135

M

magic, 35, 45–46, 57–58, 63–64,
    71–72, 142–45, 147–48,
    166–67, 225, 227, 255, 260,
    295–96
magician, 46, 57
Mahayana, 74, 129
Malinowski, Bronislaw, 46, 166
Mara, 73–74, 76, 215, 218, 232
Masai, 268
materialism, 26
Maxwell, L. E., 4
McGavran, Donald, 6, 69
mediums. *See* magic
Milarepa, 76
military, 5–7, 17, 161, 261–62
    imagery, 15–16, 19
    model, 4, 7, 17
Minear, Paul S., 11, 13
ministry, 28, 33–34, 40, 58,
    61, 70, 82, 86, 89, 92, 101,
    111–13, 116, 151–52, 195–96,
    235, 239, 241, 247, 249–50,

265–66
cross-cultural, 27, 249
miracles, 37, 151, 197, 239–40,
    243, 246–47, 249
mixed response, 239, 243, 247,
    249
missiology, 70, 94, 240
mission
    agencies, 5, 8, 17, 20–21
    organizations, 5, 7, 19–20
    burnout, 19
Mission Aviation Fellowship, 8
missional religiosity, (MR),
    89–90
missionary, 4–5, 7, 18–19, 21, 33,
    35, 37, 43, 58, 69–70, 90, 92,
    132–33, 203, 249, 255, 268
    short-term, 134
    workers, 20
Mongolia, 43, 48, 51
    Mongolian, 44, 48–50
Moses, 52, 59, 248
mullah, 48
Muller, M., 205
Muslim, 10, 19, 48, 56, 69, 189,
    198, 244
Mustard Seed, 8, 223
Myanmar, 43–44, 69, 91, 175,
    255–59, 261–64, 266–72, 274
Myint, Saya, 259

N

Nagasena, 57
Nat worship, 255–66, 268–74
Ndembu, 168–69
Nehemiah, 85
Nevius, John, 25–26

New Age, 76, 197
New Testament, 4–5, 11, 13, 16, 20–21, 26, 53, 92, 137, 240, 244, 251, 263
nirvana, 44–45, 55, 106–8, 176, 179
Northeast Thailand, 284
Nyunt, 258–59, 267

O

Obeyesekere, Gananath, 206, 219–20, 229–30, 232
Old Testament, 21, 53, 92, 137, 244, 251, 263
Oliver, Roland, 7
oral learners, 25, 27–29, 31–32, 35, 38–40
    tradition, 27
Otis, George Jr., 84
Ott, Craig, 136
outreach, 20, 113, 128, 131

P

pagan, 87, 90
Pali, 74, 176, 182, 187, 209–10, 222–24, 255, 267
panentheism, 78
Passiko, Ehi, 56
Paul, 13, 16, 19, 21, 59, 79, 86, 92, 178, 263, 266–67, 272
Pentecost, 39, 93
Pentecostal, 75, 82, 84, 93, 173, 233, 235, 239, 241
Pentecostal-Charismatic movement, 277, 282–84, 287–89
people movements (PMs), 69, 80, 91–92, 94

Persia, 52
Petchsongkram, Wan, 287
Peter, 13, 32, 38–39, 86, 248
Phan, Peter, 134
Philemon, 13
Philippines
    Filipino, 69, 71–72
Piper, John, 4
Plato, 102
Platt, David, 39
Portugal, 6
Pott, P. H., 163
"power brokers," 295
power encounters (PEs), 69, 73, 75, 83, 94, 152, 186, 240
Protestant, 6, 124, 131, 135–36, 140, 142–43, 173, 194–95, 242, 255
    Vietnamese Protestant approach to ancestor veneration, 135–36, 140
priesthood of all believers, 93, 280, 282
prophecy, 53, 62, 263–64, 292–95

Q

Qi, Zhou, 54

R

Reformation, 6
    post, 6
Reichelt, Karl, 90
repentance, 34, 78, 85, 247
    identificational, 85
Rgyalrong, 155–57, 164–66
Rgyalrongwa, 155–56, 163
rituals, 28, 50–51, 74–75, 78, 88,

125, 127, 130–31, 137–39,
142, 144, 155, 157–59, 163,
166–69, 176, 178, 184, 187,
189, 206, 220–22, 224,
226–29, 231, 233–35, 258
folk, 163, 221, 226, 235
Rockstad, Ernest, 84
Roman Catholic, 6, 124, 131–36,
140, 173, 183, 233–35, 255
Vietnamese Catholic approach
to ancestor veneration,
131, 140
rural, 32–33, 35, 38–39, 48, 57, 62,
69, 91, 93, 156, 183, 234
Russian Orthodox, 6

S

Samarin, William, 7
Samuel, 52
Sandford, John, 84
Sandford, Paula, 84
Satan, devil, 4–5, 10, 13–16, 19,
21, 26, 29–30, 32, 34–35,
37–39, 54, 56, 72–73, 76,
82–85, 139, 223, 258, 274
Saul, 52
Saxons, 6
Schrempf, M., 160
Scott, David, 212
secularism, 10, 78, 82, 163, 196
shaman, 43, 45–46, 49–50, 57, 80,
160, 163–64, 169
Shaw, R. Daniel, 71
Shenk, Wilbert, 6
signs and wonders, 69, 82, 91,
239–41, 243–44, 246, 249–52
Silvoso, Ed, 84–85

Sinhala, 187, 206–7, 212, 215–16,
220, 228, 235
Sinhalese, 74, 76, 173, 180, 186,
188, 205, 207–9, 211–15,
217, 220–23, 225, 231–34
Skreslet, Stanley H., 11
Smith, Ed, 83
soothsayers, 43, 46, 57, 232, 235, 264
South America, 6
Spain, 6
spiritual
enemy, 25
forces, 4, 15, 45, 47, 63, 82, 158, 187
opposition, 40
oppression, 30
powers, 15, 28–29, 45, 47, 52,
84, 143, 159–60, 164, 166,
169, 231
reality, 28–29, 32, 38–39, 142,
150, 163, 166
struggle, 29, 37–38
warfare, 3–4, 29, 84, 235, 240
Spiro, Melford, 256, 259, 261-62
Sri Lanka, 74, 173, 175–76, 183, 185,
187, 205–7, 209, 213–15, 222–
23, 225–26, 229, 231, 233–36
Stephen, 291
Stephens, Bill, 48–51
Suhard, Emmanuel-Célestin, 6
supernatural, 26, 33, 45, 57, 69–
70, 73, 142–44, 148, 150–51,
196, 200–1, 224, 241, 243–44,
247, 250, 269, 274
superstition, 25, 91, 126, 130, 134,
143, 150, 207
Swearer, Donald, 163

syncretism, 58, 72, 80, 86–87, 134, 136, 208

T

Taoism, 90, 129
Taylor, Steve, 281
Teraphim, 52
testimony, 139, 199–200, 247–48, 264
Thailand
  northeast, 25
  Thai cosmologies, 141
theological contextualization (TC), 70, 80, 86, 88, 94
Theravada, 173
  almsgiving ceremony, 173, 224
Tibet, 155, 157, 163
  Tibetan, 50, 74, 76, 155–57, 159–64, 168–69
Tienou, Tite, 71
Timothy, 13
Tippett, Alan, 87, 240, 247
Titus, 13
Tomlin, Jacob, 279
Torah, 91
Trans World Radio, 8
transformational spirituality (TS), 70, 88, 94
Turner, Edith, 169
Turner, Victor, 168

U

United States of America
  America(n), 18
Urim and Thummim, 52–53
U.S. Center for World Mission (USCWM), 4

V

Van Doan, Nghiem, 137
Van Gennep, Arnold, 58, 168
Vedic, 73, 207, 209–10, 219
Vietnam, 123–24, 126, 128–31, 133, 136, 138
  Vietnamese, 123–24, 126–31, 133–38, 140
Vinaya Pitaka, 55
visions, 26, 47, 53, 58, 196–99, 201, 232, 241, 243
Visser, Marten, 242–43

W

Wagner, Peter, 4
Wallace, Anthony, 8
Walls, Andrew, 86, 244–45
war
  American GIs, 8, 18
  Cold War, 9
  imagery, 4, 9, 15–16, 21
  rhetoric, 5, 8, 16–17, 19, 21
  Second World War, 4, 8
  U. S. Civil War, 9
warfare, 3–4, 15, 17, 19
  imagery, 4, 15–16, 21
  rhetoric, 5, 16, 19, 21
  potential pitfalls, 17
  terminology, 3–4
Western, 8, 28, 30, 37, 45, 64, 90, 101–105, 111–12, 114, 129, 166, 187, 196–97, 202, 269, 272
  Westerner, 28, 111–14
Wheatley, Margaret, 76
Wijesekara, Nandadeva, 207

Wild Camel Protection Foundation, 48
Wink, Walter, 78
Winter, Ralph, 4, 7
witch, 74
  craze, 6–7
  doctor, 46, 57
  masters, 255, 260–62
witchcraft, 220
Womack, Stephen, 4
World Relief, 8
World Vision, 9
Wright, Chris, 251
Wycliffe Bible Translators, 4

Y
Yong, Amos, 103, 113

Z
Zambia, 168–69
Zaw, Aung, 261
Zehner, Edwin, 151, 243, 286, 292

SCRIPTURE INDEX

Old Testament

Genesis 1:26–30, 31, 116, 185

Genesis 3:5, 53

Genesis 11, 115

Genesis 12:3, 93

Genesis 18:2, 87

Genesis 27:29, 87

Genesis 31:34, 52

Genesis 33:3, 87

Exodus 4:31, 248

Exodus 5:21–23, 248

Exodus 7:3, 240

Exodus 19:6, 93

Leviticus 16:8, 53

Numbers 27:21, 53

Deuteronomy 6:1–11, 93

Deuteronomy 6:22, 240

Deuteronomy 10:14, 14

Deuteronomy 16:16, 93

Deuteronomy 17:14–15, 80

Deuteronomy 31:8, 29

Joshua 7:14–18, 53

Joshua 18:6, 53

Joshua 21, 93

Judges 8:24–27, 52

Judges 17:5; 18:17, 52

1 Samuel 10:20, 53

1 Samuel 15:23, 52

1 Samuel 28:6, 53

2 Kings 23:24, 52

Ezra 9, 85

Nehemiah 1, 85

Esther 3:7, 53

Psalms 22:18, 53

Psalms 23, 60

Psalms 23:4, 273

Psalms 25:8–9, 273

Psalms 103:12, 102

Psalms 135:9, 240

Proverbs 3:5–6, 116

Ecclesiastes 12:7, 139

Isaiah 1:10–18, 89

Isaiah 34:17, 53

Isaiah 58:1–12, 89

Isaiah 64:8, 115

Daniel 9, 85

Daniel 10:12–13, 52

Daniel 10:14, 52

Amos 5:21–24, 89
Amos 5:25–27, 247
Jonah 1:7, 53
Micah 6:6–8, 89, 91
Malachi 1:11, 87

New Testament
Matthew 1:2–; 2:12–13; 8:3, 26
Matthew 3:17, 31
Mathew 4, 30
Matthew 4:1, 29, 31
Matthew 4:1–11, 29–30
Matthew 4:3, 30
Matthew 4:4–7, 30
Matthew 4:4, 7, 10, 29
Matthew 4:8–11, 30, 54
Matthew 4:11, 29
Matthew 4:24; 8:16; 9:32, 26
Matthew 5–6, 60
Matthew 5:16, 89, 139
Matthew 5:41, 185
Matthew 7:12, 89
Matthew 7:21–23, 89
Matthew 8:14–15, 32
Matthew 11:20–24, 247
Matthew 11:25–30, 39
Matthew 12:1–14, 247
Matthew 12:38–39, 248
Matthew 14:28–30, 38
Matthew 15:1–9, 131
Matthew 16:1–4, 248
Matthew 16:15, 264
Matthew 16:16–17, 38
Matthew 16:21–25, 38
Matthew 16:23, 38
Matthew 18:19–20, 89
Matthew 22:37–39, 89

Matthew 25:31–46, 89
Matthew 28:18, 26
Matthew 28:18–20, 39, 91
Matthew 28:19, 26
Matthew 28:20, 29
Mark 1:12–20, 29
Mark 1:14–20, 31–32
Mark 1:41, 26
Mark 3:1–6, 247
Mark 3:13–15, 91
Mark 3:22, 26
Mark 5, 78
Mark 8:11–12, 248
Mark 10:42–45, 91
Mark 11:22–26, 60
Mark 15:32, 248
Luke 1:11, 14; 7:10, 26
Luke 4, 30
Luke 4:1–13, 29
Luke 4:6–7, 85
Luke 4:18–19, 91
Luke 4:41, 26
Luke 5:1–11, 26, 38
Luke 6:6–11, 247
Luke 8:44, 86
Luke 10:1–23, 34
Luke 10:6, 80
Luke 10:13–15, 247
Luke 10:25–37, 89
Luke 11:16, 29, 248
Luke 12:12, 115
Luke 14:25–34, 38
Luke 16:20–31
Luke 17, 247
Luke 22:33–34, 54–62, 38
Luke 22:49–51, 248

Luke 24:21, 37
John 1:1, 115
John 1:14, 27
John 1:35–37, 32
John 1:50, 248
John 2:11, 249
John 3:16, 31, 185
John 3:25, 36, 32
John 4:21–24, 89
John 4:40–42; 21:24–29, 26
John 5:17, 248
John 6:30, 249
John 8:30–31, 249
John 10:32, 37–38, 248
John 10:37, 248
John 10:38, 248
John 11, 247
John 11:15, 248
John 12:31, 30
John 13:34–35, 89
John 14:6, 115
John 14:11, 248–49
John 14:16–17, 26, 31
John 14:17–18, 29
John 14:26, 115
John 16:12–15, 70, 79, 82
John 19:24, 53
John 21:10–22, 38
Acts 1:15–26, 53
Acts 2, 31
Acts 2:18, 263
Acts 2:22, 240
Acts 4:30, 240
Acts 5:15, 86
Acts 6:1, 93
Acts 7:42–43, 247

Acts 10:38, 89
Acts 14:17, 79
Acts 15:23, 12
Acts 16:10, 53
Acts 16:31, 111
Acts 17:6, 92
Acts 17:11, 79
Acts 17:22–23, 79, 203
Acts 19:12, 86
Romans 4:2–6, 267
Romans 5:8, 31
Romans 8:1, 139
Romans 8:9, 263
Romans 8:14–18, 12
Romans 12:1–2, 14, 137
Romans 12:4–5, 12
Romans 12:9, 16
Romans 13:8–10, 89
Romans 14:1–15:7, 82
Romans 14:5–8, 13
Romans 15:4–5, 11
Romans 15:18–19, 91, 240
1 Corinthians 1–4, 82
1 Corinthians 1:18–2:5, 78
1 Corinthians 2:13, 115
1 Corinthians 2:14–16, 12
1 Corinthians 3:6–8, 12
1 Corinthians 4:9, 12
1 Corinthians 4:14–16, 11
1 Corinthians 7:17–24, 92
1 Corinthians 7:18–19, 80, 86
1 Corinthians 8, 86–87
1 Corinthians 8:9–13, 87
1 Corinthians 9:19–23, 86, 92
1 Corinthians 9:24–27, 11
1 Corinthians 10, 86–87

1 Corinthians 10:32–33, 87
1 Corinthians 12:7, 116
1 Corinthians 12:12, 116
1 Corinthians 12:13, 115–16
1 Corinthians 12:15, 116
1 Corinthians 12:21, 116
1 Corinthians 12:22–24, 116
1 Corinthians 12:25
1 Corinthians 13:8, 79
1 Corinthians 13:12, 12
1 Corinthians 15:22–23, 266
1 Corinthians 15:29, 87
1 Corinthians 15:57–58, 16
1 Corinthians 16:1–4, 93
1 Corinthians 16:13, 11
2 Corinthians 1:21–22, 12
2 Corinthians 2:14, 16
2 Corinthians 2:14–16, 14
2 Corinthians 4:5, 12
2 Corinthians 5:11, 13
2 Corinthians 6:18, 115
2 Corinthians 7:6–7, 11
2 Corinthians 10:2–5, 11, 19, 86
2 Corinthians 10:8, 13
2 Corinthians 12:12, 240
Galatians 3:14, 93
Galatians 3:29, 93
Galatians 5:13–23, 89
Galatians 5:16–26, 14
Galatians 5:22–23, 115–16, 263
Galatians 6:1–2, 89
Ephesians 2:1–3, 30
Ephesians 2:1–7, 14
Ephesians 2:8–9, 114
Ephesians 2:10, 14, 16
Ephesians 2:19, 12

Ephesians 3:10, 78
Ephesians 3:14–15, 35
Ephesians 4:3, 115
Ephesians 4:11–16, 91
Ephesians 4:12–14, 11
Ephesians 4:14, 11
Ephesians 4:15, 88
Ephesians 5:1–20, 14
Ephesians 5:8–14, 12
Ephesians 5:23, 267
Ephesians 6, 19
Ephesians 6:10–11, 16
Ephesians 6:10–18, 11
Ephesians 6:10–20, 14
Ephesians 6:12, 15, 26, 187
Ephesians 6:13, 16
Ephesians 6:17–18, 86
Philippians 1:27–28, 11–12
Philippians 2:1–11, 14, 87
Philippians 2:1–15, 20, 115
Philippians 2:12–16, 14
Philippians 2:17, 12
Philippians 3:13, 83
Philippians 4:3, 12
Colossians 1:13, 139
Colossians 1:14, 14
Colossians 1:16, 115–16
Colossians 1:27, 13
Colossians 1:28, 20
Colossians 2:13, 12
Colossians 3:5, 88
Colossians 4:5–6, 78
1 Thessalonians 1:9, 79
1 Thessalonians 5:6–7, 12
2 Thessalonians 3:6–13, 93
1 Timothy 4:4–5, 86, 89

1 Timothy 4:8, 15
1 Timothy 4:14, 264
1 Timothy 5:8, 114
1 Timothy 6:11, 11
2 Timothy 1:11, 11
2 Timothy 2:1-2, 91
2 Timothy 2:3, 15-16
2 Timothy 2:12, 16
2 Timothy 3:16-17, 89
2 Timothy 4:9, 13
Titus 3:12, 13
Hebrews 2:4, 240
Hebrews 3:6, 35
Hebrews 10:21-23, 35
Hebrews 10:24-25, 89
Hebrews 12:7, 11
James 1:27, 93
James 2:14-26, 89
James 4:7, 15
James 5:14, 86
1 Peter 2:2-3, 12
1 Peter 2:4-5, 12
1 Peter 2:9, 12
1 Peter 2:9-10, 91, 93
1 Peter 2:11, 12

1 Peter 2:12-19, 12
1 Peter 2:16, 12
1 Peter 3:15, 70, 78
1 Peter 3:18-19, 266
1 Peter 4:12-16, 11
1 Peter 5:1-3, 91
1 Peter 5:2, 12
1 Peter 5:2-3, 13
1 Peter 5:8, 15-16
1 Peter 5:8-9, 14
1 John 3:9, 12
1 John 4:1, 264
1 John 4:18, 89
1 John 5:4-5, 11
1 John 5:19, 15
Revelation 1:3, 264
Revelation 1:17-18, 264
Revelation 2:19, 12
Revelation 5:7, 115
Revelation 7:9, 115-16
Revelation 12-13, 78
Revelation 12:7-17, 5
Revelation 19, 15
Revelation 19:10, 264